Fishy Tales

&

Bunny Trails......

Harry W. Burdick, M.D.

Contents

To my wife, Sandy Burdick

whose graciousness has allowed me

sufficient freedom and time to accrue the information that I

am relaying to you, and whose constant

encouragement enabled me to finish this book.

Note from Sandy

Have you noticed that fishermen always know how many they caught? Read the gospels. It has been going on for a long time. So, I have heard lots of fish stories whether I wanted to or not. One day I just said to Bill, "You need to write those tales down. And soon. We are getting old, you know." We are octogenarians.

He started writing in the winter when it was too cold to fish. So here we go. The stories are funny and full of Gpa Doctor's own made up words. One grandson says he keeps a list of his sayings, like "slicker than snot on a door knob."

And if you are a fisherman, the tales are wisdom from the aged. And about worms. Do we really care about their mating practices? I guess scientifically minded people do.

Our daughters, Beth Kuiper, Sue Comfort and Amy Anderson and I enjoyed the fishing trips, too. We went shopping with our only girl grandchild, Maddie. We shopped, stayed over at a hotel, ate out and girl talked. Oh, how I miss those trips.

If I could really edit the way I want to, I would clean up the language and some of the subject matter. This is really rated PG as Gpa is talking to grown up grandchildren. However we have eight greats coming along and they will learn how it was back in the early and mid 40's in a small town in Michigan.

Bill and I pray that the legacy we pass along is one of loving Jesus, our family and friends. He is the one who saved us and our marriage and to Him we are eternally grateful. Someone was praying for us.

Sandy Burdick

Introduction

I enjoy fishing. I enjoy camaraderie. I especially enjoy the camaraderie that fishing can provide. I have related my first recollection of the fishing adventure with my father, and the joy that event evoked. As I started to recall other fishing stories, I was simply amazed at the amount of detail my brain had recorded. To me, that meant that these were mostly enjoyable occasions and trips. What started out to be a selfish exercise as I recalled many pleasant memories changed as I felt God tugging at my heart, saying to me, "You have experiences and stories about your relationships with other men that have greatly benefited you and those joys need to be shared."

As I invited my own grandsons and other men to join me in the pursuit of fellowship, mainly through fishing, I was blessed by their response and by the fellowship we enjoyed with each other: a brotherhood of men.

As I have traveled these many years through the world of fishermen, I recall many of their stories. Like myself, they were searching for meaning, reality, and meaningful relationships. I'm sad to say I cannot recall a single story wherein the storyteller had a truly gratifying relationship with his father. True that I heard stories where the father was perhaps glorified somewhat, but there was always a telltale story of a desire for more. I am one of those men.

My wife is acting as my editor and doing a marvelous job. She has pointed out that along my life path there have been significant men who have spoken to me in one way or another. I always wanted my father to be more for me. Even as I say that, I recognize that my father did not hate me. He tried to supply my needs. He did more than an adequate job materially, but was handicapped in that he never really had a father figure who modeled well for him.

As I have listened to the stories of my fellow fishermen, I found many men with whom I shared the desire for more from my father. But God is gracious and has provided for many of us, father figures who have tried to point the way to manhood and fatherhood that we all so dearly treasure.

I have come to better realize that each of us has only one truly good and perfect Father, and He has provided us with a number of men who have been surrogates for Him to us. It seems like it's only a matter of looking around and recognizing these friends for who they are and what they have provided in our lives. I am thankful for each and every one.

Thank you for reading this book and sharing your life with me and others.

Love,

Bill, Grandpa Doctor, Gpa,

Harry W. Burdick M.D.

.

1

Why I'm Telling My Story

I just had breakfast with my friend Jim Visser. He has read some of my stories about fishing with my grandchildren and others. He stated that he got to know a little about my family and my grandchildren, Austen, Jeremy and Parker. I have also received comments about the stories from grandsons Andrew and Preston, who has not had the good fortune of fishing with his brothers or cousins; just with me, Jim and Bill Stoub. Some of the stories need to be shared because they strike an all too familiar cord; a failure of men to establish meaningful relationships with one another. Relationships are too important to be hidden by silence. This book is my attempt to share some of my experiences with other men and boys who are becoming men.

One of my first memories of my father and his attempt to establish relationship with others, was his penchant for assigning nicknames to his friends. Huck Dean was a farmer who raised blueberries. Milky King had almost milk white hair. Oily Mead drove oil and gas trucks. Skinny Lawrence who worked with me at Andy's Grocery and Market, ate a lot of sugary snacks, but was underweight. "The Senator," Walter Eidson, once ran for the State Senate but lost, was my father's cardplaying and whisky drinking 'backroom buddy.'

It came as no surprise when my wife asked me if I had nicknames for any of the grandkids. I realized I had several.

Jeremy Kuiper, 'Germy,' Andrew Kuiper, 'Scooter,' Austen Comfort, 'Auney.' These are phonetic nicknames so spelling is inconsequential. Parker Comfort, 'Porker,' Madeline Comfort, 'Maddie or Zip,' Erik Anderson, 'Eeker,'. Joel Anderson, 'Joely-Poley,' Ryan Anderson, 'Rye -Rye.' I don't recall nicknames for Preston Comfort or Seth Anderson. Not because I didn't feel they were special, but their names in themselves were so unique I didn't have to subtitle their names.

Then Jim recited the times he could remember when he did something with father figures. Almost a canoe trip with one uncle that was rained out; sad. Another time he actually went fishing and hunting with another uncle. Also, lake fishing with Fred and Louise, and finally one other time fishing with Fred Mylan. I remember Fred, because I did disk surgery on him shortly after I arrived in Kalamazoo, in the mid-sixties. I was impressed that Fred was a very kind person. The operation must have worked because Fred died just this past year and I never heard a word of complaint about back pain.

I think back on my own story. My father was an angry man who was usually in control of his anger, but when drinking, his anger sometimes showed through. Oddly enough, I was never afraid of my father. I knew what would anger him so I avoided things that would do that. I read my mother quite well, and being able to read both mother and father and being a 'nice little boy,' I avoided conflict with both of them most of the time. Like every other kid I knew, I wanted to be liked by everybody, so I was quite compliant growing up. I remember only two fights of significance.

The first one was with a younger, skinny kid called Billy Robertson and I gave him a bloody nose. I truly felt sorry about that and so tried to avoid fights; I didn't want to hurt anybody else. The other significant fight was with Big Dick Chamberlain who was significantly bigger than I. We had a minor skirmish which I deemed a draw. I got a bloody nose and he got a couple lumps on his forehead. After that we were bosom buddies until we went away to college. Oddly enough, I went to the same college that he did; DePauw University, Greencastle, Indiana. On our high school graduation trip to California, Dick and I drove through DePauw University and I was so impressed that I enrolled on the spot. Upon my return from California, I learned that I had been accepted and was given a Schwallen scholarship because of my position in my graduation class, number two out of twenty-eight.

When we got to college, he joined the party boy fraternity, and I joined the singing fraternity, Lambda Chi Alpha. From that point, we went our separate ways. It's interesting to note that both his father and my father were alcoholics. As my wife encouraged me to write about my upbringing, I'm thinking of my other high school friends. Dick Chamberlain's father was a pharmacist and an alcoholic, and his mother was an RN, a lovely person. Jim Huss had a father that we never knew, neither he nor I. His mother married one of the town's drunks, Lester Sunday. She promptly divorced him and moved to Eau Claire. Les Spaulding had a mother who was crippled with rheumatoid arthritis and who never stopped talking. His father was a farmer who quit farming, moved to town and sold real estate. I later learned that he played cards and cheated. I also later learned that he taught Les how to cheat at cards; now I know why Les Spaulding always won. I also suspected his father of being a closet alcoholic. Chuck Reinbold. I never knew his father but his mother had remarried and so Chuck had a stepbrother.

I do not remember any of these guys ever speaking kindly or otherwise of their grandfathers. I find that statement striking. I had two grandfathers. My maternal grandfather, Harry Melvin Keefer, had been a farmer, and I assumed had failed as a farmer, moved to Benton Harbor to a large house and he too, sold real estate; not very successfully. Grandma took boarders in their large home and I think supplemented their income that way. Later, Grandma and Grandpa Keefer moved to a little house on Kephart Lane in Berrien Springs. This was on a ten acre parcel of land where he had a couple of small fruit trees, built a chicken coop and chicken yard, and there, with a walk - behind tractor tilled a couple of acres for vegetables. I remember spending many happy hours at Grandpa's little farm. I could climb the big cherry tree, gather eggs from the hen house, and in season, would walk around the garden with Grandpa. We would look for tomato worms, which were very large green caterpillars. They would be eating the leaves on the tomato plants. I would grab them, throw them on the ground and squish them. I can still feel the thrill of squishing that worm under my right heel. Is that all boy or what!

Grandpa Keefer was a very kind and quiet person and definitely was that kind of a father figure for me. As far as I can remember, he never came to any of my sporting events; four sports for four years, but that never seemed important to me at that time. He was always there and always kind. As I am remembering the brief time when we were without a home in Berrien Springs, we moved in with Grandma and Grandpa Keefer for a few months.

I remember my mother and father arguing a lot during that time. That obviously had a serious deleterious affect on me as I was between the ages of five and ten. I sought comfort from the stress that I felt because of their constant arguing and bickering. I was very fearful of a divorce between my parents. In my need for comfort, I found that tickling my nose with a human hair was soothing. I remember crawling around grandmother's living room looking for hairs on the carpet with which I could tickle my nose and feel comforted.

I quickly cleaned the carpet of human hairs and found that my own hair would suffice. Therefore, I started pulling hairs out of my head and using them to tickle my nose. It was comforting for a little kid who was fearful his parents would divorce. I pulled out so many hairs, that I developed an area of baldness. In medical school I learned this condition was called alopecia ariata. That is what I had and was taken to our local doctor to find out why, only to hear, " He'll grow out of it."

17

I wonder how many times that I have placed my own children in a similar situation. And, how many times have my own grandchildren been placed in a situation like that. My conclusion is we have all failed our children and watched our children fail their children. I am aware of that apprehension following me all the way into my early married life. How much significance have I attached to that? I don't know, and can only wonder how so many of us seem to be functioning satisfactorily. The stories behind our lives are numerous and seemingly unending.

My paternal grandfather, William Isaac Burdick, was an alcoholic as long as I knew him. He had a sister, my great aunt Ann who was also an alcoholic. My father had two full sisters and a half sister. My aunt Alma was a controlled alcoholic, as was her husband Ray Garrett. My father's other sister, Florence was married, divorced, was also an alcoholic. My father's half-sister, Beth Burdick, married, divorced, remarried, and I think all of them were alcoholics. I cannot remember any mentoring relationships with any of my mothers' or fathers' relatives.

I'm thinking back in time about my relationships throughout my lifetime that have given me support and sometimes encouragement. Before Junior High and certainly Senior High, I really had never given thought to friends and relationships and parents. Once I got into high school athletics, I was surrounded by buddies on all of my teams. My bonding to them seemed much more important than bonding with any of my family; father, grandfathers, or uncles. My social and support world were my buddies. Throughout high school each of us surrounded himself with buddies, and they were almost always there for us. As I look back, most of us were in similar situations. We did not have a responsible, caring father figure in our lives; we bonded through mutual needs. For me, this carried right on through my college years. This was especially true for me because of my buddies, Jim Chamness and Joe Freund. We were fraternity brothers and all three of us pre-med.

Medical school at the University of Michigan was different in that we were much busier in class studying and in our outside work. My bonding here was first with Dick Hodgman, later my roommate Jim Jacobs and then Chi Omega's cook, Ruby Stewart. As I'm writing, I can't help shedding tears as I remember the joy and feeling of security while working with and under Ruby's tutelage. I felt sad when I quit working for Chi Omega and became the steward of our Phi Chi fraternity house.

That is until I met this beautiful, great dancer from Chi Omega whose name was Sandy Cook. When we married nine months later, we started a relationship that has slowly cemented into the firm bond that most of us are seeking; 61 years of marriage. In my wildest dreams and imaginations I could never have anticipated anything as glorious, difficult, trying or as wonderful as this marriage.

I had no time or opportunity for any other relationships until I started my residency training at Blodgett Memorial Hospital, Grand Rapids, Michigan. For two years, I enjoyed a level of camaraderie with one of my teaching staff members, who himself had recently finished the training program I had just entered; Dr. Marshall Patullo. He was a very kind, conscientious and willing mentor. Both he and his wife were more than gracious and kind to Sandy and me. Although I did not fully understand at the time, Marsh was laying the groundwork for my willingness and desire to be a mentor of men.

I was very much enjoying my residency training and had no thought about the future, except I wanted to go into the practice of orthopedics, when God threw an enormous curve into my life. It came in the form of a summons to report to active duty in the U.S. Navy effective July 1,1959. I panicked! I had two darling little girls and I did not want to leave them and be put on a battleship in the middle of the Pacific ocean. So I hurried down to the Air Force recruiting center and volunteered. It worked! I was accepted into the Air Force and was to report to Montgomery, Alabama for my four week indoctrination program. There I met Carl B. Nagel, MD, who introduced me to big time fly fishing.

Once settled in our new officers quarters at Ernest Harmon Air Force Base, Newfoundland, Canada, I launched my new secondary career of fishing for Atlantic salmon. Carl and I mentored one another in fly fishing and in fly tying. My one mentor from Newfoundland was Dr. W. Duncan Rowe, ortho-pedic surgeon from Corner Brook, Newfoundland. Again, he was very kind and very helpful and showed me a level of prac-ticality in dealing with orthopedic problems that I would never forget; do what needs to be done in the best way that you know how to do it. My Newfoundland tales I recorded elsewhere but as I am recalling those days, I certainly learned a lot more than

I realized in my two and one-half years living on the Base; many good, some bad.

We returned to a house rental in Grand Rapids, Michigan, January, 1962. My bosses had acquired a new partner, James Roger Glessner, who taught me practical orthopedic techniques that helped me to become a skilled surgeon. Kindly Charlie Frantz, the senior partner in that group was phasing out. But the next in command, Alfred B. Swanson, turned out to be a genius of an orthopedic surgeon. But Big Al, was a terror in the operating room, in the clinics, on the wards and around the hospital in general. About three weeks into my training program, big Al and I had a confrontation. That ordeal raised the hair on the back of my neck and I found a level of anger I never knew existed in me. I said, "No" to big Al. I suspect he was not used to the word 'no' to his requests or demands. He was non-plussed. He simply walked away and left me alone, basically for the rest of my training program except if he needed something done in the hospital.

I had just learned what anger could do for me. Anger became a tool and a weapon that I struggle with even today. It has helped me get a lot of hard work done. And it has caused me an unknown amount of grief. Anger, or better stated, the energy which anger engenders can be used very beneficially, but only if used wisely. My word to the wise is, "Beware! Anger is a double edged sword. Use with caution!"

When I entered the private practice of orthopedic surgery September 1, 1963, my mentor and mentoree status changed significantly. Gordon Blossom, our pastor at first Baptist

Church, Plainwell, Michigan, mentored me as best he was able in understanding God's word. He was handicapped through no fault of his own because of his upbringing and severe abuse. However, God used Gordon Blossom to move me along. In addition to learning some good things, I learned a lot about how to avoid some bad things. It was a mentoring of sorts but I have learned that God can use even fallen men to teach His Word.

Gordon Blossom invited Dr. Vernon Grounds, President of Denver Theological Seminary, to our local church to teach a Bible series. Having no better place to house the good doctor, Gordon prevailed upon my wife (I was not yet a believer), to provide accommodations for Dr. Grounds. At this point in life my thinking was, "If this guy is an example of what a Christian can be, I'll give Christianity a second thought." For two years, Dr. Grounds continued to send me good Christian reading material with little notes of encouragement. That was a perfect example of mentoring.

The next outstanding example of mentoring came through Dr. Stanley D. Tousaint, professor of New Testament Theology, Dallas Seminary. Stan had preached a whole series based on the book of Revelation. The pastor of our new church, Westwood Baptist, Richard Gilaspy, made his recordings available to me. Richard quickly demonstrated his feet of clay, evidence, again, that God can use even a sinner to achieve his work. Stan and I still maintain a friendship even across the miles. We visited several times while our son in law, Greg Comfort, was in seminary at Dallas and I have seen him several times as he travels through the Midwest on speaking engagements. For me, the highlight of our friendship came when he joined us old guys for a fishing trip on Wintering Lake. I know that all of my friends hold Stan in very high regard as do Sandy and I, and Greg and Sue.

I have two other spiritual mentors who have played an important part in my life. One is Sydney Hawthorne. Sydney had no theological degree, but was one of the best teachers of God's word under whom I sat. Unfortunately, a divorce effectively ended his very meaningful preaching career. My last mentor, was probably my finest mentor. Not only was he a good and faithful teacher of God's word, but his whole life, attitude and action exemplified a true Christian mentor, Roy Clark. As I write this, I would have to honestly say that I cannot imagine a single person who would disagree with me; Roy Clark is one of the finest mentors that anyone could ever hope for.

I acquired a mentor of unusual background considering my own life and life style. After I had purchased my fishing cabin in Baldwin Michigan, with Jim Glessner, I was introduced to my wife's great uncle by marriage, Lloyd C. Cook. Uncle Lloyd had married Catherine Cook who was the sister of my wife's grandfather, Harry Cook. It turned out that Lloyd was an ardent fly fisherman and knew all about the Pere Marquette, where he had fished for many years. For several years he shared his life and fishing skills with me and told me about an era around Grand Rapids that I could never have imagined. I wish I had written down much more than I can now remember.

How many people do you know who, by their own wisdom and hard work became millionaires twice. That was uncle Lloyd, and he was one of my dearest mentors.

As I started writing Fishy Tales, I felt a compulsion to share some of my stories and wondered why? Does my ego need to be fed? I didn't think so. I'm a pretty happy guy and satisfied with who I am and where I am. But I have been blessed by a whole lot of relationships with interesting, exciting and wise people. Could I not pass along some of these blessings to others? Most assuredly, I could try. And that's what I'm doing. I have already had sufficient feedback from my wife, my grandsons and my friends to realize I need to work hard and fast to finish this before I die. I am now 86 years old and have lived longer than any man in my family.

I feel since I had been so blessed in life I should share some of what I have enjoyed. I developed a friendship with three guys who I invited to my cabin for the opening of trout season one year, in the early 60s. They were up at the crack of dawn on Saturday morning and thrashed my middle branch of the Pere Marquette for hours with worms and spinners. It was very cold that morning, and I had learned better. I slept in! I got up about nine, started coffee and breakfast. They straggled in, cold, wet and tired. I fed them breakfast after which they died all over the cabin. About 11 o'clock, the sun was out and there were a few flies fluttering around the water. I put on my waders, grabbed my little fly rod and went out with my number twelve Adams and caught three nice brown trout. When I returned to the cabin and showed my nice little catch to my fishing buddies, you would have thought I had thrown a bomb in the door. They were up, grabbing lunch, scurrying around and back to the river. For them the day ended as it began, cold, tired and fishless. As we spent the evening together, I became enlightened. All three of them were alcoholics. They were needy alright and what I had to offer them would never suffice.

From that point on, I learned to pick my friends more carefully because my concept of mentoring changed significantly. Yes, I could learn from older men and older women. But I could also be mentored by my equals as well as by some who are younger, who have more experience or wisdom. Mentoring became more sharing than just teaching/learning. I feel that it has become a way of life for me, which brings me more satisfaction than I ever could have imagined.

As I mentioned above, I could not remember any of my friends who had a really good mentoring relationships with a father or a grandfather. I think I remember a few boys and girls who had a good relationship with parents, but for the most part we were on our own. But we had a small town, and a small school and so we all had a lot of meaningful friendships. That seems to have been the best that any of us could have hoped for.

The breakfast with Jim, retired college professor, who is so faithful to pursue me, meet regularly and fish together, brought up all these memories. I am grateful for the time we spend together. I am writing this to encourage men to be men and mentors, and remember those who have invested in our lives and do the same for others.

2

How I Got Started
Fishing in Lemon Creek

My fishing career began in about 1934. I was born in Benton Harbor, Mercy Hospital, November 1, 1930. At that time my father worked for the Great Atlantic and Pacific Tea Company better known as the A&P, in Benton Harbor, Michigan. From what I now understand about 'the great depression,' he was fortunate to be employed anywhere. My father and mother both had attended Olivet College and I never learned why they both quit after two years.

My parents moved to Berrien Springs shortly thereafter, where my father became the manager of the local A&P store in 1931. There he remained until he purchased the local Red and White store, later to be known as Andy's Grocery and Market in 1941. That was a very notable year. My dad quit the A&P, bought the Red and White store and the Japanese bombed Pearl Harbor. Many early childhood memories revolved around the activities that stemmed from association with that wonderful little store, especially because of the food rationing and my job as delivery boy. But, I stray from the greater theme; fishing.

Many lakes, rivers, ponds, streams and creeks surround Berrien Springs, my hometown. Water has always been an important part of my life. Therefore, it is not a total surprise to most of my friends that one of my early recollections is that of fishing. I am painting a picture of my first known fishing trip, based on a mind's eye picture that is still with me and the interjection of suppositions that have in fact, historically been proven to be mostly true.

I feel that I was very small; about four years old. I am standing on a sand or gravel shore, not a bank above the water, but rather close to the water itself. I am facing a tall earthen bank across the water, probably a distance of no more than five or six feet. The water is flowing from right to left, in a tight semicircle with me in the center of the half circle. I have in my right hand a fishing pole, placed there by my father, who is standing on my right. The fishing pole felt like it was about nineteen feet long. It was actually eight feet long and made of split bamboo. There was a wheel like thing clamped on to the bottom of the pole and a line ran from this wheel out toward the end of the pole through some loops that appeared to be attached to the pole.

The line was orange and thicker than a piece of string. At the end of this line that stuck out beyond the end of the pole, was a piece of plain fairly stiff line that my dad called a leader. That in turn was tied onto a shiny thing, which spun around. My dad called it a spinner and to the end of the spinner was fixed a very sharp thing he called a hook.

That hook was very sharp, pricked my finger and I bled.

My father was not very consoling. He said something like, " Be tough, be a man." That was a real challenge especially for a four year-old. Onto that hook my father had attached a large gob of worms. Up to that point I don't recall ever having handled a worm. It was kind of icky to me. That was how my dad fished in those days, in fact, all the days of his life. He never changed! I often wonder if he ever thought about what he was doing, if he could really do it differently or better.

Using the rod to propel the spinner and worm, he threw it into the current with the spinner and worm on the end of the line. I remember the current pulling on the line downstream to the left of my dad. He handed me the bottom end of the pole for my right hand and gave me the line to hold in my left hand. I remember hanging on to the fishing pole that I just described; split bamboo rod, automatic wind fly reel, spinner and worm, standing on the edge of Lemon Creek.

I remember something pulling on my pole. Somehow my next memory was that of my dad holding up this funny, silver wiggling thing, on my hook; a shiner. He was very excited that I had caught my first fish at the age of about four. With that very episode my fishing career was launched.

Was I excited? Considering that I didn't know what I was doing, I had no concept of catching fish as a sport. Was I having fun? I don't really remember. My father was excited about the whole thing, so I was excited too. I had followed my father's instructions; that made him happy. I had caught a fish; that made him happy. So was I happy? Well, my father was happy and that was good enough for me.

I digress to talk about the pole and to tell you how we all fished in those days. In 1934 there were no synthetic poles or rods: no fiberglass, no graphite, no composite material. We had cane poles, in reality, bamboo rods in almost any length, up to sixteen feet; tubular steel rods, including telescoping casting rods and split bamboo rods for fly fishing or bait casting.

Fishing line was rather simple. One line for fly casting and another type for bait casting. Bait casting line was braided linen or cotton, in different thicknesses (strengths), usually black. It was put on reels with simple, single wind capacity and no level wind mechanism. The art of bait casting was really an acquired talent; there were no naturals. Casting rods could be as short as you wanted to make them, but three foot long rods were usually the shortest used. Most commonly used were four to five feet, however longer rods were made as well.

The bait or plug to be cast was either wooden or metal, usually shiny, a spinner or spoon and had some weight. The weight at the end of the line made all the difference between bait casting and fly fishing. I will talk about fly fishing later, hopefully. At my age, saying I will talk about it later, carries an inherent risk; will I be there later? Will I remember?

The technique of bait casting is rather simple. Rear back with the rod and the plug attached to the line by a snap swivel and usually a braided steel leader and throw that darned weight as far as you could. One of several things was possible, depending on your state of consciousness and awareness:

1. Forget to release the thumb that held the reel in check. That darned weight could swing back towards you and;

a. hit your buddy,

b. hit your dad,

c. hit your self.

2. Forget to thumb the reel. Backlash; the origin of the term backlash came from fishing.

The concept of bait casting is quite simple, really. The bait casting rod is flexible, and as such provides you with a whip action whereby the weight of the plug causes the reel to un- wind at a fairly rapid rate. As gravity and inertia set in, the speed of the bait or lure slows down. But the spin of the reel continues unabated. The skilled bait caster, with his thumb, will apply some pressure to the spool of the reel, such that he will have the reel spool stopped at the same time the plug hits the water. Simple, right? You need to find a really old guy to tell you about old-fashioned bait casting and backlash. With our present-day spinning rods and reels, backlash is a thing of a bygone era, thank God! I'm going to all the trouble of explain- ing this so that you young people will have an appreciation for the hardships that we grumpy old guys have experienced in an effort to make your world better.

3. Try to stop the plug early, thumb hard on reel re- sulting in;

a. Snap back of plug into your ear.

b. Broken line; retrieve plug fast, if it is a floater, before a bass hits it and you get that sinking feeling that you just screwed up.

c. A perfect cast. Dropping the plug right where you wanted it.

It was always my hope that I would do that and a bass would see it coming and hit the plug before it hit the water. It actually did happen once, at least I think so. It happened at night. Fishing at night is a whole new and different world. Sight isn't very important but sound becomes king.

The sequence goes something like this. I rear back, take aim at an imaginary spot between lily pads, and heave the plug out. The reel sings out, more a whir than a sing and I sort of hold my breath waiting for the splash of the plug hitting the water, not a lily pad. Spaloosh! A lunker bass just hit my plug, before it even hit the water! My anal sphincter tightens; I hope my urinary sphincter doesn't give out. My heart jumps into my throat. I snap the rod back to set the hooks and reel in as fast as I can, I'm ecstatic. My buddy, Dick, nets the fish and brings it into the boat. It is huge; it is the biggest fish I have ever caught! My heart is pounding. My joy couldn't be greater. This is the fish of a lifetime. I'm twelve years old. Dick says, "It's not as big as mine!" The process of bait casting separated the men from the boys in a big hurry.

Here are some of the things I had to consider in the early days as I launched my pursuit of fishing as a sport.

Lines for bait casting. Realize that spin casting as we know it today, was not available until the early 1950s and neither was the fiberglass rod. The early casting reel was a simple direct drive reel; one turn of the handle equaled one turn of the reel. So to bring in one foot of line you had to turn the handle about ten times. This could wear a guy out, even a young stud like me. What to do?

Use a bunch of cheap line called backing to increase the diameter of the spool, thereby increasing the efficiency of the retrieve. So instead of having one to one efficiency you increased it to three or four to one. Then wind on the good line as the final or finish line, until the line would just fit under the cross rods that held the reel together. With a three or four to one ratio, every turn of the reel would bring in four to five inches of line. What a good deal. How could life get any better?

Fly Lines. They were different in that they were finished with a coating of waterproof substance which enabled the line to float, somewhat. I think it was called enamel. When the coating cracked, then the line would fill up with water and sink. So it had to be dried and coated with a grease substance, later, silicone. Fly fishing was a lot of work in those days.

The Leader. The fly leader in those days was catgut. Dry catgut was very brittle and so catgut leaders had to be kept moist. I remember my dad had several flat aluminum leader cases. They were about 3/4 inch thick, about as round as a softball with a hinged lid. Inside were two or more felt pads that would hold water. The leaders were coiled and kept inside these cases. Just to be certain that the leader was moist and knotless it had to be drawn through ones mouth before being tied on to the line either over the tongue or between teeth to check for kinks, knots or unusual curls. Think of all the crap each of us ingested several times a day and we never ever got sick let alone died.

Terminal Device. The terminal device hasn't changed

33

much. A hook is still a hook but the quality of the metal is much better these days. Before the hook could be tied on, my dad always put on a small spinner, especially when fishing for trout. I was reminded of that fact when recently fishing with my friend Bob Bailey. He always used a Christmas tree configuration of multiple spinners.

This was a fisherman's lot in the olden days. Modern equipment has revolutionized and simplified fishing today.

3

All You Need to Know About Worms

Again, my first recollection of fishing was of the episode that occurred when I was four years of age. Using the information and knowledge that I have accrued about fishing with my father and his rather antiquated methods of pursuing the fine and genteel art of fishing, I would propose the following rendition of the event of note.

There per-chanced to be near the small village of Berrien Springs an equally small creek called, for reasons totally unknown, Lemon Creek. I have two distinct recollections of events or happenings that occurred in my life in relationship to Lemon Creek. The first was the first incursion into the wonderful world of pursuing Pisces.

This first event must have occurred on a Wednesday afternoon or a Sunday because my father was the manager of the A&P store, which to the uninitiated, was a chain grocery store. To the very young, this was an era wherein people lived reasonably sane lives and took time to smell the roses.The entire town of Berrien Springs closed down on Wednesday afternoon and every Sunday, even the local drug stores.

How we got to the creek I can only surmise. Dad did have a car but I don't remember it very well. It was close to a model T. I remember that is what he drove when he ran over my little red wagon. I cried. The axle was bent and had to be fixed. Any purchase of an item like a wagon was an event. You didn't just throw it away and go to Walmart and buy a new one. We fixed, saved and used everything. Trash collection was done by each family and once a month we would take the disposable goods to the local dump in a small container. The trash containers we have today would have lasted six months.

Somehow Dad and I got there. We had no such things as spinning rods; no fiberglass or graphite rods. We had fly rods, which were all made of split bamboo. For that day the rod du'jour was an old bent, split bamboo fly rod.

Onto the rod was affixed a reel. One could use a single-phase reel or an automatic fly reel. I remember one or two single-phase reels in my father's collection but he preferred the lever action automatic reel. These ran by a spring made of flat spring steel all wound like a clock spring. To start using one the user would have to wind it up. That could prove to be tricky.

If you wound it too tightly, you couldn't pull out much line at one time. Then you would have to turn the release rim and hope you still had enough spring left to pull the line in when you hit the wind lever. If you didn't wind it tight enough, then in your effort to pull in a fish with the wind lever, you might be stuck with the fish six or eight feet from the boat, or shore, and no good way to bring him in.

It was a source of unimaginable frustration to a wee lad such as myself. At that time I knew little of the possibilities available to fishermen. All I knew was my dad had given me the worlds greatest tackle, his own, to start my fishing career; his old bent fly rod and an old semi floating fly line.

If you wanted to fish under the water surface you had to devise a method to get this somewhat floating line down to the bottom. If you had an old fly line this was no problem. It had so many cracks in the surface that it soaked up and held the water; it would sink quite well, like a rock. This was great for fishing in a lake or fishing a stream with bait. But if you wanted to fly fish you had to coat the fly line with some kind of grease to keep it on top of the water. After a while the grease would pick up tiny particles of dirt that would break the surface tension of the water or the line would crack and the cracks in turn would pick up more water and soon you were back to square one; a sinking fly line that was difficult to handle, a sore arm and no fish. And my dad wondered why I wasn't enamored with the fine art of fly fishing.

There were three accepted methods of dealing with this most unpleasant situation. One was to wipe the entire line off with a clean rag. I have never known a fisherman, especially a kid, who had a clean rag to use to clean the dirt and excess wax off of the line. In my early years this was never an option.

Number two was to false cast the fly until the line had dried somewhat. This involved standing up, usually in a boat, waving your arm with the rod firmly affixed, back and forward in a slightly circular manner, like a lunatic. Failure to utilize this slightly ovoid pattern would usually result in one of three un-desirable choices. First would be resemble a backlash in a cast-ing reel. At this point few people reading this have any concept of fishing with a casting reel so I am speaking a foreign lan-guage. Those few of you who do understand know that this is called a bird's nest. No self-respecting bird would even look at this mess let alone consider using it. The second option is catching the fly somewhere in or on the rod. This usually re-sults in a sharp crack and a frantic search through the fly box to replace the recently departed fly.

The third happening, although rare, is of such impact that it needs to be noted by all would be fisherman. Although the fly has whistled past the fisherman's ear on many occasions, little notice has been given this gently whooshing sound. The very next forecast is accompanied by a very gentle thud, a piercing feeling in the upper lobe of the right ear and then followed by a piercing scream, multiple expletives, frantic activity such as dropping the rod, another scream when one realizes that the falling rod embedded the fly more deeply into the ear, then cut-ting the line to free the rod from pulling on the line again, a loud splash as the rod falls out of the boat, a few more exple-tives and finally frantically rowing the boat to the nearest shore, never mind that the car is on the other side.

Next is a rapid and erratic trip to the ER interrupted by a friendly police officer who is merely inquiring about your good health, especially since the drugs you must be taking are im-pairing your driving ability so severely, when he spots the blood streaming down from your right ear. He turns pale and bids you safe trip. Your arrival at the ER involves the usual Q and A including your mother's name and mother's maiden name.

After only an hour or two you are rushed into the room where the doctor will appear as soon as he pulls the bait casting plug out of a seven year-olds left foot. If you are lucky, the doctor is a fisherman who knows the Swedish method of hook extraction. If not, you will probably not go back to the lake to dredge for your fly rod.

What is the third method of getting one's fly line to float again, you reasonably ask? The explanation of number two was so long and laborious that I forgot what I was going to say. So, I am going to have to make one up. What I used to do when I fished with Doug was to get up early in the morning, pull the line out from the reel and string it between two Tag Alder bushes to allow the line to dry and then re-coat it with some kind of preservative. Early on it was bear grease and later it was silicone. Then the excess had to be wiped off. It was a very laborious process.

The line is much too thick and cumbersome to attach the fly directly so we must add a leader between the line and the hook. You say "no problem" and today you can say that. Seventy years ago, guess what kind of leader material we had to put between the thick, highly visible line and the hook, which was to fool the fish by holding a delicious piece of food.

That lo-viz but tough substance was none other than catgut. You've got to be kidding. No, I'm not. Have you ever tried to bite through the "casing" of an uncooked Brat or sausage link?

That is gut, cat or otherwise. It is soft when wet and tough. The operative word is wet. When dry, catgut, pig gut or any other gut is hard, unpliable and brittle. It had to be moistened to be used in order to regain its pliability and strength; rarely did we have a piece longer the three feet. Real fly fisherman would keep their gut in a small aluminum container about the size of a hockey puck filled with a moist cotton pad. Let me tell you that the old time fly fisherman was a dedicated soul.

Well, at this point in this rather laborious story, we have a bent or crooked split bamboo rod, an unpredictable automatic reel, a waxed, woven linen fly line and a three foot piece of cat gut and a partridge in a pear tree. Today, next in line would be a fine wire hook; all of my grandkids know this. But in the olden days that would be wrong because my dad was just like his dad. "We always do things this way." That phrase and, "What will the neighbors think?" ruled my parents lives. It is a wonder to me that my dad had the smarts and guts to buy a little Mom and Pop grocery and meat market and make it work. He just fit in with the times. Don't ask questions, just follow the crowd and don't make waves.

So what comes next? A spinner. A what? A small double bladed spinner. You have never seen a double bladed spinner? It has a fixed loop at the upper end and below the spinner is a hard wire loop, held closed by a small sliding spring that holds the free end of the wire next to the shank to keep the hook from falling off. All of the kids have had enough trouble getting a 6 pound test line through the eye of a fine wire hook. How big would the hook have to be to get it over the wire loop of a double bladed spinner? HUGE! So now we have added this double bladed spinner and a huge hook. It had to be at least a six, the kind that Bill Stoub used when we started fishing together. And now that I think about it, that is basically the way Bob Bailey fished for blue gills in Warner Lake.

So what comes next in the order of fishing? Bait. What is it that we all had access to that was cheap and readily accessible? Worms. But not at the local hardware store, gas station or bait stores. Then where for pity sake are they to be found?

In your own backyard. Sounds like a great title for a story or song. Nonetheless that is where my dad told me to look later in this truncated story. To the young and uninitiated we used to get our own worms. My father told me to dig for them and he told me where to dig. I have always suspected he wanted to plant a garden, better spoken that he wanted me to plant a garden.

I was not very big at that time and using a square ended shovel was not very easy in spite of what dad told me. At that point in time I suspected he didn't even know which end of the shovel to grab. But I gave it the old college try, or rather the old grade school try. It was hard work and unproductive. A lot of grunt for a few scrawny worms. I would work a week for 1 days fishing; the juice to squeeze ratio was poor.

In other words I had to build a better mousetrap. I knew a little about mousetraps because I had just read 'Trigger Berg and His Ten Thousand Mouse Traps.' So I went about looking for a better way. In the process I learned a lot about worms, especially the ones I wanted to use for bait; night crawlers.

Night crawlers! A reasonable knowledge is imperative to any and all budding fishermen. Night crawlers are very interesting creatures. I certainly didn't know this at age ten or so but I remembered my earlier experiences as I went into Biology 101 at DePauw University. The result of which is a compilation of useless information, which I shall endeavor to relate to my long-suffering grandchildren.

Night crawlers are bisexual. That is a whole lot different from homosexual, queer or fagots. God created some species to be bisexual. That does not mean they can fertilize themselves, but rather they mutually fertilize one another. My discovery of this created an indelible impression on my young mind. At about this age I had some knowledge of the difference between boys and girls. Even though what I had experienced was not verified until I reached college, I had a strong idea of what was going on.

How does one find night crawlers? As I have said, we did have bait stores, but crawlers were expensive, about ten cents a dozen. If you had a dime, where would you rather spend it, on a Red Ryder movie, or a dozen crawlers? No brainer. Let's find a way to get crawlers free.

Crawlers live in the ground close to the surface. I know this in spite of what our maid in Newfoundland told us. She told us that night crawlers come from the sky. When I asked her how she knew that her response was simple, "They are all over the street and ground every time it rains." I really had a hard time refuting that piece of 'Newfie' folklore, so I didn't. I simply agreed with her and wondered if I was really very smart at all.

Why do they come out at all? Their whole life could be spent underground and they could die happy never having seen the sun or a robin. The first reason is in the Newfie tale. They breathe air and in a heavy rain, their hole becomes flooded and they must leave the underground temporarily. On a few occasions I remember the rain was so hard they came onto the road and sidewalk, I was in hog heaven running around and simply picking up the hapless creatures and popping them into a can of dirt. My dad told me to put in some sand so it would toughen their hides. He also had me throw in some coffee grounds for food. To this day I'm not sure about either trick. I really think that my dad fully expected the worms to get hopped up on the caffeine and be much more active in the water to attract the fish.

I still haven't answered the question. But here is what you have all waited to learn, it's all about sex! You have to be kidding, worms and sex? That's preposterous! I didn't catch on right away since I was quite young when I discovered this but it is quite logical. Why do they come out of their holes when it hasn't rained and its night? What else, sex. You older guys will understand. You younger guys just file it away as I did. This little tidbit will come in handy later on. I have a file called useless misinformation where I have an abundance of worthless rat-facts. Just wait, you'll get it all later.

But here is the drill. When you expect to go fishing and you know that you will need worms, you get out the hose and hook up the sprinkler during the day. Usually after noon rather than morning since the sun dries out the grass too fast; make it late afternoon. After dark get out your good flashlight or put new batteries in the old one, get an empty tin can, preferably one that had early June peas in it, well rinsed out (worms don't like early June peas—they like the older tougher ones). Go to the part of the yard where the grass is the scantiest, and the dirt the darkest. Worms like rich dirt and a lot of grass, but I can't see them in a lot of high grass, so I go to scant grass or freshly mown grass. And since I didn't like to mow the grass just to go fishing, I simply chose scant grass. You must walk very softly. Worms can't see or hear well but are very sensitive to vibration, so walk softly and carry a big light. Beware; they're out there

Train your flashlight on the ground just ahead of your feet and look for them. They will be stretched out on the ground and will glisten in the light. As soon as you spot one, lunge for him or her as the case may be. Grab fast, they are light sensitive and will pull back into their holes when they sense light. I know I said that they can't see but they can sense light, so move fast and grab hard. Then lift up the worm slowly. His tail will be in his hole and he will be pulling hard to get back in the hole. If you pull too hard you will end up with a crawler head and the rest will pull into the hole and die. The tail without a head will die. However, the head without a tail will live and grow a new tail. But to wait for a new tail to grow just to go fishing is too much to ask. Pull slowly but steadily until the tail gives up and you have the whole crawler. Put him in the can and don't tip it over.

But I still haven't explained why the worms are out of their holes at night. Back to worm sex 101. Worms are truly bi-sexual. They can't fertilize themselves but they can fertilize one another. If all this sex talk is too much just skip to the next paragraph. How did I learn this at such an early age? I used to have good eyesight. Once I grabbed one crawler thinking I had his head. I didn't have his head; I had the middle of the crawler. How do I tell the head end from the tail? The tail is paler than the rest of the crawler and the head darker. The most striking part of the crawler is the clitellum. The word means saddle and that is what it looks like, a saddle on a worm. That is the external sex organ. What I saw that night is etched indelibly on my mind. The worm was none other than two crawlers, end-to-end, clitellum to clitellum. And as I lifted the one crawler, I saw two, not one, very tiny organs between the two clitellum. Those were worm penises. The crawlers come out at night to copulate with each other. Like Solomon said, "So what's new?" Did I understand what was happening at my tender age? You bet!

The other method of getting the worms out of the ground is as follows. One takes a metal rod about two feet long. Take an extension cord and cut the receptacle end off. Tape the bare wires to the end of the rod and make a handle out of electrical tape. Stick the rod into the ground and plug in the other end to a 110 V. outlet. Walk around the end of the rod and look for very wiggly crawlers. There might be a little tingle as you pick up the crawler but it is not too bad. There are two things that you don't want to do at the same time. Water the lawn before hand and go barefoot. Or pee on the rod. Nuff said?

In summary, gather crawlers at night, use a flashlight, move slowly and quietly, go for long worms, doubles, and beware of the tail in the hole, that's the worm's ace in the hole.

4

Berrien Springs, Michigan
My Home Town

My home town Berrien Springs was a village of about two thousand people who, it seemed at that time, were all poor. There was only one fairly wealthy person in town, Guy Heim. He was not only wealthy but also very smart as I was wont to learn later in my childhood. He was a gentleman farmer and insurance salesman and goodness knows what else. I remember him telling my dad that he kept a metal box in the basement in which he placed one hundred dollars for his wife when she ran out of grocery money. To me that was an incredible amount of money since bread was about ten cents a loaf and a pound of hamburger was twenty-eight cents. Gum was a nickel a pack and there was no such thing as a candy bar that cost more than five cents. The movies cost fifteen cents and my Grandpa Keefer smoked Marvel cigarettes that were only thirteen cents a pack while all others, Lucky Strikes (my father's brand) and Camels (Uncle Ray's brand) were fifteen cents a pack.

At my earliest recollection there were (what must seem as prehistoric) some things which I must relate to my grandchildren. Our milk was delivered, not purchased in a grocery store or gas station, by a milkman who wore a white uniform. The milk came in glass quart bottles with cardboard caps and was delivered door to door by the milkman from a horse drawn milk wagon. The lady of the house was always home so the milkman ran to the door to ask what she wanted. The choices were quite simple; whole milk, skim milk, cream and occasionally whipping cream. I think he also had butter. Cottage cheese came to the grocery store in five and ten pound crocks and was only one curd size. The milkman kept track of the purchases and collected once a week. If the lady was to be out she would leave a note and the milk was left on the back steps. Some of the more modern houses had a milk compartment built into the wall by the back door.

Many of the houses at that time had iceboxes and so ice had to be delivered several times a week. That was the highlight of a hot summer's day; all of us kids running after the horse drawn ice wagon hoping the ice man was in a good mood and would chip off a small piece of ice for each of us to suck on. I remember when the ice man, Al Bender, proprietor of Hilltop Ice and Coal, got one of those new-fangled motorized trucks to haul ice and coal; ice in the summer and coal in the winter. I also remember that his wife was my typing teacher and gave me my only C in high school. How could she do that to one of Berrien Springs' star athletes and students? So now you know why I waited so long to try to write this story. Thank God for computers and spell check and the 'Dragon,'

My folks had an electric refrigerator with the large cylindrical cooling unit on top. If you have seen any pictures of pre-historic refrigerators, that is what we had. The freezer compartment would hold two ice cube trays and that was all. We had no need for anything larger, there were no frozen foods. I don't ever remember any type of freezer in my Dad's grocery store. The only item that we could purchase frozen at that time was ice cream and that in quantities of 1 pint or 1 quart; you bought only what you could devour on the spot, no saving for later. With ice cream it was now or forget it. And the place to buy ice cream was the drug store.

In Berrien Springs that was the only place to buy ice cream. A few restaurants, and I use the term very loosely, carried several two and one half gallon tubs each of vanilla, chocolate and strawberry for adding to pie or cake. Only near the end of my high school days, did Buth's ice cream in Benton Harbor, introduce fudge ripple. WOW! But the action was at the drug store. There you could get fountain coke with all sorts of flavors added. My favorite was lime-flavored coke, but mind you any flavor that could be put in a soda you could stick in a coke; all for ten cents.

But my all time favorite was a chocolate malted milk. It was so thick that you had to push the spoon to get it into the malt. Sundaes could be ordered to be made any way you could imagine; five kinds of ice cream and at least that many toppings plus bananas, nuts, cherries and real whip cream. Sodas were my next most favorite; a double chocolate soda. The straws originally came in a large glass jar with a metal lid; you lifted the lid, pulled out two straws and started slurping. Later the straws came individually wrapped in thin paper. The name of that game was, 'Stick it on the ceiling.' We carefully removed the smallest portion of paper off one end of the straw, put a small piece of well-chewed gum on the other end and blew it up to the ceiling. If you were good there would be a long thin tube of paper hanging from the ceiling. It was not easy to do on a fourteen foot high ceiling. If you got caught you were banned from the drug store for a week or so. That was okay because no one could afford to buy ice cream more than once a week anyway.

Sometime during the Great War, WWII, Mr. Taylor brought a new fangled deal into Berrien Springs; a Locker Plant to be known as Taylor's locker plant. It was revolutionary. Remember I said the refrigerators had only small freezer compartments. Well, because of the war and the interruption of food chains in the USA, people had trouble buying and keeping certain food products, especially meat. My dad, in the grocery store, couldn't always plan on meat being shipped into our town; it was called meat shortages. There were many shortages during the Great War and I'll mention some as I continue but the locker plant was a means of fighting the shortages at home.

My dad figured out a way to overcome some of the problems by making a deal with 'Scummey' Castner to slaughter cattle for us; beef, veal (calves), pork and lamb. When he killed for us, we would have an excess of meat for a while and people would buy as much as they could. This was all very complicated because of meat rationing, red points and stamps, but people needed a place and a method to store excess meat.

Enter Mr. Taylor and his marvelous frozen food locker plant. It was a simple cement block building with all kinds of individual metal lockers that were rented out to people for the express purpose of saving food in a frozen form. That really pre-dates what we now have as a fast frozen food industry. The lockers were about two feet by two feet and about three feet deep. That would hold a quarter of a cow if packaged properly. So 'Scummy' would knock a cow in the head with a sledge-hammer. Bullets were also hard to come by during the war, so the preferred method of permanently anesthetizing a cow, was a sledge to the head. Mind you there was heck to pay if 'Scummy' missed but I never got to watch a miss.

The cow went down, hooks were inserted into the Achilles tendons, attached to ropes and pulleys. The cow was hoisted unceremoniously up until his, or her as the case might be, head cleared the floor and the throat was cut to allow the animal to bleed out. This was humane but with pigs they were hung while alive, and then stabbed in the throat with a long butcher knife and again allowed to bleed out. The butchering that followed would have been the object of animal rights group's protests and condemned by sanitation engineers and would not have happened today. But during the Great War, people got real hungry and could care less how they got fed.

So during the war, my dad would get a cow that didn't cost him red stamps; so the bartering began and the food lockers got filled. That is why I was a' chubby buddy' while growing up until I got into athletics. We ate well during the war and so did the gas station owners and a few others who traded in goods in short supply. There were a large number of 'black marketers,' one of whom was my father and by implication, also me. Glenn Briggs, our neighbor, was our gas station man. We never wanted for gasoline during the war for between our T sticker and Glenn's penchant for T-bone steaks, we could have driven to Chicago and back several times a year. All motor vehicles had stickers affixed to their windshields; A for peon's, B for teacher's and other semi-important people, like small business owners, C for people who were deemed essential for 'the war effort,' whatever that was. And T for all farmers and businesses who supplied goods to the peon's who didn't qualify as important. Needless to say I lived in the privileged class of Old Berrien Springs.

5

Berrien Springs
During the Great War

The day I heard about Pearl Harbor was December 7, 1941. I had just celebrated my eleventh birthday. It was on a Sunday around noon. My parents and sister, Barbara, were in our home on W. Ferry St., when we received the news on the radio.

The radios in those days were very large. The main radio in the house, frequently the only radio in the house, was always placed in the living room around which chairs were frequently arranged. We sat in a semi circle around the radio while we were listening. I believe a radio like ours was fairly common in households in those days. The radios were housed in a wooden cabinet, which was fairly ornate. It was large because radios consisted of a collection of many large radio tubes. They usually had a brass base with two or more prongs fixed to a circular base of metal and then a glass tube over the base.

When the radio was turned on all of these tubes lit up and glowed. They were all placed on a fairly large base or board into which was run an electric cord. All of this was contained on the inside of the radio. On the outside front of the radio cabinet were several knobs labeled on, off, volume and tuning. There was a face on the radio with numbers which corresponded to the available radio stations. So when you tuned the radio, you turned a knob or dial and a line radiating out from the knob showed you the approximate station to which you were tuned. All of the radio stations were AM. (Amplitude modulation) as compared to FM. (Frequency modulation). The latter did not arrive in our community until about 1944.

There were such things as short wave radios. These were fancy high tech radios. You could get messages from all over the world with one of these short wave radio phenomenons. As you turned the dials, you heard all kinds of squeaks and squawks that came out of the radio as well as funny words that were being spoken by foreigners. Listeners usually wore headsets but occasionally had these short wave radios directly wired to speakers. But only the guys who we considered to be geeks wore these headsets and operated these crazy radios.

My father was listening to the radio that Sunday, probably after somebody called him on our telephone. Telephones in those days were black and were shaped like a C and they had a phone or earpiece on one end and a mouthpiece on the other end. They sat on a cradle so that when you lifted up the handpiece, the phone was turned on. When you dropped the hand piece back in the cradle the phone was shut off. Pretty simple but it worked. There was not always a dial for dialing a number. In the olden days when you lifted up the phone, you would hear a voice on the other end saying, "Number please?" And you would give the operator a four digit number. Our number was 3731. Can you believe that? Those four digits stayed with our phone number as long as I can remember. Yes, we had to add a prefix but the suffix 3731 stayed the same until my parents died.

Occasionally I would forget somebody's number so I would say to the operator, "Dick!"

And she, always a she, never a man, would say, "Chamberlin or Wilson?"

Then she would plug me in to the right number. She would recognize my voice and knew who I might be calling. The telephone operators were always local and usually knew everyone in town. Worse yet they could tune in on any conversation. So there were no such thing as secrets in Berrien Springs, Michigan. You always had to be careful what you said on the phone if you didn't want the whole town to know it. If you think I'm talking gibberish, listen to an old Fibber McGee and Molly radio show. It went like this; "Hello operator, give me number—. Oh is that you, Myrt? What's new today? No! You don't say. No, really, oh, you don't say. Did his mother know? What did she do?" And so on. That was small-town USA in 1941.

So Dad turned the radio to WGN or WLS or some similar station. He listened a short time and said in a very loud voice, "Pearl Harbor has been bombed." So I thought to myself, "What does that have to do with the price of eggs in China?" Fortunately for me I didn't mouth that; my father wasn't too tolerant of wise guys or wisecracks. Of course, at age eleven, I did not have a very large world view. I had no idea what Pearl

Harbor was or where it was. But when he said, "The Japanese have bombed Pearl Harbor," I realized that probably wasn't a good thing. All I knew at that point in time was that we shipped a lot of our scrap metal to Japan and they in turn sold us a bunch of crappy little knickknacks and toys with little American flags on them. Had I been wiser, I would have realized how hypocritical the whole thing was.

I was told the Japanese were imperialists and that we would have to declare war on the nation of Japan and we would have to do the same on Germany. I had no idea the impact that day would have on our world and particularly the United States of America.

Today, I just looked up on Wikipedia to learn the estimated death toll throughout the world during the time of the events leading up to and including the war. It was estimated to be between sixty and seventy-million people or roughly two and one-half percent of the worlds' population. That is the largest known death toll from any war in the history of the world. The impact that World War II had on the United States in less than four years, in retrospect, was truly phenomenal. I write this to help my grandchildren understand the tremendous change that I have witnessed in the United States during my lifetime. We went from a nation of one hundred thirty-five million, struggling to come out of the great depression to the nation that was on the doorstep of becoming the world's greatest superpower with a population of three hundred thirty-million people.

When I was born in 1930 the United States was struggling to come out of the depression. Jobs were very hard to find. The economy was stagnant at best. Men comprised probably ninety-five percent the workforce at that time. Women's place was in the home raising children, not working in the labor force. As the war in Europe began to grow in the late 30s, the United States was contracted by Great Britain to supply many of their war needs. So the economy by 1940 was improving. Once we were attacked and declared war on Japan, Germany and Italy, the United States changed forever.

Men volunteered for war, were drafted and left the labor force. The war effort, that is building supplies for the war, required many, many more people in the labor field.

For the first time in the history of the United States, women went to work in factories and virtually everywhere. There were women's branches of every service; the Army (WAC), Navy (WAVE) and Air Force (WAF). Although none of them, to my knowledge, saw combat, they were vital in the support of our fighting men. Many of the factories in the United States that were barely getting by in the 30s, changed their production and became a vital part of the war industry. Most companies in the United States went to work shifts. Some of the more important industries worked around the clock; three shifts a day. The overall benefit to the United States was a booming economy. There were many millionaires created during that period of time. But almost everyone prospered.

WWII Information—The greatest generation.

Population of the USA on or about December,7. 1941: 130 million.

Date of attack on Pearl Harbor, Hawaii; December 7.1941.

The war was declared on Japan, Germany and Italy that day or shortly thereafter. The war was declared over May 8, 1945, for Germany and August 15. 1945, for Japan.

During that brief three 1/2 years, the United States of America produced the following:

22 aircraft carriers

8 battleships

48 cruisers

349 destroyers

420 destroyer escorts

203 submarines

100,000 fighter aircraft

98,000 bombers

24,000 transport aircraft

58,000 training aircraft

93,000 tanks

257,000 artillery pieces

105,000 mortars

3,000,000 machine guns

2.5 million trucks

millions of M1 rifles

There were 16.1 million persons in uniform and all of this in three-and-one-half years.

My father, Andrew Sprague Burdick, had just purchased his new Red and White Grocery Store which would become very important for my family and me.   Much of our activity centered around our involvement in running the grocery store during the war.

It is there I learned more than you can imagine and more than I can remember. Some was rather mundane but some of it has impacted my life much more than I ever realized until I sat down to write this little story. I'm now going to list some of the things that I learned. I was given my first job at age eleven bagging potatoes in a peck bag; sixteen 2/3 pound per peck. So I became a potato pecker. Back in the days of my youth, pecker was a naughty word.

In those days there was no such thing as a plastic bag. Everything was brown paper bags, in various sizes and named according to the weight it was supposed to carry. We had two pound, five. ten, sixteen and twenty pound bags. A twenty pound bag was the biggest we had because paper wasn't that strong. If you try to put twenty-five pounds of material in a twenty pound bag, especially if you put eggs in the bag, guess what? You got scrambled eggs.

We bought potatoes from a wholesaler in one hundred pound burlap bags. When it came time to put the potatoes into peck bags, we dumped a bag or two into the potato bin. The bin was made of wood and was about four feet wide about four feet deep and about four feet high. It had a lid on it so we could store groceries in cartons over the potato bin. At age eleven, I needed a little help to dump a bag in the bin. After we had dumped several bags into the bin, I had a large scoop made out of heavy gauge wire with which I would scoop potatoes up and put them in the bag until the twenty pound bag was nearly full. That was considered a peck. Did I weigh them? Are you kidding? When I said it was a peck it was a peck! That was my first touch of real power—a peck was a peck! Actually, I would weight the first few pecks until I had an idea how many potatoes ought to be in the bag; that was my way to peck potatoes.

Well, you think, that's a pretty simple story. You might think that, until you found out if you dumped too many hundred pound bags into the potato bin and left them there too long; they tend to go bad. That's called a rotten potato. And let me tell you, they did stink! After the second time I had to empty the complete bin, in which there were several hundred pounds of potatoes, search for the culprit, hope that there was only one, find it and throw it out, wash all of the rest of the potatoes, and scrub out the bin; that is when I learned to dump in only enough potatoes for a week. No more rotten potatoes for me, buddy. So when you hear that childhood rhyme, "Last one in is a rotten potato," that is really something to avoid. Rotten potatoes really stink. And it is hard to wash the rotten potato stink off your hands with only cold water; you have to wear it off. My father made me go home after I cleaned out a rotten potato bin because the girls who worked at the store couldn't stand to be around me.

As I am writing this section of the story about rotten potatoes, I'm listening to a jazz recording of Benny Goodman and Harry James and recalling the impact their style of music had on my generation: sock hops, dancing in the gym after every home basketball and football game, Saturday night at the American Legion club for teens, and hanging out in Dick Chamberlain's basement, with a knotty pine paneling. No booze, no drugs and no smoking, although many, or perhaps most of our fathers smoked cigarettes and were alcoholics. And that same story held true for our entire high school. Oh yeah, a few of the farm boys would sneak out to their cars for a smoke at lunchtime, but that was really the exception, not the rule.

"Cherokee" by Billy May is being played. That song became the standard for all of the cowboy and Indian movies which comprised about ninety-five percent of the movies I saw until I was fourteen.

I digress to tell a few of our childhood adventures in our local theater, which was called "Our Theater." Friday and Saturday night was our time for the 'moving pictures,' as they were called. There may have been a few chick flicks during the week, but Friday and Saturday were reserved for Cowboys and Indians. The cost of the movie was ten cents, one thin dime. A group of us would go in together. If we thought it would be crowded, we would stack our coats in a pile and put a hat on top to make people think there was an extra person in our row so they would not interrupt us. The seats in the movie theater where soft and covered with fabric, not plastic or leather. One of our favorite pastimes was to quietly sneak out a big fart, so we would not be heard, and then in a few seconds later we would bounce up and down on the seat to spread the smell. That never failed to elicit some crude remarks from the people around us. Needless to say, adults did not often frequent the theater during cowboy and Indian time at the theater.

Back to work; although bagging potatoes was my first job, as soon as I was strong enough I took on more chores. Many of my chores around the store were rather simple as one might expect; a daily sweeping of the floors, dusting shelves, stacking or stocking shelves with canned goods. There were virtually no glass containers of food, nor any such thing as a plastic jar full of nuts. There were also no such things as freezer foods. We had a small 'produce' display rack, and it was my job to artfully display produce once I was old enough to bring it out of the walk-in refrigerator. At the end of the day I picked up the remains and put them back in the walk-in refrigerator. That was a daily chore six days a week.

The store had a front door and a backdoor and there were screens that barely functioned to keep out insects. You could imagine what happened to the store in the summertime since there was no such thing as air-conditioning in those days. We would accumulate quite a number of flies, a few bees, and numerous other insects. After-hours it was my job to position the electric spray bottle on the top of a ten foot ladder and spray the entire store.

That was a very onerous job, so I frequently went next door to Chamberlin's drugs owned by my best buddy's father and we would read comic books which were in those days sold in drugstores, and sneak cokes, or even ice cream. The drugstore sold pills, prescription drugs, alcohol, comic books, ice cream, and was home of the soda fountain. Oh! By the way it also functioned as our local inter-city bus stop. It also had three booths where the local thugs, Dick and I and our friends, would hang out while drinking soda drinks from the fountain or eating ice cream.

An interesting observation on the times and my age; I had

no concept of alcoholism. Only later did I learn that both my father and Dick's father were alcoholics. I would think that being next door shopkeepers would endear them to one another. However the opposite is true. They had a speaking acquaintance only, and had nothing to do with one another as far as I knew the entire time that Dick and I were best buddies in high school. Not just downtown neighbors but in fact we were back-to-back neighbors where we lived.

Another almost weekly chore was washing the windows. There were two very large windows which ran from a small bench at about two to three feet up off the floor, to the ceiling which was about fourteen feet high. This required that I clear the bench of last week's special, return it to the shelves and wash the inside and outside of the windows with a long handled brush and ammonia water and then squeegee it dry. After which I had to set up the next special. I soon learned the special was not a special price, it was a special in the light of the fact we needed to get rid of this stuff. My father usually determined what was special and I got to decide how to set up a display. One day he said, " You pick out the special." Was I ever excited! Another moment for self-expression and control. I chose baked beans and toilet paper. It did evoke the hoped-for response from the local patrons.

My father was somewhat entrepreneurial and would try various and sundry methods to sell products. One of these adventures was to purchase a large, perhaps four foot high, wooden barrel of sauerkraut. It had a wooden lid on it and inside we placed a fairly large cup with a long handle. We would sell sauerkraut by the bulk in wax cartons. And I must say it was quite good. The habit of most of us employees was to walk by the sauerkraut barrel, lift up the lid and with our bare fingers take a pinch of sauerkraut. In such small quantities I found it to be quite tolerable. Otherwise I can hardly stand to eat sauerkraut. It must have taken us three weeks to get rid of that sauerkraut. Just think of an open barrel of almost raw, minimally processed cabbage. The only inhibition to the varmints and flies was a wooden lid.

Today that grocery store would be closed in about three hours. But that kind of activity and sales went on throughout the whole village of Berrien Springs. Another such venture was a similar size barrel of very large dill pickles. In those days I wasn't fond of dill pickles but today I can see that could be a real winner. The only bad deal that I remember my father indulging in was to purchase large cardboard boxes full of cookies, Fig Newtons with flavored icing on them. They were awful and we had eight gezillon of them. I'm sure by the end we were giving them away just to get them out of the store.

Another tale my father told me about and I'm sure it happened, but it was before I could remember. Stover's market bought a barrel of pickled pork chops. I guess my father thought that was a good deal because he simply bought his own large barrel of pickled pork chops. And that started the war. I'm not sure the starting price of these pork chops but it was probably less than 25 cents a pound. As the story goes, once they realized there was a competitive sale going on, they started dropping the price.

We had in our town, as I'm sure is present in every small town, certain peculiar people. One of our peculiar people was 'Deafy' King. Guess why? 'Deafy' was obviously deaf and could not speak but he was very bright. He would routinely make the tour of all the grocery stores in downtown Berrien Springs and report what the various prices or sales were in the various stores. So as near as I could tell, he single-handedly fired up the sale of pickled pork chops in the village of Berrien Springs. He would come into our store, grab my dad, point to Stover's and write down ten cents. Whereupon my father would post a sign on our pork chop barrel; nine cents a pound. It would not be very long until 'Deafy' returned and wrote out eight cents. And so the battle continued until both Stover's and Andy's were giving away pork chops. That was the end of the pork chop war.

Another chore I did at the grocery store was unload all kinds of delivery trucks. There were no such things as fifty-three foot long semi trucks in the 40s. Most of our trucks were single frame four-wheel trucks. Of course the deliveries came to the rear of the store which faced a dirt alley. The first door off the street was Chamberlin's drugs, my buddy's father's drugstore. We were number two. The next store to the west of us, stuck out about twenty feet further than ours. That made a big problem for even the short semi-trucks that brought goods to the other stores along the alley. That's because the alley only had one entrance which was on the east end. I spent not an in-significant amount of time helping these short semi's back into the alley around our store. Helping these big trucks in and out of the alley, for a twelve or thirteen-year-old kid, was a real hoot. It was a real trip. It gave me a sense of being or belonging to the community. I was a real help. I had worth and that was very important for a kid who had little affirmation from mother or father or grandparents.

Unloading trucks for the most part was just sheer labor, hard work. But I did it and I loved it. Dollies, or trucks, were unusable in our alley because of the dirt composition and many pot holes and mud puddles. The trucker would bring the boxes and cartons to the rear of the truck and put them on the tailgate; they had to be carried inside. I simply lifted as many as I could and carried them into the store. Of course I knew where everything belonged, because that was my job. I remember the first time I encountered a wheeled ramp. I thought to myself, "What will they think of next." You simply placed the box on the upper end of the ramp, and gravity carried it all away to the other end of the ramp, where I would be waiting to place it on a dolly and move it around inside the store. Was that great or what?

Stocking the shelves sounds like a drag. And for the most part it was. As I wander through a grocery store today. I marvel at the variety of goods at one's fingertips. In the olden days we might have three brands of green peas, two types of corn, cream or whole kernel, one type of asparagus, one type of carrots and so on. I think all of my grandchildren have seen the type of shelving I have built into our storage rooms in our home. Our store shelves were of the same design except that we did not have plywood in those days; the shelving was solid wood one by eight, side-by-side. The shelves were painted white and the uprights were, of course painted red i.e. Andy's Red and White grocery. When we put food on the shelf, it would be a whole case of twenty-four containers at a time. There was no room in the back of the store for part lots of canned goods or jars of food.

So Ma, my mother, who frequently worked at the store as soon as my sister was old enough to take care of herself, would say to me, " I need a case of peas and whole kernel corn." So I would go to the back of the store, find the case of each, carry each out, and put it on the shelf. I would then 'knock the box down' and added to the stack of collapsed cardboard boxes in the rear of the store.

Even in those days we were conservation minded. But for different reasons. There was a war on, 'you know.' So all during World War II, 1941 to 1945, we re-cycled cardboard, newspaper, tin cans and collected fat or grease in containers for the 'manufacture of munitions,' whatever that meant. Since we operated a meat market, the US government designated us to collect fat, grease, cooking oils and anything else that could be remotely conceived of as contributing to the 'manufacture of munitions.' The fat and grease sat around in various types of containers until it was collected once a week. Boy! Did that stuff stink. But we all could be proud because we were contributing to the 'war effort.' Today, it is inconceivable to me that this present generation could experience the feeling of patriotism that I experienced growing up.

The shelves were approximately fourteen inches high, which allowed for most cans to be stacked two high. The shelves reached a height of about five feet, and then on the top shelf were placed very light items, such as breakfast cereal and other breakfast foods. Many of the brands that you see in the store today, were present in those days, and a great many of those put Battle Creek on the map. Toilet paper and paper towels were available a roll at time, no handling of six or twelve rolls at a time. We had wax paper, but no foil (war effort) and paper bags. There was no such thing as a sandwich bag, a quart bag, freezer bag nor the plastic carry out bags from the grocery store. All these had yet to be invented. We carried our lunches in a tin lunchbox, or a paper bag.

6

Andy's Red and White Market

Except for my athletic endeavors, I spent almost all my spare time working in the grocery store. At the time I viewed it as a task or a chore. I did not realize the benefits I would ultimately derive from having been placed in such a position of responsibility at my age from eleven to seventeen. Occasionally my father and my mother would become ill for a day or two and I was basically left in charge of running the store. At the time it didn't seem like a big deal but as I mentioned my age at that time, it really was. When I returned from my graduation trip to California in June of 1948 and learned my father had sold the store, I was very upset. Working in our store had become a way of life for me and I felt somewhat lost and very sad not to be able to go back to work in the store.

Cheese was a department by itself. We bought cheese in bulk in the form of a fairly large wheel. The wheel was about a foot and a half across and between four and six inches thick. We kept this wheel on a round wooden plate. It was covered with a large lid that was transparent so that everyone could see it. Cheese lovers would come in and ask about the wheel of cheese. Many of them would wait to buy cheese until there was a layer of mold on the cheese.

That's right! Plain old-fashioned green mold. They asked to sample the cheese and if the mold had been there long enough and was strong enough they would buy a slice of moldy cheese. We were well known for our moldy cheese and people would come into the store just to buy the moldy cheese. What you think would happen today if you walked into the butcher shop and ask to see their moldy cheese?

What did we keep in the walk-in cooler? Everything, when you consider in those days there was no such thing as air-conditioning. Stores like ours had refrigeration for the meat display case and the walk-in cooler. That was it. Freezers? What were those? Everything that had to be refrigerated was kept in the walk-in cooler. At the front of this cooler were three glass double walled doors where we kept certain foods on display: milk, which was pasteurized but not homogenized, coffee cream, (not half-and-half) and whip cream were all in one compartment.

Next to them were such things as butter which was packaged in one pound units, cottage cheese in large crocks that had to be weighed and put into waxed containers, a few bricks of various types of cheese which could be sliced, eggs, small rings of baloney and all of the loaves of sandwich meat. People didn't ask for this or that, they just came around the meat display case, opened the door, took out what they wanted and put it in a basket, usually their own. We did not have carts.

70

Inside this walk-in cooler we kept the extra milk in quart bottles, butter, eggs and cheese. The other two walls were layers of meat hooks. At some time or other you may have heard someone referred to "putting your meat hooks into" something. That is where we hung the carcasses of the animals which supplied our meat.

Our meat supply consisted of a hind and front quarter of a cow, sometimes extra pieces of desirable meat such as steak, and chuck roast, parts of a calf which was called veal, at least one half a pig and parts of a lamb. Lamb had to be distinguished as young versus old which was called mutton. Young lamb had a very distinct and pleasant flavor. Old lamb, mutton, had a very strong and sometimes undesirable flavor. People knew the difference and would make sure they were buying young lamb and not mutton.

Before and after the war, we had access to processed meat. That means we would buy from a packing house where quality control was reasonable. But during the war, travel was severely curtailed because of the gas rationing. Food stamps along with meat rationing was in effect so we would resort to local farmers and/or slaughterhouses to buy some of our meat. Such was Merle 'Scummy' Castner.

I remember going out the 'Scummy's' farm and watched him butcher pigs. If I described what happened you probably would vomit. You may want to skip the next line or two. These pigs were not delicate. They ran from one hundred to two hundred pounds each. 'Scummy' would sometimes hit the pig on the top of the head with a large hammer or mallet to knock him out. He would then put a large meat hook in the region of the Achilles tendon in a hind leg. The other end of the meat hook would be attached by a chain, which would then pull the pig up with a large overhead pulley.

At this point the pig would not be dead but stunned, so at some time in this process it would start squealing. If you've ever heard the expression 'squealing like a stuck pig,' this is where it came from. Once the pig was safely impaled, he was hoisted to an overhead position where the head of pig was about knee level. I often wondered why 'Scummy' wore knee high boots and a leather apron. I was about to find out.

He then took a very long sharp knife and stuck it in the front of the pig's neck. The blood shot out like it was coming out of a faucet onto the concrete floor and down the drain. The drain ran the blood to the outside of the building into a 'pig trough.' And yes, the pigs outside the slaughterhouse, ate the blood as it flavored other parts of the undesirable portion of the butchered pig. "Do you really like pork chops and pork sausage?"

But that was part of growing up in my era. Fortunately, 'Scummy' would dress out the pigs, and that was a good thing. Dressing out a pig is a real bloody, slimy, messy job. Pigskin is just like it sounds, tougher than nails. It takes an extremely sharp knife to cut through the pigskin. And then the fat, which is very slick, must be cut away from the skin. The skin itself is sold and used in manufacturing. The fat is cooked, or pro-cessed, and then packaged and sold to us as lard. In the olden days, many people used this pig fat for cooking purposes without any processing at all. My dad was curious and so one time we tried to process our own pig fat. Fortunately, he got cured with one batch and we never tried it again. We sent it off to be processed by a proper company. But we used lard for cooking and still use it in the finest of pie crusts. If you don't believe me ask your mother or your grandmother.

On the outside of the back of the walk-in cooler was a two by six board, about seven feet high, and sticking out about three feet. It had adjustable meat hooks for hanging animals. Sometimes we would buy a whole calf and hang it from the meat hook and George Stover or Maynard Teed would skin it. I really wanted to learn how to skin a calf, but a hole in a skin diminished its value. We could make money from the calfskin, but if it had a hole in it, it was worth a whole lot less. So my dad never let me 'skin a calf.' On occasion a hunter would ask to use our store to dress out a deer. I did get to skin out or at least partially skin out a couple of deer; that was fun.

In the olden days in which I grew up, there was always sawdust on the floor of the meat market. I always wondered why because it didn't look good, it didn't smell good and it was occasionally slippery. But there was a good reason why there was sawdust on the floor of a meat market. Can you guess why? To soak up the blood from animals that were being skinned, from fresh meat that was being cut and from scrapings from the butcher block that got away from the scraper or the scraping brush. Sawdust in a butcher shop was a necessity.

So here is the routine for the butcher. "Hi, Andy! What you got for steak today?"

"I've got some fresh round, some well aged porterhouse and T-bone. What would you like?"

" Let me see the round."

" Okay."

My dad would go into the walk-in cooler, pick up a big leg of beef, carry it out and put it on the butcher block.

"How's that look?"

"Kind of fat isn't it?"

" I'll trim it for you. How thick do you want it?"

"Three quarters of an inch."

My dad would then pick up the large steak knife and skillfully cut off three quarters of an inch of the round steak down to the bone, pick up the saw and complete the cut. He put the steak on a piece of wax paper, weighed it on the scale, figured the price and told him how much. If he agreed, Dad would wrap the meat in butcher paper, mark it with a pencil and hand it over the counter. Sounds kind of antiquated, doesn't it? That was life in Berrien Springs during the Great War and for several years thereafter.

One of my very favorite jobs was making hamburger and sausage. Today, as I go through the grocery store and meat market and look at the labels on some of the hamburger and sausage, I have to laugh; seventy percent lean, thirty percent fat or eighty percent lean and twenty percent fat. How do those people know that? I used to make hamburger and I had no idea of the percentage of lean or fat in the hamburger. I don't believe the people today have any better idea of the percentage fat and lean than I did seventy years ago. My dad would say, "It's time to make hamburger." So I would start my search. When one of the butchers, my dad, Maynard and occasionally me would cut the meat for steak or roast or any other special cut, we would always trim the piece.

When we were done, the trimmings never got thrown out; they were saved in a waxed container and stuck in the walk-in cooler. So we always had scraps of beef. I would gather them all together, pile them up on the workbench and try to assess what I had; how much fat, how much lean.

We always kept a quarter of a beef in the walk-in that was second rate. It was an old cow, probably tougher than nails and we used it for special circumstances. I would find a portion of that quarter of beef and cut off enough lean meat to make the hamburger look reasonable. I would then set up the meat grinder and run all of the meat through. When I was done I would look at it and decide if I could add more fat or needed to add more lean which I would do. Then I ran the whole batch through the grinder again and when finished, placed the hamburger in a serving tray and put it in the meat display case. I was pretty careful about the way I did it because I didn't like some old lady coming into the store and saying to me as I stood behind the counter, " Young man, that hamburger looks very fat!" I took pride in my work and I wanted everybody to think that the hamburger looked good, so I worked hard to try and make it look good.

A couple of points to put this meat cutting business in proper perspective are as follows; I never wore gloves, nor did anyone else in the meat cutting business in the olden days. We would occasionally wash our hands with soap and water, but we didn't have any running hot water in the store. That made hand washing unpleasant. As I said, we did occasionally wash our hands, but more often than not we would wipe them off on one of our butcher rags. It didn't add to the cleanliness of the meat handling but at least it striped some of the grease off our hands so we were less likely to drop a piece of meat.

You might be tempted to ask at this point what happened if you dropped a whole steak on the floor in the sawdust. I cringe even as I think about my answer today. However in those days and at that time I felt no compunction about picking up the piece of meat, walking to the back of the store and washing off the sawdust and anything else that might have been picked up by the meat. I would then wipe off the piece of meat with another butcher rag and return it to where it had fallen. I would like to reiterate, to the best of my knowledge nobody ever died or even got sick after having eaten piece of meat from our store.

I spoke also of making sausage. Generally the same process was followed. I would take pork scraps, assess the relative amount of fat vs lean and try to reach a balance from a piece of pig hanging in the walk-in cooler. In addition to grinding, re-assessing and re-grinding I was able to add seasoning to the sausage, to my taste. Again, as I'm dictating I must have realized the power that I felt when my father told me to go make hamburger or sausage, trusting me to do it the right way. I never did mention, even to my father, that I would occasionally add pork to the hamburger or beef to the sausage. After all, it was going to the same place, who cares.

Chicken every Sunday. That's the name of a book or play or something. But that was real life in Berrien Springs. We had fried chicken every Sunday as long as I could remember. And it was my favorite. My part was the drumstick. So I had a drumstick, mashed potatoes, chicken gravy, frequently noodles and usually canned green peas. Keep in mind there was no such thing as frozen vegetables. So everything came out of cans or out of the garden. They were called Victory gardens during the war and every household had one.

Occasionally, in the summer, we would have fresh peas, corn, lima beans and rarely, fortunately, green beans. As I recall broccoli had not been invented yet, but we occasionally had cauliflower. Creamed onions were a delicacy to yet have been discovered by my wife. Dessert was frequently brownies or cake, and in season, apple pie. My favorite dessert growing up was Huckleberry pie.

What is Huckleberry pie? Huckleberries are wild, uncultured blueberries. They're very small, very tart and very hard to pick. Each summer my mother would can twelve quarts of huckleberries each one ending up in a most delectable Huckleberry pie. Other things that were frequently canned were strawberry and raspberry jam, grape jelly, apples for pie, peaches, pears and occasionally apricots. Keep in mind the following; there was no such thing as frozen anything, and women did not work in factories, they stayed home and cooked. My mother, Jeanetta, kept the house clean and the food pantry full of home made goodies. She belonged to the Home Extension Group and learned a lot of tricks for being a good homemaker.

My grandpa Keefer had a favorite trick he would pull when he killed chickens. Even after he moved off the farm, to 808 McAllister in Benton Harbor, he still maintained a small garden and a chicken coop. So when it came time to butcher chickens he would go out to the chicken coop, reach into a nest where one of the old biddies was trying to hatch an egg, grab her by the feet and drag her outside. He would then swing that chicken in a circle six or eight times, until it got dizzy. With his left hand he would flop the chicken down on a block of wood and almost simultaneously swing the ax down on the chicken's neck. This obviously would decapitate the chicken. He would then throw the chicken up in the air with blood spurting in every direction and watch it come back to the ground and run around in a totally crazy pattern. The chicken would run until she ran out of blood and then collapse. It only took one such experience to realize from whence came the phrase, 'running around like a chicken with its head cut off.' I witnessed this numerous times and can assure you this was a totally weird experience.

Every Saturday we had chickens for sale at our grocery store. I don't remember how much my father paid for them but they were supplied by the local farmers. They had to be spring chickens, not layers. I'm sure you've all heard of the phrase 'she's no spring chicken.' That refers to the fact that spring chickens are much better eating than old, fat laying hens.

Here is the sequence of events at Andy's Red and White Grocery and Market on Saturday morning. Old George Stover was the master of chickens. The farmers delivered chickens outside the back door early Saturday morning. When the weather was decent, George would take a large metal barrel out back, reach in the chicken cage, grab a chicken by the head, twist the head backwards, cut the throat and throw the chicken into the barrel where it would flop around until it bled out and died.

In the meantime in the back of the store, he would have a barrel three quarters full of boiling water. When all the chickens were dead, George would grab one by the feet, cut off the head and dip it into the boiling water and then strip the feathers off the bird. It smelled very bad. The bloody, stinking chicken feathers were all placed in another barrel. When they had all been plucked the next phase was entered; they were drawn. Do you have any idea what drawing a chicken entails?

If so, bear with me. if not, try to follow along. George would take a boning knife and stick it in the chicken's rear end, just under the tail bud make a slit. He would then reach inside the bird and pull out all of the guts. You may think it's revolting to read about it, but you ought to really have been there with George and experienced it. That was absolutely the worst smell I've ever experienced in my life. So now when you go to the store to buy a dressed chicken be grateful that you don't have to go through the experience of drawing a chicken yourself. We've come a long way baby.

How did we sell those chickens? Not cut up. You bought the whole chicken or nothing. In the summertime, when migrants came out of the South to pick fruit, we learned that they would boil chicken feet for soup. So we would cut the feet off the chicken, package and sell them separately for about a nickel a pound; Africans dearly loved them.

Allow me to try and describe the physical appearance of Andy's Red and White Grocery and Market in 1941. The height of the ceiling was at least fourteen feet with the ceiling made of hammered tin which was so common in those days. There were three large ceiling lights and fans in the front two-thirds of the store and one in the back. The front of the store was made up of two very large glass plates. They weren't windows, just two very heavy pieces of plate glass separated by a vertical steel pole. They were framed in by a wooden frame.

The front door was set at a forty-five degree angle to the glass and its recessed piece was part of a door frame to an upstairs apartment. On the East side of the store, the wall was recessed to allow for the stairway upstairs. Along this wall were displayed bags of flour, sugar and some other large items. That wall recessed around the door to the basement and from there to the back of the store That wall was covered with wooden shelves, each being high enough to allow two cans of stacked fruit or vegetables. The picture regarding this story tells a lot about what that store looked like. To the West of the entry door was a shelf about a foot and a half high that ran across the bottom of the front windows. It was on that shelf that I would make the display of the week. On the West side wall was positioned our vegetable/fruit rack. This was a rack about three feet in depth, probably ten feet long and tilted at a thirty degree angle. So with that we could display the various vegetables and fruit. It was situated as though it were the top of a table. Under this table, in orange crates, we would display fruit and the pecks of potatoes.

Apples were packed differently in those days and this is important because empty apple and grape crates became boxes for my grocery deliveries. These wooden boxes were constructed of wooden end pieces approximately four inches high and a foot-long, and were connected by a single thin 18 inch long board on each side. When filled with Apples they were packed with paper or pressed cardboard with a wooden lid. The lid could be removed and disposed of but the boxes were quite sturdy, therefore they became our grocery delivery boxes.

Other citrus fruit came similarly packed. Non-citrus fruit, which was grown around Berrien Springs was displayed sparingly because there was so much local fruit that local people had their own special orchard from which they picked or purchased their own fruit.

Beyond the fruit display began shelves that were approximately two feet deep and sixteen inches high, supported in the back by a piece of one by two nailed to the wall, and in the front by two by two uprights outside the shelving. There was nothing glamorous about the shelves, they were strictly functional. The shelves were painted white and the upright boards were red: Andy's Red and White store.

On the top shelf were stacked lighter objects because they could be stacked higher, mostly cereals: Wheaties, Rice Krispies, Shredded Wheat, Oatmeal, Malto-Meal, Cream of Wheat and Kix. Is there nothing new? I walked around the grocery store today specifically to try and remember some of the soap products from 1941. Here are a few that I remember: Duz, Rinso, Chipso, Lux, Ivory Flakes, and Fels Naphtha. It is interesting that I have not seen one of these in many years.

Shortening or spreads were interesting. Of course we had butter and oleomargarine. And that was the exact word that we used, oleomargarine. It came in rectangular packages just like we buy today. However it was white like lard. It was contained within a clear plastic or waxed bag. In one corner would be a small capsule of yellow or orange coloring.

Since oleomargarine was not refrigerated it was soft and one could squeeze the bag to mix the coloring throughout. For people who use oleomargarine that was important because it told them, it wasn't lard. It was oleomargarine.

We also had lard in fifty pound buckets. Lard is congealed and processed pig fat. Doesn't that sound just scrumptious? We would sell the lard from the fifty pound buckets by scooping it out with a wooden paddle, putting it into a waxed tray, covering it with wax paper and selling in bulk. Lard was commonly used as shortening for cooking and 'greasing the skillet.' We had vegetable oil or cooking oil, but it was expensive. Thus many people used lard for cooking.

In the village of Berrien Springs in 1941, we had several grocery and markets: Ed Botham and his Royal Blue Market,

Schroeder's Grocery and the A&P store, none of which, had meat markets. Stover's Grocery and Market and Andy's Red and White Grocery and Market had meat markets. They were all in business and apparently all earned a living. It wasn't until several years after the end of the Great War that Kenny Sill came home from the war with some newfangled ideas and decided to start a supermarket.

It was called Schroeder's Supermarket and it put everybody else out of business. Fortunately for my father he sold his store in June, 1948, while I was traveling out west with Dick Chamberlin. So he didn't lose his shirt; he got out while the getting was good. Unfortunately, he decided to go out on his own and sell insulation. I say unfortunately because it was asbestos insulation and you all know about asbestos. That failing, he went to work for West Michigan Electric selling appliances and did very well.

I didn't fare quite so well. I had lost my job at the store but I managed to get hired on as a 'gump' for Dan I. Porter Concrete Construction Company. That sounds like a really big deal. It was and it wasn't. Dan was elderly, probably in his late 50s or early 60s and supervised only. His main job was keeping the barstools well polished at the local VFW. His son Royal was the real deal. The other employee was Dick Van Dyke, who married Dan's daughter. She was several years older than I and in grade school I had a constant crush on her. It was only years later that I learned that Dick Van Dyke was a spousal abuser, and he had abused a girl I was madly in love with when I was in grade school.

But Royal and Dick were the real worker bees and excellent carpenter; we built houses. Concrete was just a sideline. Dan had two other sons. Les who did full-time concrete work and Bob who never did work for his father.

Let me set the picture for my job as a 'sub concrete contractor.' We, I mean Dan, would contract to build a house. Once he had surveyed the lot, he would lay out the lines for the footings. We needed to dig ditches, sight the elevations and pour the concrete. In those days there was no such thing as a backhoe. Footings were just ditches with dirt for the bottom and sides. Stakes were set for elevations, and the cement was poured in the ditches. Dan would call Consumers Concrete, not really! Consumer's Concrete was not even a figment in somebody's imagination at that time; we poured our own cement.

I would position the concrete mixer which was called a 'half bagger,' fill the gas tank, pull the ripcord and off we would go. Putt, putt, putt. Sand was piled on one side and bags of mortar were stacked on the other. My weapon of choice and of necessity was a spade.

If you've ever looked at a deck of cards and wondered where the term spade came from, it came from the tool used to 'charge' a cement mixer. The spade had a very long handle which was needed to put sand and mortar into the hopper; fifteen shovels of sand, five shovels of mortar. Next I add -ed water from a bucket or a hose until I deemed the mixture to be proper. When ready, I turned the crank on the hopper barrel down and poured the concrete into a wheelbarrow. Finally I wheeled the concrete to the designated site and dumped it. It would be either too wet, too dry or okay, 'Lightning' which was their favorite nickname for me on the job. Guess why?

Mixing mortar for cement blocks was very similar except that we use mortar mix instead of concrete. The sand had to be much finer and the final product had to be much drier. Mixing concrete and mortar and delivering it to the worksite was preferable to digging the ditches for the footings; that was the worst.

However, I was more than amply rewarded for my labors. When my dad paid me for grocery work, I got thirty-five cents an hour. When I stepped up to do hard labor with Dan, my salary went up to eighty-five cents an hour. One day early on in my servitude, Dan picked me up to go to work and started the conversation with. "I understand you're going to college."

I replied, "I certainly am."

" Well, I have an engineering problem for you to solve."

And I thought. "At last I am being rewarded for my intellectual achievements." He then said, "Remember that footing ditch you dug yesterday?"

I certainly did because it was in clay and the hardest ground I'd ever shoveled. " Well," he said, " I want you to figure out how to move that ditch three feet to the south."

I guess you could call that a kind of wry sense of humor that I did not appreciate. But in those days I was lucky to have a job, so I re-dug the ditch.

Working for Dan had some good, long-term effects. I lost nineteen pounds and ended up at hundred and sixty pounds of pure tiger meat. When we unloaded bags of cement, eighty-six pounds each, I would carry one on each hip. Occasionally, I would show off by carrying three bags. Although it certainly toughened up my muscles, I think it was probably very bad for my back. Readers beware; avoid foolishness when lifting. The results may not be obvious at the moment but carry a possible long term detrimental affect.

Running a wheelbarrow full of sloppy cement up and down a two by ten contributed to my balance, which has served me well long term. All of that shoveling of cement and sand similarly contributed to my muscle bulk, but I'm sure had a long-term ill affect on my back. As I look back over my life and consider how much enjoyment I received from building things, I have to feel that my experience with that construction job played a large part of my appreciation for the building trades and orthopedics; it spurred my interest in both.

An interesting sideline to this job was the fact that cement powder sticks to sweaty skin like glue. Thus it serves as a very fine sandpaper. If you rub a portion of skin covered by this cement powder you will end up with a nasty sore that really hurts. I found this out the hard way. After a long day of work in the hot sun, I had shed my shirt. I had lost a significant amount of weight and my pants had to be held up by a belt. The belt slipped up over the top of my pants. With my repetitive bending, the belt rubbed on my back which was covered with powdered cement. I developed a sore on my back the size of my fist; it was as sore as a boil and lasted a week.

I needed to wash the cement off my skin but soap and water wasn't working. I consulted my boss who said, "Oh, didn't I tell you? You have to wash the cement off with vinegar."

"Okay," I said. Whereupon I found my mother's vinegar jug, soaked a rag with it and wiped off my back. Do you happen to know the active ingredient in vinegar? It is acid, acetic acid. At this point in my life my knowledge of chemistry was zero in spite of the fact that I intended to become a chemical engineer. I had not yet connected all the dots. But by the time I had stopped screaming and my eyes had stopped watering, I had a fair grasp of the situation. I knew what had to be done.

Heretofore, our house had one bathroom with one bathtub. That was pretty much standard fare for the average household, especially in Berrien Springs in 1948. Showers inside a home were very uncommon. There were a few showers at the beach in the bathhouse but aside from that I didn't know anyone who had a shower in his home. I explained my situation to my father who was quite understanding. He knew a plumber who rigged a shower in the basement right next to the washtubs. Overhead the plumber hung a ring about two feet across to which we attached a sheet that served as our shower curtain. On the floor, I fashioned a small cement curb allowing the water from such containment to run into the floor drain. I had just invented the first home shower in Berrien Springs. I don't really know if that was true but it makes for a good story. Thereafter upon arriving home from my cement job, I went to the basement with a bottle of vinegar, rubbed down my entire body with a vinegar swab, stepped into my brand-new shower and soaped off all the vinegar and cement. Life was good.

7

My Jobs at the Store

Another one of my regular chores was that of 'egg boy.' Most of our eggs were purchased from a supplier and came in 'egg crates.' Like everything else these were made of wood. The two ends and middle piece were three quarter inch cheap wood, thin slats for sides and a little thicker slats for the bottom. There was a removable top which was also wood. The eggs were separated by formed cardboard similar to the containers seen at Aldi's grocery store today. In each side of the egg crate there were six layers of three dozen eggs each.

As in egg sales today, we had choices of large, medium and small with a fourth category called pullet eggs. These eggs came from chickens that were called either pullet or bantam hens and were much smaller than standard eggs. Berrien Springs was in the middle of an agricultural county; a lot of our people had their own farms or truck gardens as they were called during the war. No matter what their major agricultural product was, most of them had a variety of farm animals; a couple of cows for milk and some for beef. A few would have sheep and goats and almost everybody had a large garden and a chicken coop. Since most farmers had a bunch of kids, they needed their own milk and egg supply. When the kids grew up and got married the parents still had the chicken coop and a bunch of chickens: Rhode Island Reds, Barred Plymouth Rocks and Leghorn chickens were the most common. Those chickens supplied me with a lot of feathers with which I tied flies to catch trout and salmon.

As the need for eggs diminished the chickens had become pets. Then the farmer finally realized he could sell the eggs as fresh farm eggs. But cars, travel and roadside stands had not come into being. So what was a poor farmer to do with a whole bunch of eggs? Sell them to Andy's or any other store that was dumb enough to buy them. I say that because buying eggs from a farmer was a crapshoot.

We had no idea how long those eggs had been sitting around without refrigeration. A non-refrigerated egg from a barnyard is usually fertilized and a chicken starts to grow in the egg. If our customers bought eggs from us and tried frying them only to find a partly grown chicken in one of the eggs, they found another grocery store.

The eggs would come to us in all sorts of containers; some of them were cracked, dirty and frequently covered with chicken poop. Those eggs became my problem. I had to wash and sort them for size and color. Finally, I would have to candle each egg. The candling process was rudimentary. The candling machine was a simple cardboard box with a light bulb on the inside and a fifty-cent piece size hole in the top. I simply turned on the light, carefully placed an egg on the hole and viewed the contents of the egg. A fresh egg would appear as a homogeneous mass and therefore edible and salable. Frequently I would see something other than a homogeneous mass such as a dark spot or some other abnormality. Those eggs usually ended up in a carton that went home so my mother could break each one and take a closer look. Our home egg supply consisted of my castaway eggs. The partially developed chickens in those eggs were usually edible for the most part, so we scrambled them. After all it was no worse than my grandfather's favorite breakfast; scrambled eggs and scrambled brains.

Color was also a problem because, unlike today, brown eggs were considered inferior. Today a smart marketer gets brown eggs and touts them as being superior in quality. If you doubt me go to Mejier's and look for specially priced eggs; there you will find brown eggs are no different than white eggs. An incidental note, eggs are sterile therefore highly edible. They are an excellent media for the growth of various bacteria and perhaps viruses as is evidenced by their use in clinical laboratories. You would think they would be highly susceptible to contamination. That in fact is not true; they are highly resistant to infection, therefore are a very safe, edible commodity.

Bacteria and viruses that might infect the eggs usually kill the chickens; that stops egg production. It's highly unlikely for anyone to get sick from rotten eggs. Rotten eggs are usually rotten because they are secondarily infected. Again I say, eggs are a very safe food provided they have been reasonably refrigerated. Even being cracked, if the lining is intact, that egg is not contaminated. Enough for your biology lesson for today; I had 30 hours of zoology in college.

Delivery boy was my highest calling at Andy's Grocery and Market. We had two telephones in our store. They were private lines, not party lines like many people in Berrien Springs had to live with, especially country folk. If you lived in the country, you would find out the telephone company ran one line along your road for, let's say two miles, and everybody in that two-mile stretch, who had a phone, had a common line. Each customer had distinct ring: one long, two shorts or two longs, one short. When you heard your ring, you, picked up the phone and talked to whoever was on the other end. You hoped that no one else on that line picked up her phone also, because they would hear everything that you heard; that was a party line. Secrets in Berrien Springs were rare! Everybody knew everybody else's business. There were no such things as smutty calls, porn calls, or harassment calls, because everybody recognized everybody else's voice.

One of the favorite kid tricks in the olden days was to make a phone call to the drugstore and ask, "Do you have Lydia Pinkham in the bottle? "

" Yes, we do. "

" Well, let her out! "

The other trick was to call the grocery store and ask, " Do you have Prince Albert in the can? Well, let him out! " Prince Albert was a pipe tobacco . As I am writing about the telephone era of the 1940s, I just realized that with emails, texting, tweeting, and Facebook that today everybody is doing the same thing but is proud of it.

We, at Andy's Grocery and Market, would receive a phone call from an infirmed person, who would relay a grocery/meat order to be delivered. Whoever answered the phone, would write the order on a small order pad with a pencil. Ballpoint pens had not been invented. For pens, we used ink out of a bottle. One would put the point of the pen into the bottle, lift the stylus on the shaft of the pen that sucks ink into the pen; replace the stylus and you are ready to write. In those days, writing with an ink pen was an art and a distinct hazard, so much so that we did not use them in the grocery store; to be inked was really bad news.

The items ordered, except for meat, would be collected and put in a grape box. We frequently put a cardboard or paper liner in the bottom of the box to keep small things from falling through the cracks in the boards. After the order was filled the amount of the bill was tabulated on an old-fashioned adding machine which had a crank handle. The customers name would be written on the slip and placed in the bottom of the delivery box. After the order was filled the box was set in a row along the base of the shelves so that I could read the name and plan my delivery route for the morning or afternoon.

It was my job as the delivery boy to figure out the most efficient route, who would pay cash, figure out how much I had to carry as change and then load the boxes accordingly. During the school year, I arranged my classes so I would have a study hour in the morning and in the afternoon, during which time I ran the deliveries. Most days the job was easy with only a few stops. But in bad weather the number of deliveries increased considerably. Remember, many people did not have cars and walked to the grocery store regularly. With inclement weather my job increased significantly. On Saturdays and holidays I would have as many as thirty stops. On those days the girls were very busy, and I filled my own orders.

I really had to get to know the people on my route. I learned the name they wanted me to call them, what door to come in, where to put the groceries, heard about some of their family and cleaned my feet always. Because some of them were confined to wheelchairs or just couldn't get around, I had to put the groceries away. Then I gave them the bill, collected the money, and wished them good morning, good afternoon, and Merry Christmas, etc. and say you're welcome, because people used to thank me profusely. On slow days I would take time to speak with the people, most of whom were elderly or in-firmed. I would be the only person they saw all day or even all week, especially in the winter time. Days and nights were very long for those who could not get out of their home. With no relatives in town, no neighbors who could or would call on them and only a radio and books to keep them company, I was more than welcome in most of these homes.

My means of transportation was the Red 1939 Chevrolet panel truck with four on the floor: a clutch, a brake, an accelerator and a starter pedal. The side mirrors were fixed. If you wanted to change them you had to get out and move them. The rear windows were so small that the inside mirror showed you only the inside of the back of the truck. There were two seats in the front of the truck and nothing behind these seats. So when I loaded up a bunch of buddies to go sledding or other activities, they would sit on the floor. Occasionally we put some benches on either side of the back of the truck. I hauled a lot of kids around in those days without incident and without safety belts.

The bumpers were spring steel and were fixed to the frame by two rods front and back. That left a gap between the frame of the truck and the bumper. I was always scared to death that I would slip getting in or out of the rear of the truck and my leg would fall inside the bumper; I might fall over and break my leg. I had friends who had done just that. The thought of that happening, gave me 'willies' as I was climbing into bed at night.

My 'Delivery Boy Job' is why I had to learn to drive at age fourteen which was a double-edged sword. It meant a lot of work but it also meant that I got to drive the delivery truck; not only for making deliveries but also as my personal runabout vehicle. What a big deal for a fourteen-year-old boy. I was the envy of every kid in school, except for the country boys, all of whom had been driving vehicles since they were ten. For them driving was no big deal. As a matter of fact, every fourteen-year-old kid that I knew had a driver's license. The big deal was, we had two vehicles: a car and a panel truck.

In that time and in that era, the rule was one car per family. Even though every kid age fourteen had a driver's license, there was not necessarily a car available to drive. It was wartime; gas was rationed, there were no such things as new tires so nobody drove anywhere that was unnecessary. By the end of World War II, we were all driving on a bald or retread tires. My first winter of driving the delivery truck, no tread at all. I had to carefully plan my trips, so that I would not have to go uphill from a dead stop, because I knew I could not drive uphill from a dead stop. Driving on snow-covered streets was a real hazard, but we had no choice. There was one snowplow in the village of Berrien Springs; we were always driving on snow covered streets.

Driving a truck like that today would present a real challenge but in those days we were just grateful to have wheels of any kind. There was usually one tail light on the drivers side, no turn signals, no backup lights and one dim brake light. If you were driving and wanted to make a left turn, you cranked the window down by hand and stuck your left arm straight out. If you wanted to turn right, you stuck your arm out , bent your elbow and hand up. That was a right turn. Sudden braking was a real hazard because the brake light was not very bright There were no head rests on the seats so if you got whacked from behind, you had an automatic whiplash injury. Head-ons were usually better for the driver because the steering wheel kept him from flying through the windshield. The right front passenger frequently did just that, fly into or through the windshield which was usually fatal.

Driving the truck presented numerous opportunities and several challenges. With a stick shift and rear wheel drive, one could do wheelies on snow, gravel, wet payment or even dry pavement. However the biggest challenge in the days of the

Great War was driving on bald tires. There were no such things as new tires; retreads were common but after two or three times, there was no tire left to retread. So we all learned to drive quite carefully: no potholes, no ruts, no fooling around. When driving in snow, I never parked without appraising the height of the ground, so I would start out going on the level or downhill.

Back to the store; sweeping the floors in the store is simply to note that we had wooden floors like so many people are putting into their homes today. Except, when these floors were put in, one hundred years ago or longer, there was probably only a poor finish applied to the wood, which was usually oak: plentiful, cheap and sturdy. By the time it became my turn to sweep the floors they were all dark brown from years of hard usage and no care. We simply spread a slightly oily compound on the floor and then swept with push brooms. This prevented dust from rising which would have covered everything in the store.

Running the cash register was an awesome task for a twelve year-old boy; so I didn't get to do that until I was thirteen. The cash register was a large mechanical device with a pull down handle which sprung the door open, revealing the interior. The front trays had sloping fronts and held coins up to half and silver dollars. The second row had compartments into which were fitted bills; one dollar, two dollar, five, ten and twenty dollar slots. Each had a spring wire device to hold the bills down. There was one last slot for any larger bills, which I never saw. There was an additional slot for checks. Most people paid by cash, but a few of the middle class and up had money in the bank on which they could write checks. There was no such thing as debit accounts, debit cards or credit cards. Most people paid by cash or check.

There were a few of our faithful customers who would run a credit line at our store. The information for each person was maintained on a large table. It was a mechanical device, which held all of the accounts of the various customers. All entries were manual: pencil or pen. There was no electronic system of keeping books on the accounts. Needless to say it was tedious and onerous but many people did not carry cash or even have cash except on pay day. We knew when everybody's payday would be due and most people would come in on or after payday and settle their credit account. This sounds very antiquated, and it was. It was also tedious and time-consuming, but necessary; as I mentioned, a lot of people simply did not have cash to pay bills on the spot.

I need to talk about the butcher shop; the place I first picked up a knife. When my dad bought Andy's Grocery and Market, he was strictly a grocery man. He had no concept of butchering. So we hired and paid a butcher. The first one was old George Stover, a very kindly old gentleman who lived just around the corner behind the store. So for him getting to the store was just a short shuffle. I never saw him walk rapidly; his was always a steady shuffle. He started out doing all sorts of butcher work, but slowed down so much that he had to be retired to cleaning chickens. He was replaced in turn by a gentleman by the name of Maynard Teed. Maynard had a heavy hand and had to be rebuked frequently. But he was a good butcher and taught my father and me the butcher trade

Let me describe for you the appearance of our butcher shop. It was located at the back of our grocery store. In the center was a small display case with sliding doors in the back, a pair on each side. In the middle between the sliding doors was located our one and only meat scale. A divider wall sat behind this counter covering a quarter of the width of the room on each side. Between these two half walls were located the butcher block on one side and the slicing machine on the other. About 3 feet back behind this area was a walk-in cooler, not freezer but cooler.

The butcher block was a very heavy chunk of wood. It was composed of slabs of hardwood approximately two inches thick and about three feet long. These were glued together and bolted to make a square top three feet by three feet. The wood was probably eighteen inches thick and was supported by four very stout legs. It was virtually immovable and it had to be because a lot of hard, heavy work was carried out on its surface.

When it was new, the butcher block was flat. As the meat was being cut on the block, scraps of meat stuck to the top. So this top would have to be scraped off with a metal plate stuck into a flat wooden handle. Obviously you would scrape up small fragments of meat and the plate would have a gummy, fatty surface which needed be cleaned. The method for cleaning the scraper was simply to wipe it on the edge of a cardboard box. At the end of the day the butcher block was thoroughly cleaned, and I used the term thoroughly cleaned loosely, with a very heavy-duty wire brush. This required two hands on the block and would be brushed off in two directions and then wiped off with a clean cloth. We processed food on that block so we couldn't use soapy water on it, just plain water. So when I say clean it's all a matter of relativity, less contaminated than other parts of the store.

What were the tools used on the butcher block? First of all there was a meat saw. It was like an overgrown hacksaw. It was probably three feet in length and had a large gap between the blade and the shank. It was stored by hanging it from a hook, which was overhead of the meat block. The other items used on the meat block were a series of knives, some of which were as small as a paring knife, others as large as a 'butcher knife,' that being about sixteen inches long and two ½ inches wide. You can imagine it was a formidable weapon.

Other knives would be skinning knives, which had a curved arc cutting blade; these were used for actually cutting the hide or skin off animals and had to be extremely sharp. There were also boning knives which had a very narrow blade. These were used to cut the meat off larger bones. The purpose of these knives was to obtain meat that was to be used in hamburger or sausage. There were usually several mid-sized butcher knives. But the most formidable weapon in the meat department was the cleaver. The meat cleaver was mostly used to chop bony meat. Sometimes it would be used to soften meat, that is to precondition it to softness before cooking. We also had what looked like a square headed hammer about two by two on a wooden handle. The head of this hammer had grooves cut into it so that when you pounded a piece of meat, it would indent small areas of the meat. The use of this device was to tenderize meat. Some patrons would ask us to routinely pound their meat before we weighed it and packaged it.

Another interesting device was a cubing machine. This machine consisted of two rollers with teeth which opposed one another almost coming in contact. The teeth were offset from one row to another. The purpose of the entire machine was to take a fairly flat piece of meat, put it in the slot at the top, and run the meat between the two rollers, which were turned by a crank handle. The result of this process would be basically to partially cut the fibers of meat to make them tender. The result was called cube steak. This process was basically reserved for poor grades of meat which ordinarily would be very tough. The cubing process tenderized the meat to make it really chewable and edible. Many people claimed it added flavor but if it did so, it's only because the teeth had accumulated a lot of meat which had gone south, and which in turn could impart a certain flavor to the meat, 'Au rotten.' We cubed both beef and pork.

I alluded to the slicing machine which is a very necessary part of every butcher shop. We had many types of processed meat in the forms of loaves just like grandma's loaves of homemade bread all of which were suitable for sandwich meat. The same types of loaves with the same types of seasoning are still available in the butcher shop today. But we bought the meat in chunks or loaves and had to slice it according to the patron's desire,"How thick do you want it?"Most patrons knew the number of the thickness they desired and would tell us. I do that even today, " Cut that on twenty."

The names of the meats were quite interesting: pickle and pimento loaf, homemade loaf, olive loaf, bologna, barbecue loaf and several others. There were a few kinds of cheeses but we never had any prepackaged cheese or sandwich meat. It was always bulk. The machine itself was quite simple. It was a circular very sharp blade with no teeth, on a motor; it had guards and guides. There was a handle by which we could set the depth of the cut.The slicer was almost my whole domain; I was the sandwich king. We had never heard of Quality Control. Clean was always a relative term and sterile was an unknown word. It's amazing that none of us died from 'ptomaine poisoning.'

8

Adventures on Lemon Creek

I have been at this for two weeks and have lost my train of thought; I'll try to pick it up. We were on the edge of the stream. My dad baited the hook with crawler. The hook was large and attached to a spinner. He tossed the bait into the stream and let the current take it downstream. My dad carefully pulled line out from the automatic reel and fed it down stream. He let me hang onto the crooked bamboo fly rod as the line was traveling downstream. I felt something pull the line and make the pole twitch.

My dad told me I had a bite and to 'set the hook.' I had no idea what setting the hook was all about. He said, "Jerk the rod."

I got the picture. So we pulled the line in and re-baited the hook.Then we did it all over again. I felt something funny on the rod so I jerked. I had a fish on. My father pulled the line in hand over hand, as one must do with a fly rod. Lo and behold there was a fish on the end of my line. I was now a fisherman at the age of four. It was of little consequence that it was a chub, inedible, but it was a fish and I had just caught the first of a million fish that I was destined to catch in the ensuing eighty years. I was ecstatic and my daddy was proud of me. That's all that mattered!

Event number two. Fast forward eleven years; the same Lemon Creek. My dad had made the acquaintance of one Al Brett, formerly of Chicago. I remember well because he talked funny. I was to learn later that all people from Chicago talked funny; it was like a foreign language. I didn't know what a foreign was, it was just different. My dad said that it was okay that I talk to him. Besides, they had a very interesting car. Al called it an Oldsmobile hydromatic. All of us had to learn to drive a stick shift or four on the floor. Today that is some sort of sports car. In 1941 four on the floor was all we had. There were a few newer cars that had a small shift lever on the steering column. This Olds had one of those funny shift levers and the Bretts talked about driving all the way from Chicago over to Berrien Springs without having to shift. Incredible! What would they think of next? That was the first automatic shift car that I had ever seen. And that model was the first one sold in the USA, Olds Hydromantic.

The Brett's had a cottage on a nice bend on Lemon Creek. I thought it might be fun to fish for trout there and they agreed that I could do that. So one day in the middle of summer I drove my dad's delivery truck out to the Brett's summer cottage. It was a hot summer day but cloudy. I had borrowed one of my dad's crooked fly rods. Come to think about it, all he owned were crooked fly rods because we used them for every kind of fishing that we did. My dad did not understand about split bamboo fly rods or how to care for them. So I hauled the rod out of the closet where he kept all his fishing gear. I then took out his one and only tackle box. In those days all tackle boxes were metal. We had no such thing as plastic. And they were all heavy and rusted. I rummaged around until I found an automatic reel that worked, a few hooks and sinkers and of course some spinners. I didn't get worms at home because that meant I would have to shovel a lot of dirt. I knew that Al kept a pile of leaves at the end of his garage and that is where I would find worms. Yes, indeed, a wet pile of leaves was worm heaven. So I grabbed a tin can and went on my merry way.

The Brett's had a spacious parking area around the garage and there I parked. I announced my arrival and asked permission to fish. Permission granted with a couple of cookies added. I proceeded to the leaf pile next to the garage, peeled back wet leaves, a few at a time and gathered a bunch of red worms. I have always wondered if red worms were baby crawlers or professional red worms. These were not leaf worms even though I got them from under the leaves. Professional leaf worms are smaller, redder and are found in very wet circumstances, like piles of apple pumice.

What is apple pumice? In the old days when people made cider, they would squeeze the snot out of the apple. The left over skins, seed and pulp, would be discarded in a pile but not into the garbage cans. There weren't many people with garbage cans. Most city folk had garbage cans of sorts and once in a while we would take the garbage to the city dump. If you had a lot of money you could pay to have someone pick up the garbage but mostly we took care of it ourselves. In the country you just dug a hole and threw the garbage in. The trick was to remember where you last buried the garbage so next time you wouldn't 'dig up old garbage.' And that is the source of that old saying, 'digging up someone else's garbage.'

Apple pumice was a treasure. You cared for it well. It was carefully piled away from all buildings and not buried. It was left to ripen a little and then came the worms, leaf or red worms. We called them 'pummey worms.' They were okay, but small, very active and quite fragile; one bite from a fish — gone. It took a lot of them to catch a mess of fish. Needless to say it took a strong constitution to gather pummey worms. That warm summer day I settled for the professional midget crawlers, red worms.

So I walked up along the stream because my dad had taught me to always fish downstream with a worm and spinner. No wonder he didn't catch many trout. When I had trudged up stream far enough, I carefully made my way to the edge of the stream. We didn't have waders in those 'good old days,' only hip boots and my father wasn't about to let me use his one and only pair in Lemon Creek and risk a snag and tear. So I had to fish from shore. The technique for this type of fishing down-stream is as much an art as fishing upstream which is a better way to catch trout.

What's the difference, you might ask? Well, I'm glad you asked because I really want to explain. The more you know about your quarry, the more likely you are to succeed in catching or killing him. Fish live in the water so they must gain oxygen through a different mechanism than we do. We extract oxygen by our lungs, from the air that is eighty percent nitrogen and twenty percent oxygen with a trace of other gases and chemicals. Fish extract oxygen from water that is H20; two parts hydrogen and one part oxygen. To do that, they have gills that act a lot like our lungs to extract the oxygen from the water. To do this, fish take water into their mouths, allow it to flow through the gills and out under the gill cover, the operculum. The operculum controls the flow of water through the gills. The purpose is to speed up or slow the flow of water to allow more or less extraction of oxygen from the water, and that depending upon the temperature of the water and the relative oxygen saturation.

All of this is to say the trout must face upstream almost all of the time. They can swim down stream for short periods but the faster the stream, the more often they must stop and turn around to face the current to renew their oxygen supply. This can be observed in Steelhead or Atlantic salmon returning to the sea after spawning.

Realizing trout are always facing upstream to 'breath,' what else do I need to know to be a successful trout fisherman? More than I can tell in one book.

Trout don't have ears; they have a lateral line which is a pressure sensing mechanism running the full length of the fish's body. This can be observed in some fish as a different colored line, usually darker, along the side of the fish, half way between the back and the belly. This functions as the ears for the fish. However the pressure they perceive through this line is infinitely more sensitive than our hearing. A blind fish can avoid predators and find prey therefore stay alive using his lateral line.

Seeing is actually the fish's best defense and offense. Their visual acuity is almost beyond belief. They are very sensitive to light and dark and their sense of color is better defined than ours. They have monocular vision which means each eye sees independently and has an arc of 180 degrees. Because of the shape of their head, they have almost no blind spot; just a small area above and behind the head. Smell or olfactory perception is even more acute than their eyesight or 'hearing.' If I am above the fish, especially when in the stream, it is very tough to fool the fish. He can smell my feet (boots), see my moving arm and feel my leg motion because the current is bringing everything, including food, to him. Why would he face downstream? He wouldn't and doesn't.

Thus coming up from below increases my chance to fool him. He has a blind spot, smell is being carried away form him and the current dampens the pressure or noise I make as I move upstream. At night I have caught trout literally at the top of my boots. Why would I ever fish for trout downstream? Because my dad told me that this was the way to do it. Only after fishing with Doug Wendzel did I gain most of this knowledge.

The technique for fishing for trout in those days was quite simple. I stood on the shore or concave edge of the stream where sound or vibration is less likely to be transmitted to the fish. I needed to put the worm on the other side of the stream where the current was stronger and the creek deeper. That is where the fish live, usually in the deepest holes and runs, in a small creek. It is to be noted that where they live and where they feed may be different places. The trout's first instinct is self-preservation, like every one of us. On bright, sunny days deep and dark is where they will be found . In order to catch them, you must get the bait to them. It's not like a pizza parlor that acts like a magnet to teens. It's more like delivering a pizza to the wrong house; they may or may not eat the thing. The operative word is delivery; in the delivery comes appeal.

Why do fish bite at all? The usual assumption is they are hungry and you have just presented to them a T-bone steak, or as Robert Traver is want to say, "a pork chop." But what if they aren't hungry? Will they still bite? The answer is yes, but the reason is beyond our understanding. Perhaps they are angry with the intruder and want to teach it a lesson; their only weapon is their mouth, so they bite it. Bang! It bites back and they are hooked. The other thought that is plausible is that the spinner is bright and shinny and attracts them. They come up to take a look, spy the worm and bite it to eat. H. C.—'who cares.' It catches fish.

The next step is to move as close to the water's edge as possible, pull out and coil at your feet a reasonable amount of line. With an amount of line equal to the length of the rod, swing the spinner and bait across the creek so that they land near the other shore. Allow the current to pull it downstream into the hole or the run.

Here comes the art of downstream fishing. When using a spinner, one can feel the gentle pulsation of the spinner. Of course the line must be kept tight. The rod is held in the right hand and the line in the left. With the line held tightly, the rod tip is lifted gently up, a couple of feet of line is released by the left hand, the rod tip dropped slowly and then lifted again a few inches; always feeling for the throb of the spinner. This drops the spinner and worm downstream. The rod tip may be moved upstream and back several inches either way, giving the fish the impression that there is an idiot on the other end of the line.

This reminds me of the saying, "a fishing pole is a stick with a worm on either end," or "a fishing pole is a stick with a worm on one end and a fool on the other." Either is quite appropriate.

After having let out sufficient line and having no bites, one is not surprised. In spite of the lack of success, one is compelled to do something. He can repeat the same exercise, which is considered to be futile or move a little downstream. I suppose he could move upstream, but I consider that to be more ludicrous than what I am about to tell you. Do not repeat the same maneuver in the same place. If a trout doesn't wop the bait the first time through, move on. At this point I must digress from this somewhat enlightened treatise on down stream fishing in general.

There are some very good reasons for and methods of fishing downstream. For example, Steelhead, Atlantic Salmon and, may their name be cursed, Black Bass. Small mouth bass are not quite so bad as large mouth bass. In fact, small mouth bass are good fighters and a very good sport fish not to mention that they are quite savory.

On the other hand, large mouth bass are fairly good fighters, but very easily caught; evidence the number of sport fishing shows hosted by 'red necks' saying, "Golly, this a good'un. Yes, sir, this is a real fish." Only to witness him pulling in a twelve inch long large mouth bass with the apologetic comment, "He sure was a fighter!"

My recommended method of treating a large mouth bass is to hit it quite a few times with a stiff object, such as a hammer, leave it out in the sun while you continue to fish. Upon returning to shore inquire of your wife as to her favorite rose bush and proceed to partially uproot it in order to plant the bass under it: they make wonderful fertilizer.

Small mouth bass are frequently found in rivers that lead to my comment that down stream fishing for them is reasonable and fun. I would love to digress a bit and talk about fishing for steelhead and Atlantic Salmon, but those subjects are deserving of a separate treatise.

Back to the story of fishing for trout in Lemon Creek at Al Brett's cottage on a warm summer's day. I had patiently and methodically moved down stream, fishing as I have above described and had a number of bites from what I considered to be small fish. This was borne out by netting several chubs and no trout. The sky began to darken and in the distance I thought I heard some overhead jets.

But remember, in the 1940s the only jets in the air were German and they were experimental. Had they been in production and if Werner VonBraun had invented the V-2 rockets a few years earlier, the Germans might have won the war. Or at the very least, our victory would have cost us many more casualties. If not, it would have cost us a lot more casualties to ultimately win. As it was we won, we stole Werner VonBraun and Grandma's uncle, Richard Cook, went to work for him at the Huntsville Space Center as the number two man on campus: just so you kids can be proud of your ancestors.

It turned out this noise was nothing other than an old fashioned summer thunder storm. I quickly worked my way down stream so that I was very near Brett's garage and lean-to shed. I checked my bait to make sure that I had a bodacious amount of leaf worms on the hook, heaving it out to the opposite shore, which at that point was a deep hole. Immediately there was a huge thunderclap, followed shortly by a bright lightening strike.

I moved almost as fast as that lightening. Now, if my memory does not fail me, light and lightning travel at the rate of ninety-six millions miles per second. I was a little slower but adequate in my quest for cover, the shed. This hasty retreat was motivated by my knowledge that sound travels at the rate of one thousand eighty feet per second. When you see the lightning and start counting, one thousand one, one thousand two and so on, by the time you reach five, you know that the lightning struck one mile away. On that day I didn't ever start counting when the thunder pealed all around me. Nuff said? I skedaddled to the shed, dropped my crooked bamboo rod with the load of worms at the end and left the bait at the bottom of the hole on the opposite side of the creek.

A few minutes after the rain had started, it stopped abruptly.

I considered myself very fortunate to be alive and dry. I commenced to idle over to the stream side when I noticed that my rod had changed positioned. My pace quickened. I knew that although the rain had been hard, it was not strong enough to move my rod. There could be only one reason, a fish!

This is a short digression to further educate you all in the fine art of angling with a worm. This must not be taken lightly since this bit of knowledge could one day save you from starvation. Trout are always hungry. They do not always eat or feed but they are always willing to consider the opportunity to eat. A rainstorm provides that opportunity.

After the usual hard rain, worms can be found in abundance in the stream. Where did they come from? As I already mentioned they might be considered to have come from the sky during the rain. I have mentioned that our 'Newfie' cleaning lady would buy that story but the explanation is much simpler and very plausible.

Remember that I also said that the rain floods the worm holes and the worms need air, so up they come and they move around looking for dryer soil. Once they have pulled up stakes and have no tail in the hole to anchor them, they are at the mercy of prevailing circumstances, that being little rivulets of water flowing downhill. Downhill in nature is frequently a trout stream.

After an unusually hard rain millions of worms are washed into the stream. The fish don't actually know about rain and its effect on the worm population since they haven't read this treatise. But they know a good deal when they encounter it. Thousands of worms flowing downstream, helpless to defend themselves against marauding schools of hungry trout. I hate to disclose all of my trade secrets but I feel that I don't have enough time left to tell each grandson, individually so here it goes.

In a situation like this, the trout go bonkers! Trout are super cautious and stay out of sight and even under cover about ninety five percent of their lives. In this situation, they throw caution to the winds. They move out from their cover into the center of the stream. Realize the stream is now dirty and the trout cannot be seen from above. Their sense of smell, olfactory perception, is dulled by the speed of the current and all of the debre that is flowing downstream. Besides they are very hungry. They sit in the middle of the stream and snarf up any thing that remotely looks like food, especially worms.

They become gluttons. They don't just eat until they are full, they continue to gorge themselves to the point where they can't actually put any more in their stomachs. I have caught trout that are so full, that as I grasped the fish to unhook him, I have actually squeezed several worms out of his stomach.

This whole scenario is so well known to ardent wormers that they will do virtually anything to 'catch the rise.' To miss the rise is to fail their calling as ardent wormers.

When I first started fishing with Doug Wendzel, he told me of hearing a thunderstorm in the middle of the night and awakening with a severe need to go the bathroom. I thought he was talking about the phenomenon common to all old people; running water gives us the urge to micturate (pee). But he explained otherwise. He was a very wise wormer and I learned most of what I know today about worming from Doug. A thunderstorm meant that 'the rise' was eminent. After he would empty his bladder, he would grab a can of worms from the refrigerator, jump into his International Harvester Scout, and head for his favorite stream, no matter the time of night. He always kept his worm gear in the truck so he was mister 'Ever Ready' at the drop of a hat, or rain as it were.

To miss the rise and arrive at the stream when the stream was near its peak was to fail. The trout feed so ravenously that within an hour or two of the onset of the gully-washer they are done feeding and in fact, they may not feed again for several days. So you see the importance of recognizing 'the rise.'

I must further digress to acknowledge there is another 'rise;' this rise is known to fly fishermen. During this time, trout are rising to the surface of the water to engulf insects that are in or on the water as a result of a 'hatch.' Since the discussion of the fly hatch is so much different from the rise heralding a worm feeding frenzy, a lengthy discussion must be postponed to a more opportune occasion.

Lest even I lose track of the reason for the somewhat erudite discussion, I shall return to the scene of action that stimulated my brain to recall all of this; back to Al Brett's house. After the storm, I returned to my old bent bamboo rod. It was jerking madly in a downstream direction. There was only one conclusion to be reached; I had hooked a fish! Rather, a fish had hooked himself. Regardless, I had a fish at the end of my line. I grabbed the rod and lifted the tip. There was no slack line so I did not have to set the hook; it was already set. With a fly rod, the cork grip of the rod is grasped with the right hand, or the left if you are left handed. I hope that you are not left handed because this makes for a lot of extra work with a crank reel. You have to take the reel apart, reverse the chrome line guides of the reel and install a left handed clicker mechanism. As I said, it's a lot of work and right now it is unnecessary because I just remembered that I didn't even use the reel to catch the fish.

I simply hauled the line in with my left hand, catching each loop with the index finger of my right hand until I had the fish at one-rod length of line away. I had no net and even if I had I would not have known how to use it. So I very unceremoniously lifted the fish out of the water and dropped him onto the driveway. It was a fourteen inch brook trout. That was and still is the biggest brook trout I have ever caught in the state of Michigan. I ran screaming into the Brett's house where they duly oohed and awed over my fish but I realize now that Al didn't know a trout from a porcupine. Nonetheless I was overjoyed, excited and ebullient. My father even congratulated me and we promptly cooked and ate the fish. No catch and release for me; it was fillet and release.

I have finished the brief reminiscences of fishing on Lemon Creek. I have alluded to the village of Berrien Springs, but I have shared none of my childhood memories about the Village itself. I will tell you that next.

9

Watermelons

The setting was old Berrien Springs. It was very late summer or perhaps early September; it had had to be 1945. The watermelons were ripe and we all knew it: Big Dick Chamberlain, Little Dick Wilson, Les Spaulding, Jim Huss, and his step brother, Little Dale Sunday, Ralph Locke, Eugene (Skinny) Lawrence, Chuck Reinbold and his half-brother Jim, and me; all "townies." The farm kids would never have needed to pull off such a stunt as this. They all had their own watermelon patches. But in those days none of us had gardens and it was watermelon season; we all liked watermelon.

I was fourteen and had my drivers' license so that I could drive the delivery truck for Andy's Red and White Store. In exchange for that chore, I was allowed relatively free access to the 1939 fire engine red panel Ford truck. Oh, I should note, in big white letters on the side of this red truck was ' Andy's Grocery and Market.' That was of no concern to us because our activities were going to be centered outside the city limits of Berrien Springs, where there were no streetlights and our activity was planned for after dark.

Some of the information that I am now supplying may have been available to me at the moment of that dark hour, but only later did I really fully understand some of the circumstances of the existence of this particular 'cult.' The House of David and its nearby neighbor, Mary's City of David, were both part of the cult called, 'The House of David.'   At that time, all I knew was that they had a farm adjacent to the town. On the farm they had all sorts of animals: horses, cows, sheep, goats and chickens. I know they had a few orchards where they grew fruit, common to the area: apples, pears, plums, cherries, strawberries, raspberries, peaches and grapes. Almost all of those fruits would be available to any and all of us, since our mothers would buy them in bulk and can them for the winter. But no one canned watermelon so we had no in-house supply.

The inhabitants of the House of David were a little bit different. They did not cut their hair nor shave their beards. They all wore bib overalls. I don't think any of them smoked or chewed tobacco, but they smelled bad enough to make us wonder. They were peculiar looking as you might imagine from what I've said. We had them pretty well pegged as weird. They seldom came into town and I don't ever recall seeing any of them in my father's store, but I heard a number of stories from my grandpa Keefer, and his neighbor, Henry Shippy, better known as the Whistler. He whistled so loudly, that I could hear him whistling all day long an acre away from my grandfather's house.

Later in life, I became curious about the House of David and so did some research. That is when I learned they were a cult somewhat similar to the old fashion Shakers: the shaker men and women lived in separate buildings. The House of David went one step further and they lived on separate farms. Needless to say, their sex lives were really screwed up. I know they had children, and I do know how that happens, but I can't explain it in terms of their living arrangements. I can only surmise there was a great mixture of heterosexual and homosexual activity in that communal living. However, at that point in my life I was a whole lot more interested in the sweet tasting watermelon than I was in knowing about weirdo's and their screwed up theology.

The local headquarters for the House of David was Benton Harbor. They had built an amusement park which had a number of interesting displays, activities and sideshows that would draw customers. But for me the big draw was the miniature locomotive or steam engine on which you could take a ride through and around the entire park. It was a huge thrill for a little kid. They made the best ice cream in the whole world. They had a baseball team that played in the semi pro leagues around our area. I knew little about baseball and cared less, but my grandfather was greatly impressed with the first baseman for the house of David team. He claims that guy could play big league if he would give up the house of David. All I could think of was his long beard getting in the way of fielding a low, hot grounder.

The plans for our adventure were hastily devised. Although, most of us could drive, and had drivers' licenses, my family was the only one to have a spare vehicle. We planned to meet at a location to which we could all walk. That would be the local high school building. It was a dark, there would be nobody around and everyone lived within six blocks. Now that's my definition of a small town. We met and devised our strategy. There were two accesses to the House of David farm: the Baroda Road and the Bridgeman Road. We were all eager to participate in this 'grand theft.' As we talked about it and how we were going to do, Skinny got cold feet and started whining. I quickly relinquished my job as the vehicle driver of the getaway car to Skinny.

Skinny was a year older than I and had a drivers' license, at least that is what he told me. He was given explicit instructions; drive the vehicle slowly past the farm, then speed up so that you could turn around quickly and drive back the other way. Give us 10 minutes head start, because we knew the watermelon patch was between the farm house and the Bridgeman Road.. We needed to sneak our way into the patch, thunk out the melons, until we each found one that was ripe, pick it and sneak out. We had all visited the house of David farm and knew its general layout.

There was a low early evening glow emitting very little light. Our mission could not help but be successful given our stealth, wise planning and those dumb farmers. Skinny drove carefully to the West End of Ferry Street, and noted no traffic on any of the streets that led us to Baroda Road. It's hard for anyone this day and age to imagine such a deserted area that time of night. Gas rationing was still present; there had not been a new car on the street for four years. Everybody's tires were worn bald including my red truck and so who would be out at ten o'clock at night. Right! Nobody.

We drove past the farm carefully observing all things and noted no lights, no activity. Skinny drove past the farm, turned around and drove us back slowly. When opposite the farm, Skinny stopped. We all got out and carefully did not slam the door. Skinny moved back toward Ferry Street, and we climbed over the ditch and made our way into the melon patch. We had no flashlights but we could see silhouettes in the evening glow. We could see cornstalks in the distance and get a hint of the farm to the east of us. We were sneaking around; all separated looking for our own melon. I found mine and carefully thunked it. Whoopee! It was dull and that meant dead ripe. I picked it up and started for the road.

Through the chaos of the next moment, I have a mind's eye picture that will stay with me until I die. As I was making my own hasty retreat from the watermelon patch I glanced to my left and to my amazement I saw little Dale Sunday. He was three years younger than the rest of us and about five foot two. He was lugging one of the biggest watermelons that I saw that evening, and he was really trucking. Head down, hopping over watermelon plants, running like a scared rabbit; he beat me out of the patch by a country mile and I was no slouch.

The chaos of the moment began with several shotgun blasts, followed by hollering from adults, not kids. These were clearly the farmers who had been alerted and were waiting for this attack. I don't recall how many watermelons we actually got out of the patch but the most important part was all of us escaped unscathed but with the crap scared out of each and every one of us. I don't think we celebrated anything that night. We all went back to the point of embarkment, and debarked. I drove the red panel truck home very quietly vowing to not tell a living soul of this fiasco.

Fortunately my parents were already in bed and so nobody asked me where I'd been or what I'd been doing, so I just quietly went to bed and slept rather fitfully. I may have had a few nightmares, but I lived through them and the next day started out perfectly well. After breakfast I went to work at the store. As I walked in the back door, I saw Skinny standing there with a sheepish look on his face.

My father then accosted me with the fact that he had heard all about our misadventure. I have no idea of the sequence of events except that Skinny ratted us all out. We were caught. We had to make retribution. So I gathered all the guys together and that night we drove out to the house of David farm where we were greeted by some very somber faced old men in bib overalls, long beards and long hair. After we confessed our sins, they asked for retribution; money or labor.

Mind you the year was 1945. A nickel bought a pack of gum and a pack of cigarettes was fifteen cents unless you smoked Marvel's as my grandfather did; they were only thirteen cents. A good grade of hamburger was twenty-one cents a pound. We all had jobs, but we sure didn't earn much. I think my father was paying me thirty-five cents an hour. Anyhow, we reached into our pockets and pooling our resources came up with two dollars and forty-three cents. The farmers grumbled a little amongst themselves then they broke out with the biggest smiles I've ever seen. They got two dollars and forty-three cents for the most fun that they had all summer. They cut open a few of the ripest, most delicious melons I have ever seen or tasted. We all sat around, joked, laughed and ate our fill. Those old weirdos weren't so bad after all.

As I commence this next tale, I have serious doubts about my own IQ and my memory. It was probably a year later on a Saturday evening. We were all working at the store cleaning up as we needed to do at the end of a busy Saturday. This was one of the few times during the week that we made an effort to clean all the meat cutting tools; both saws, cleavers and all of the knives were actually washed with soapy water. We carefully wiped clean the cutting blade on the slicing machine. I think that would be the only time all week that water would touch any of those blades. But you know what? Nobody died; we were a tougher lot in those days.

A number of my dad's old cronies would stop by late in the evening to greet my father and pass a few words. I'm sure that some of them were invited to the back room where they would share a shot of whiskey with my father. One of the guests that evening was Ally Macomber. My father mentioned Ally spoke highly of his watermelon crop that year; it was the best he had in many years. Incidentally he was going to leave town after he left the store. My father supposed that evening might be an ideal time to inspect Ally Macomber's watermelon patch.

He discussed the matter with Skinny Lawrence as well as me. We reluctantly agreed we might take a run out to Ally's watermelon patch after we closed the store and before we went to my house to have our late-night snack and play cards with my parents.

You might think since you've just read an account of my unsuccessful watermelon cooning efforts, I would be on high alert. Especially since our proposed caper included Skinny "the rat" Lawrence. Nothing could have been further from my mind than the fateful night a year prior. We drove the now famous red panel truck out to Ally Macomber's farm. Since we were really out in the country we left the car lights on all the way to the patch. We drove up to the end of the two track, turned around and faced the highway. We were parked on the edge of the watermelon patch where it met with a small woods.

We got out of the truck and quietly closed the doors. We were not particularly afraid of anybody being there because this was truly out in the country with no farmhouses remotely close. So we casually sauntered around the watermelon patch searching for large ripe melons. About this time, I began to get a little suspicious. As we searched through the patch, I eased my way toward the edge of the woods. I was in no hurry and was searching for a really good melon when it happened again.

Shotgun blasts, screaming and hollering. This time I realized that it was all a trap. But for a few anxious moments I was not quite sure. So I snuck into the woods and hid. As the noise continued I finally recognized the voices because I'd heard them both earlier that evening; Ally Macomber and Les Glassburn, two of the roughest and toughest characters in all Berrien Springs. And they were friends of my father who put them up to this scheme and was probably laughing his butt off as we were out there sweating in the heat of the night wondering, "What the heck is going on." After I had realized what my father had pulled off, I came out of the woods, readily acknowledge my guilt and took a couple of the melons that the guys offered me. We all had a laugh and parted company.

As I had expected, my father and mother were waiting up with big grins on their faces asking how my evening went. We all laughed and ate steak sandwiches as was our Saturday night custom and played cards. I won.

10

The Cistern

The Cistern Tale was one of the funniest things that I remember while growing up. I'm guessing that I was approximately twelve years of age when we moved into 421 S. Main. This was the fifth house that we lived in during my childhood, all of them in Berrien Springs. The house was big; at least I thought so at that time. It was a two-story square cement block house. The outside of the block was contoured supposedly so it wouldn't look so awful even though it was. About twenty feet from the southwest corner of the house was a circular piece of concrete about three feet across. In the center was a three inch hole that went to nowhere or China. I asked my dad what that piece of concrete was. He said it was a cover to an old 'sister.' I thought she must have really been naughty until I finally understood that he had said cistern not sister. I had no idea what a cistern was, but any answer satisfied me in those days. All I knew was we could walk on it, jump on it and nothing would happen. I found out though, that the concrete was hard and if I fell on it, it hurt.

On a very sunny day a couple of my buds and I were fooling around with firecrackers. Back in those days firecrackers were real and if you held on to one too long it just about blew your fingers off. So we were really careful about what we did with firecrackers. I remember using them to blow up stick bridges, move rocks and occasionally blow up a frog or a toad. That was real fun. And as chance would have it one of the guys said, "What's that?" pointing to the cistern cover. I said all I knew was that it was the cover of an old cistern, like I really knew what was going on.

He asked, "I wonder what would happen if we drop a firecracker down there?"

Of course, I didn't know, so I said, "Let's try it. But suppose there is water down there. The firecracker would get put out and nothing would happen."

Its now time for a little lesson about septic tanks and the like. In the olden days when sewage from a home had to be processed, it was drained into a single holding tank called a cistern. Nowadays in remote areas where water flows out of the toilet and out of the house it goes into a large concrete bunker or septic tank. In some cases there is a pipe connection to a second bunker or septic tank.

If it doesn't go to a second bunker, then the drain-pipe at the top of the septic tank flows out into a drain field which is constructed of a series of pipes that flow from one central point, from the drain pipe, out into the ground. These pipes are loosely connected so that the fluid can leak out between pieces of the tile. Most drain fields are loosely connected tubes of tile or just plain half tiles. The theory behind all this is rather simple. All of the crap that flows out of your house flows into the top of the septic tank and hopefully sinks. There exists in nature multiple types of bacteria, algae, and fungus and other stuff. These bacterial forms work on the solid material to break it down. The drain-pipe out of the septic tank is at the top so theoretically material seeping out is digested by bacteria and is mostly fluid. The fluid then passes into the drain field and moistens the earth.

In locations where there are septic tanks and drain fields, if the use is especially high and if the drain field is in clay or other difficult types of earth, the septic system tends to clog up and has to be pumped out periodically. This whole process is what happens in some areas where there is not city water and sewer. Before this modern-day septic system came to pass and before we had concrete readily available, people would dig their own holes in the dirt and build inside these holes a circular structure made of brick or block. Mortar was used sparingly or not at all. Because these bricks were in a circular fashion they tended to be stable from outside pressure. Once the circular structure was completed, the outside of the hole was packed with dirt or sand, and the hole would be covered, either with a very strong wooden structure or in the case of my house, it was covered with a circular structure of poured cement, with a hole in the middle to allow the escape of gases produced by the process of degradation.

Now keep in mind at age twelve one is not well versed in the process of sewage disposal. All I knew was there was a hole in the top of the concrete and water from rain could seep in and perhaps partially fill this, whatever it was, down there. My dad called it a cistern. So we couldn't simply drop a firecracker down there because the water would snuff out the firecracker. So what would you do in a circumstance like that when you just needed to drop that firecracker down the hole to see what would happen? The obvious solution was a short piece of string, one end of which is tied to the firecracker and the other is tied to the middle of a stick that's just a little bit longer than the hole is wide, say five inches long. We measured the string so it wouldn't be longer than one foot figuring that there couldn't be that much water in the hole. Calculating this whole thing was a hoot; one of us held the cracker and lit it while the other held a stick over the hole. The firecracker was dropped into the hole and we all stood back, not far enough as it turned out to be.

What happened next was beyond our wildest expectation. There was not a simple little crack or pop from a zebra cracker. There was a very loud explosion, following which or almost simultaneous with, the cistern lid flew about five feet into the air, did three or four di-dos and fell back on the hole slightly ajar. Fortunately we were far enough back so we didn't get hurt but our hearing was impaired to the point that we could hardly hear my mother screaming like a banshee, out the back door, "What have you done? There is 'fecal' matter all over the floor around the toilet."

The words she used have been laundered to protect the ears of the young innocent children who will read this. It appears that somebody had forgotten to disconnect the pipe that ran from the old cistern to the new sewer pipe that ran out to the street. The force of the explosion blew material from that pipe back into the house and up through the toilet onto the floor of the bathroom. I say bathroom because, although we were not poor, most homes in those days had only one toilet in the house. That was par for the course in those days. Those days being about 1942. That is how I learned so much about cisterns and septic systems in a very short period of time.

11

Newfoundland, Canada

Early in the year of 1957, I was in my second year of residency training in orthopedic surgery at Blodgett Memorial Hospital, Grand Rapids, Michigan, when I received a letter notifying me that I was going to be drafted into the U.S. Navy. My obligatory military service, had been postponed when I entered into graduate training. I figured that I had escaped the whole mess, so when that letter arrived I was shocked, and especially saddened to learn that I would be going into the Navy. I didn't want to go to sea and be separated from my lovely Sandy and two darling daughters, Beth and Sue. So I made a few inquiries, hot-footed it down to the local Air Force recruiting center to sign up. It worked; I got out of the Navy before I got in and was ordered to my basic training at Gunter Air Force Base, Montgomery, Alabama.

I arrived on July 1, 1959, in my 1953 blue Chevrolet. Montgomery, Alabama, I learned, is just this side of hell. The lecture rooms were air-conditioned, and that was it. I worked up a sweat, at seven o'clock in the morning, walking from the dorm to the dining room, one hundred yards away. The classrooms were the best part of my day. I made a few acquaintances, knowing even then, these would last only four weeks and then we would all be sent all over the world. In that first week, I had one hour on the firing range where I was allowed to shoot a forty-five one time and that was enough for me. I turned to talk to one of my buddies and the instructor grabbed the gun away from me supposing I was going to shoot him and that was the end of my gun training.

We had about two hours of 'Phys Ed' that entire four-week period. I guess they realized that we were doctors not Rangers, so they gave up the gung-ho tactics. In my second week of brainwashing, I was notified I was going to be sent to Ernest Harmon Air Force Base, Newfoundland, Canada. I thought I was a pretty good geography student, but I really had no idea that Newfoundland was an island, or exactly where it was. When I finally found it on a map I was somewhat dismayed, to put it mildly. I was greatly heartened by the fact I could bring my wife and children with me. But, there was a catch. As a commissioned officer, a doctor, my tour of duty was two years. If I wanted my family with me, I would need to extend my tour to the full time required: three years.

Upon visualizing the town of Stephenville, where the base was located, it took me about thirty-seven seconds to realize that my family could not live in that town. We had to be on the base. So I extended to the full tour, and my wife and children got a free airplane ride to the base.

Back in Montgomery, where I was bemoaning my fate, stuck on a rock pile, a million miles from anywhere, a geeky looking nut came up to me and said, "Isn't it great! We're going to Newfoundland." I almost slugged him. I didn't want to be associated with a crazy man like that for two, now three years, on that rock pile. He invited me for a drink at the officers club so we could discuss, 'our future.' At that point, any encouragement at all would be good news. He had two years invested in general surgery training and then like me was drafted. His home was California, he was single and loved to fish. He had spent considerable time fishing the West Coast for Steelhead and Pacific salmon and knew a lot about that type of fishing. When he learned he was going to Newfoundland, he bought Lee Wulff's book on Atlantic Salmon. He shared it with me and I began to see a little light at the end of the tunnel.

Long story short, Carl Nagle, my new friend, flew to Newfoundlandand and I drove. He got there a week before I did and was firmly ensconced in his officers' quarters, complete with more books on Atlantic salmon, fly tying, fly fishing in Newfoundland and a forty ounce bottle of scotch that cost two dollars and fifty cents; that can ease a lot of pain.

My three day drive through the northeastern United States, New Brunswick and Nova Scotia to the ferry in North Sydney was really quite pleasant and very beautiful. It was all in very stark contrast to the Rocky, somewhat barren, coast of Newfoundland. It did not improve as I traveled from the south coast to Stephenville, nor did it in the ensuing two-and-a-half years. It is very rugged country, but also somewhat attractive. Stephenville, Newfoundland was like a small town in a third world country. There was no industry or commerce to be found there except to supply the U. S. Air Force Base.

As I checked in with my hospital commander, Lieutenant Colonel Norm Vivian, I received a warm welcome. I was informed that the base had just completed building a whole series of duplexes, officers accommodations and one half of one of those buildings was mine, brand new. I bought enough new house stuff to survive and moved in. The Air Force Base has to be flat and it surely was. There was a high Hill or Ridge just north of the base and the engineering corps had knocked off the top of the ridge for a width or depth of about two hundred feet with a road down the middle that was about a quarter of a mile long. The backside of the ridge went right directly into the woods, but the front side dropped off to the base and the hospital was directly below our new home. All I had to do was walk up and down a very steep fifty foot hill to go to work.

About three weeks later, Air Canada delivered my wife and daughters practically to my doorstep. Never mind that my pregnant wife had to drag two tired kids, with all their clothing, diapers, bottles, etc., plus all of her clothing. We had some stuff shipped although really we didn't own much at that time in our lives. But we were together again and I was overjoyed. Sandy remained in a state of shock for some period of time, but gradually morphed into the scene.

The accommodations were more than adequate. We had three bedrooms and full bath upstairs, large kitchen and a very large dining room/living room combined and a half bath on the main floor. In the cold but dry basement we had one large open room with a washer and dryer. There were some limitations in the building code. We could not put any nails anywhere in the house. Decorating the house taxed our ingenuity. I eventually divided the basement into one large open area and two rooms. I made the walls with two by fours that I fixed to the trusses by driving wedges between them. The walls were made of cardboard which we had in abundance since everybody who moved brought their belongings in all kinds of cardboard boxes.

Beth was 2½, and Sue was ten months old when they arrived. There were a lot of kids on the ridge and so they had to be bused to and from school every day. Those buses ripped up and down our road and scared the heck out of me. We couldn't let our children out of the house alone. So I defied the building regulations and put a thirty inch high white picket fence around our backyard. I even wore brown shoes in a black shoe society. The whole base was used to physicians who were not professional Air Force. They tolerated a lot of our junk.

In reality, the joke was on me. I tried to put the posts into the ground with a shovel. It took at least one hour for every post hole. I did end up with a very nice picket fence, which protected all three of our daughters from being run over by maniac bus drivers. By the time the fence was built, Sandy had delivered our third daughter, Amy, who was our Newfie baby.

I specified the height of the fence as 30 inches for a purpose. The first winter we were in Newfoundland we had about one hundred inches of snow, which was average for that area. The second year was awful. We had over two hundred inches and where we were positioned, we had wind all the time; all day, every day. That year the blowing snow drifted as hard pack to the top of the fence. So when I went to work, I walked on top of the fence and slogged my way down the hill to the base hospital. The snowplows became ineffective and we had to have large front-end loaders move the snow from the road and from our driveways. They stacked the snow in front of each house so high that we could not see the first floor of the house across the street.

You might be tempted to say how cozy. That was a word I couldn't use, because that year they changed base policy. They now considered Ernest Harmon Air Force Base to be a hardship station and for married people it was no longer a three year term rather a two year commitment. So I got out six months early. "Why was it so hard ?" you might be tempted to ask. Every family on the hill had at least two kids and some had more. You can't just pick up the kids and go visit your friend with two feet of snow everywhere. There were no cell phones and no radio. There were exactly two television stations, both of which were Canadian and they started in the afternoon and closed down at midnight. Library books were at a premium. Seagrams seven Crown and Seagrams V. O. were two dollars and fifty cents for a forty ounce bottle, and if you mixed a highball, the mix was more expensive than the whiskey. There was a lot of drinking, and a lot of unhappy people on the base. If there was any stress in your marriage, it was multiplied 10 times over in those circumstances.

For me it was quite different. I spent a lot of time with our very young children. I frequently fed them, bathed them, played games with them, rocked them and sang with them. We went to the beach in the summer and sliding in the winter.

We had lots of time for reading and did so simply because there was not much else to do. I read Carl's material about Atlantic Salmon fishing and about fly tying. I knew the basics of fly tying, but tying salmon flies was a whole different ballgame. A few of you understand the skill that fly-tying entails and with about six different materials one can master fly tying quite well. The classic salmon fly uses a minimum of a dozen different kinds of material. The Jock Scott salmon fly, requires twenty-six different materials and on my best day, two hours of intense work. Carl and I found a guy on base who could help us learn how to tie the salmon fly. Needless to say we did not have in our possession anything close to that amount and variety of material.

Enter W. Duncan Rowe, MD. Dunc was a native Newfoundlander, who went to England for his training, and returned to his hometown of Corner Brook, Newfoundland, which was only an hour's drive from our base. He was the acting orthopedic consultant for the medical hospital on base and I insisted that I needed his supervision; so he would come down to visit us every few weeks. He supplied Carl and me with unlimited tales of fishing for the mighty salmon in Newfoundland. He introduced us of a wonderful fly tying shop in Corner Brook. We supplied him with a bountiful supply of cheap whiskey from our base, and a few good meals. In turn, he invited all of us up to visit him and his wife Maisie in Corner Brook. The trip was always a delightful occasion.

He was our contact for guides and information the whole

time we were on the base, and after I left. He remained a valuable contact for me for eight successive trips back to fish the River of Ponds with my father.

Our first fishing season was very short and unremarkable. Although both Carl and I were fly fishermen, and had read some about salmon fishing, we really had no idea what we were doing. One of the master sergeants from our hospital had married a Newfoundland woman and knew about salmon fishing. He gave us a little advice and so Carl and I went out one day fishing the Fischell's River. As per the advice given us, we walked quite a ways up river until we ran into a rapids. We fished the runout of the rapids into the river with whatever we had. I had only some trout streamer flies which were totally ineffective. I had no idea what Carl was using. After a couple hours of threshing the water we developed sore arms and shoulders. We got our heads together and realized that were we upstream from any fish warden, so we could try something 'verboten;' a Mepps spinner. The government of Newfoundland had ruled that all artificial lures, except for flies, were illegal. I found out why. About my third cast, I thought I snagged a log. I should've known better on two counts. One, this was a Newfoundland stream and as are all Newfoundland streams, much too fast to harbor logs. Two, it was swimming, I could feel the throbbing at the end of the line. Logs don't throb. So I pulled it in and landed it. Big disappointment! It was small, thin, dark colored and not very active. I was hugely disappointed in Atlantic Salmon fishing.

This was probably the second week in September and, as I

was to learn later, this is rather typical for a late run fish. Early run fish are bright silver, strong swimmers and leaped. What I had caught I would learn to call a "slink." Had I not learned this fact, I may have given up Atlantic Salmon fishing before ever getting started. I was told by the few mentors that I could find on the base, and in the countryside, to expect much better things come spring; the fifth of June. The season closed on September 15th and would remain so until the fifth of June the following year. That gave us eight months to research the area providing local stream fishing for salmon, as well as people and stores to help us in our fly tying efforts.

We had many maps, a few friends on the base and a number of fish wardens since every stream had its own fish warden. Before the snow impaired our travel we went south from the base to every fishable river we could find. We stopped at the town adjacent to the river and inquired as to the presence of the local warden. We spoke to no less than eight fish wardens who were within a two hour drive from our base.

That winter of intense studying brought on a sense of bravado and foolhardiness I did not know existed in me. I must admit that it was greatly enhanced by alcoholic beverages. Seagram's seven Crown, at two-fifty a forty ounce bottle, may have led me to unrealistic expectations. As Carl and I read more and talked with more knowledgeable people, we gained a level of confidence in our ability to slay Atlantic Salmon, in an almost unrealistic fashion. I recall that before the season of 1960 had begun, I had wagered with a number of my compatriots in medicine, that I would catch no less than twenty salmon, twenty inches or longer and even worse, that I would catch six salmon in excess of twenty-six inches. Mind you, all of this was predicated in my state of mind and level of intoxication with no actual experience. The total amount that I had wagered in dollars and booze, would have exceeded one hundred dollars. Can you imagine what a hundred in 1960 currency would have purchased? I shudder to think the impact that Seagram's seven had on me in those ' bad old days.' Lest you worry beyond needs, I caught thirty salmon over twenty inches and eight over twenty-six inches. As I am writing this, and recall the magnitude of the bet, one hundred dollars, I recall that only two years later, I bought a brand new Volkswagen 'bug' in Corner Brook for only seventeen hundred dollars.

My parents visited us on the base in July, 1960. Dr. W. Duncan Rowe suggested that I might take my father way up north to a place called River of Ponds and camp while fishing for Atlantic Salmon. With Dunc's help, I made arrangements to drive my father up to the River of Ponds for a week of fishing, only to learn that our intended guide had just gotten a job and left us flat. I asked around and found an aspiring young fishing guide, Ralph Sampson, nineteen years old and a part-time teacher. He welcomed the opportunity to take care of the young doctor, and 'the old man.' From that point on, every person in the River of Ponds knew about my father, "the old man." My father had a way of kidding people that endeared him to everyone. Not to mention, we always carried a good supply of Canadian whiskey, and a large bottle of Lemon Hart rum, 151 proof. That would provide more attention and help than would money.

Ralph had his boat, or at least the loan of his father's boat, which we quickly loaded and traversed the first small lake. Dad and I walked up the trail to a camp and sat inside while poor Ralph dragged the boat, loaded with camping gear, up through the rapids to the big lake. We crossed the lake to the mouth of the river at which site was located the warden's cabin. We set up our campsite right next to his cabin, and commenced our week of fishing. The warden arrived a few hours later and was very remarkable in a number of ways. He always whistled as he rowed, he pushed with his oars rather than pulling, and was totally unflappable in his demeanor. He warmly greeted us upon his arrival at his cabin, and invited the 'old man' into the cabin to sit on a chair rather than a log: he was overjoyed to have a shot of lemon Hart rum. To say that they bonded would be an understatement. They would drink and talk every evening that the warden was on site. On later trips, when we were camped way up the river, the warden would make it a point to row and walk to our new camp, every time 'the old man' was on the river.

To help you understand the circumstances surrounding our fishing, I would like to point out a couple of factors. I was thirty years old and in the prime of my life. My father was fifty-five and suffering from arthritis of the spine and knees. The rivers where we fished were not sand or gravel. The bottoms of the river were rocks, from fist size to boulder size and they were incredibly slippery. I immediately learned that I could not walk on these rocks without felt-bottom waders, or felt-bottom wading shoes. Even with them, walking on the edge of the bank, I always had a stick. My father could not walk on these rocks alone. Whenever he fished, the guide had to help him out to his fishing spot and retrieve him when he wanted to move or quit. Even with all that help, he managed to fall a couple of times. A fall was always unpleasant in that the water since it rarely got above fifty-two degrees.

Prior to this trip I had fished a couple of local rivers around the base and had a number of good hits and perhaps even landed a fish. I was very disappointed that I had trouble hooking salmon even though I had hits. Hundreds of dollars in bets were beginning to loom very large. After talking around, I realized this was a fairly common problem among fisherman, especially Americans. Somewhere before this time I had heard about the so-called 'Portland Creek Hitch.' Prior to using this hitch, I simply cast the fly out at forty-five degree angle and allowed it to swing across the River. There was always twenty to thirty feet of line out with the line bellied, or sagging. So when a salmon hit I did not have a tight line, and it was possible for the fish to grab the fly and let go before I ever felt it. At least that was my concept of what was happening to me.

With a hitch in place and a raised rod, I could get the fly to travel near the surface instead of near the bottom. Theoretically, when the fish hit the fly, he would break the surface of the water and I could see him and therefore set the hook faster. So much for theory; did it work? You bet it did, it revolutionized my fishing for Atlantic Salmon. For a short line, less than fifteen feet, it was deadly. For casts longer than fifteen feet, it was less effective and by the time I was fishing a thirty foot line, it was still effective and caught a lot more salmon for me than I ever would have caught at 30 feet with a fly on the bottom.

I would start my run in a very shallow rapids, move slowly down stream to deeper water and by the time I had reached flat water at the end of the rapids, I would stop, rest and start over, maybe changing flies. The Portland Creek Hitch was simply a half-hitch tied just behind the cemented head of the salmon fly. The hitch is locked down so the line will run off from the head at a forty-five degree angle from the vertical. It sounds complicated but once you get the gist of it, a matter of a flick of the wrist and you have your hitch. If I am standing on the right side of the river looking down stream, I'm casting to my left at a thirty to forty-five degree angle. The hitch must come off the right hand side of the fly as I am looking at the head of the fly. This pulls the fly up and makes it ride near the surface of the water. I figure I have it just right when I can see the white of the water being raised just under the fly: I could never really see the fly. But I could see the course of the fly by the water being turned by the fly. When a salmon hit the fly he had to rise to the surface and I could actually see the mouth of the striking salmon. That almost always assured me of a solid hit.

As I plied my trade on this very pleasant stretch of the River of Ponds, next to the warden's cabin, my spirits were buoyed as I would hook and land anywhere from two to four salmon a day. I knew the average fisherman from the Air Force Base, would be happy to bag four salmon for the entire year. I could feel that hundred dollars burning a hole in my pocket. We finished our fishing trip on a very enjoyable note, returned to the base, and shipped my parents back home for another year. I was very happy, because I felt I had finally done something to please my father.

12

Fishing with Carl

Carl and I discussed our relative lack of success around the base and tried to learn more about the River of Ponds. We learned that the river is relatively inaccessible to all but the most enthusiastic of salmon fisherman. We made arrangements to fish there for a week near the end of August. The plans were roughly as follows. We borrowed a boat from Dunc, with a very small motor. We mounted it on the top of my car which we loaded with the appropriate camping gear and met our new guide, Earl Patey, 'They calls me Herl.' Earl was fifty some years old and had survived tuberculosis after having one lung collapsed. He was very congenial but one tough Newfie. When we loaded the boat with our gear and the three of us, we probably had two inches of freeboard. Carl and I were completely lost but Earl knew the way.

We crossed the first pond and came to a spit of land which appeared to have a small lake in the middle. So rather than unload the boat we simply dragged it across an area of sloppy mud to the lake. Much to our dismay, the lake was about six inches deep on top of a ton of mud. We could not run the motor and we could not walk the boat round the lake because of the mud. I got into my waders and dragged or swam with the boat across this little pond. We finally dragged the boat back to the big lake, got aboard and proceeded to putt along. Looking out at the main lake I could see threatening waves and wondered what this meant for us, with our two inches of freeboard.

We rounded the first point, and quickly cut behind the next point to avoid being swamped. We took on a little water but we could bail that and keep ahead of the game. We rounded another point; same deal. We repeated this maneuver several times and finally got to the place where the waves would not swamp us and crossed the lake to our campsite. Good news, Earl noted that this was an old campsite developed by, 'our hero, Lee Wulff.' There was a board floor from an old tent campsite which was level, dry and solid and there we pitched our tent and spent a happy week.

That week with Carl and Earl on the river was another week of learning. We were camped on the south side of the river and I spent most of my time fishing along that edge. It was late in the season so the water level was down. I was able to cross and try the north side of the river, which I found to be extremely difficult to wade and totally unproductive. I returned to the south side and never again fished the north side, except for the run out.

My fishing companion for this trip and for most of our two years in Newfoundland was Carl Nagel. Carl's father was a distinguished general surgeon from San Francisco. Carl was raised in a very formal family setting in which he was the dutiful, intelligent, well mannered son of a distinguished surgeon. He referred to his father as, 'Sir.' I am guessing that he had classic training in everything that he did. He read only classic literature, listened to only classical music, drank only straight Scotch whiskey and had as little to do with the common folks as he could manage. My picture of Carl was of a fairly tall, thin person, standing on a huge boulder at the edge of the river, with the nine foot long fly rod, casting as far as he possibly could in the hope of enticing a salmon to hit his classic salmon fly.

All the while, I was traveling up and down the south side of the river trying different holes, runs and riffles and flies. We both had been schooled in tying flies on single hooks and Carl persisted in this habit. I had learned about the use of a double salmon fly hooks and had learned to tie flies that were imitators, or tempters rather than classic salmon flies. I could use my Portland Creek Hitch much more effectively on doubles.

Why do salmon hit flies at all? All anadromous fish leave saltwater, or very large freshwater reservoirs, such as Lake Michigan and travel up stream for the express purpose of spawning. They stop eating as they enter the rivers, so even though they may be hungry, they are not feeding on anything. I have a theory as to why fish will hit a fly when in the process of spawning.

The female's job is to find a suitable bed for dropping eggs and cleaning it off by vigorous tail action. For the fisherman, as you look into the river bottom, you will see a whitish stretch of sand or gravel, and know that is a bed or redd. When the eggs are dropped, they fall in and around the cracks in the gravel base.

The male's job is that of a protector, as well as a fertilizer. I have watched male salmon run small trout and other predators off the spawning bed. I have also seen them pick up twigs and dead leaves and move them aside in order to keep the bed clean. So the reason a fish may hit a fly is perhaps to keep the area clean, or to run off a challenger. The other things that I have observed while fishing for Atlantic Salmon led to a third possibility and that is they are just curious or even playful.

On the spawning beds in the Pere Marquette River, I have observed the male and female action together. I have noted that when the female opens her beak and squirts eggs, the male moves alongside and squirts his milt on the dropping eggs, thereby fertilizing them.

Again, why do they hit flies? They are cleaning, they are mad or they are just curious or playful. I could care less. As long as I see them do it, I have a very good chance of hooking the fish. So while Carl was busy being a classicist, I was busy being an investigator and an instigator of new methods. Carl, with long lines and classic fly, and me with my relatively short casts, high riding fly because of the hitch, were competing all week. Score? Carl; two, Bill; thirteen.

We returned to the Air Force base and regaled our friends with many tales of our successful fishing trip. I informed all my drinking buddies of my successful season, and they paid up promptly, especially after I fed them freshly caught salmon.

Dunc heard our tales and started talking to his friends in

Corner Brook. He came to Carl and me with a proposal, which I thought was quite reasonable. He and his Newfoundland fishing buddies were thinking about putting a cabin at the headwaters of the River of Ponds. For only a few hundred dollars from me, Dunc contacted Earl who proceeded to construct a one room cabin at the river's edge, at the top end of the River of Ponds. To complete that scenario, Earl would float material in one of his boats during the spring high water, and leave it there for all of us to use. It sounded great to me and it was since my father and I used the cabin for about seven years.

Travel during the early years in Newfoundland was always difficult, because the only paved road around us was the Air Force base itself. Every other road was gravel and not well maintained. Open road driving would net you between thirty-five to forty-five MPH. From the base to the town of River of Ponds was a three hour drive. Following the drive we had a twenty minute boat ride, a half hour walk, a thirty minute boat ride, a thirty minute walk, another boat ride at the upper end and another twenty minute walk. With the cabin waiting for us at the top of the river, we could fly in a floatplane from Corner Brook to the upper pond in one hour. Had that not been possible, my father couldn't get there, and I wouldn't want to get there any other way.

This three-quarter mile stretch of the River of Ponds, I fished for a week with my father nine successive years and I felt I knew every rock and every run. The last year after my father died, I fished with Earl but with a heavy heart. Yes, we caught fish, and had a good time but it was not the same without 'the old man' as cantankerous as he was. That week I left Earl with great sadness knowing I would never be back to fish River of Ponds. But I left him with a token of my appreciation for him; my father's favorite fly rod.

Things changed at our campsite through the years, but it was the campsite that changed, the river stayed the same. I never ceased to be amazed at the number of times that people just dropped in to see the old man. We were in the middle of nowhere, but people found us. One day I was downriver at 'the runout" when a guy came walking out of the woods. He had a staff and a big backpack. Obviously he was prepared to be where he was and to do what he was doing. It turns out that he was a surveyor walking across country, doing his job. He was totally nonplussed to find me fishing alone out here. I simply invited him back to the camp to have a drink, and a fresh salmon dinner with Andy, Earl and me. I can't even remember if he spent the night in our camp, or just walked on.

To most of us landlocked fisherman, the tales of salt water fish such as Atlantic Salmon, all five species of Pacific Salmon, Steelhead and a few species of trout running up a river to spawn sounded incredible. And so it was in Newfoundland. It was rumored that at the top end of every salmon river in New-foundland, there was a large pool fed by the river coming over a steep falls. The salmon could only go as far as this large pool at the foot of the falls and were stacked in there like cordwood. I talked to many fish wardens and heard many similar stories. Carl and I read maps and decided there was one such pool at the headwaters of Fischell's River, about one hour away from the base. We talked about it incessantly which attracted the attention of some young airman.

Very early one Saturday morning, Carl and I and two young airmen left for Fischell's River. We parked the car and started walking, initially across a bog that would save us time and effort. Then we hit the river and followed it, and followed it, and followed it. We never once stopped to try and fish, we just kept on hiking. This was hiking in Newfoundland. There was no flat, level ground anywhere. It was across the rocks; big rocks, little rocks, mud and occasionally right in the river. About noon, Carl and I had a conference and decided we should have been there by now. But we were not.

At this point the youngest airman, 'little Al' decided, "Just leave me here, and if you come back, pick me up," Note; he said 'if' not when. This poor little kid was ready to die. We promised we wouldn't go much further, but we probably went another hour at which time the river was so small we could jump across. We figured we must have miscalculated somewhere or maybe somebody lied to us. No falls, no pool, no nothing.

We slogged back to little Al and we all headed back down stream. We finally reached a fishy looking place in the river, crossed over to what could be a decent campsite, ate our sandwiches, drank river water and crawled into our sleeping bags. All except me. The food and the water and sitting down revived me. I assembled my rod and proceeded to quarter cast my wet fly, progressing slowly down the rapids. The sun was down, but the sky was still light enough to reflect off the river and give me a very light background. As I picked up my fly after the run was completed, I still have a vivid memory of the following; a very nice sized salmon, suspended in the air, almost swimming upstream toward the fly that I had just snatched out of his mouth.

I felt my heart in my throat, thumping. I know I uttered some expletive, but those in the camp were so dead tired, that they paid me no heed. I carefully marked my position in the stream, backed over to the bank, carefully removed a Chesterfield, lit it and smoked it. I deftly flicked the butt to the far side of the stream, returned to my spot and methodically worked that same run. On about the umpteenth cast, he hit just at pick-up. Bingo, what a thrill! I worked so hard all day for this one moment, and here it was. I just hooked my first salmon on a bona fide salmon fly. This time I know that I screamed, and everyone woke up. The other guys were almost excited as I was, but it was too dark to fish anymore that evening. Had I not still been a heathen, I might have said something like, "Thank you, Jesus."

Our camp at the upper end of River of Ponds was always on the south side of the river, and right where the lake started running into the river. There were a couple of boulders right there where both my father and Carl loved to fish. They would stand on a boulder or a big rock and quarter the river with their casting. They would start with a very short line at right angles to the edge of the river, allowing the fly to swing across through the current and pick it up and cast again. They would slowly advance the fly one or two feet at a time until they had covered all the water within the reach of their extended line. Carl would move down river somewhat and start all over. My father would simply get off the rock, sit down, maybe change flies, rest and repeat it all. I could never fish that way.

I would start a little below where they fished and move slowly down river. There were spots that could not be fished and there were spots that never contained any fish. That didn't change in the eight years that I fished that area.

There were three specific areas where I would spend most of my day fishing. The first was located one-third of the way down the river. There was a large boulder at water's edge, above which I would enter the river. There was a very large rock at the edge of the current about ten feet below where I stood six feet into the water, from the boulder. I learned to carefully run my hitched fly across the water toward that rock. I needed to advance that fly only six inches at a time and the line length that I was fishing was only twelve to fifteen feet long. The fly was skimming across the top very rapidly and the strike of the salmon was equally quick.

If I were distracted and missed seeing the strike, I would feel a bump and that was it; no fish. I would always rest that fish for the amount of time it took to smoke a Chesterfield. I would then return and run the fly in precisely the same manner as well as I could. The strike, if it came, would be at precisely at the same spot. The salmon would come to rest in a certain spot in the river and stay there. Therefore if you could remember where you had the strike, and repeat the cast again and again, you had a very good chance of hooking that fish.

I returned to skimming the fly, and the fish returned to strike. This time I saw him, struck him, hooked him and the fight was on. Playing an Atlantic Salmon is different from any other fish that I have ever caught. They are usually fresh run, meaning they have not been in the river very long. They have the strength of an open sea salmon. If you try to hold him as you might be tempted to do with the fresh water fish, you will either break the leader, or pull the hook out of his mouth. You are always using a fly reel that has a drag, and the linen line backing the fly line is approximately one hundred yards long. So when the salmon is hooked, you make sure your drag is appropriate and hold your fly rod straight up in the air as high as you can, hopefully to avoid the line or the leader snagging on a rock or boulder in the water. As the fish tires, you slowly and carefully reel him in, again with the rod tip high in the air.

Once the fish is fatigued and comes up on his side, he is ready to be put away. We fisherman, who are landlubbers, simply reach for the net, lead the fish over the net, lift it up and land the fish. In all of my Atlantic Salmon fishing experiences I never used a net to land the fish. Instead there are two accepted methods of handling an Atlantic Salmon. One method is tailing the fish. Atlantic Salmon have a stiff forked tail that does not collapse. If you have enough strength you can grasp the fish just ahead of the tail, squeeze like heck and lift him out of the water. I said strength is important because the fish is slippery. I never had that much strength, so I resorted to a tailing rag, or a cotton glove. Either one gave me enough traction so that the fish would not slide out of my grasp. Tailing is the method of choice, for real red-blooded Atlantic Salmon fisherman.

The other method I favored whenever possible, which is most of the time, is called beaching the fish. Using the fly rod, which is flexible, apply a steady pressure as you pull the fish up upon the beaching surface. As the fish flops against a hard surface he actually propels himself with the aid of constant traction, up onto the beaching surface. Be very certain to not release tension on your line before the fish is secured. Sand or gravel makes the ideal beaching surface but it can be done over small rocks, but not big rocks.

You just caught your first salmon and it is the first day of the five-day trip. You are out in the boondocks with no refrigeration. How do you keep that fish? You build a holding pool at the edge of the river with high enough sides that he cannot jump out. Making the pool too deep will also allow him to jump out. The problem up there in the River of Ponds was we were fishing early in the year and the water level was dropping daily. So I had to check my holding pool every day. If the pool is too shallow I have to build a new one and check it several times every day.

There are critters in Newfoundland that like salmon almost as much as I do, but the only time critters got my salmon was totally unexpected. Early in the week I was inspecting the pool and found it empty. The rocks around the edge of the holding pool were all purple. Two and two. It was late in the summer, and the wild blueberries were profuse in the flat country. Who likes huckleberries as much as I do? As I asked that question of me, I heard in the distance the caw of a crow. Perfectly logical.

A crow, or group of crows, ate their dessert first. They ate the blueberries and then flew over to my salmon holding pool, pooped all over the rocks and ate my salmon. From that point on my holding pools were covered with heavy branches.

My other favorite spot on the River of Ponds was the run out of the river into the pond below our campsite. At the run out, the river widened and split into two halves. It also shallowed up with a fairly uniform small rock or gravel bottom. Of course the current was rapid and with a combination of rapid flowing water, shallowing up of the bottom and flattening out of the entire surface of the river, it created a series of wave like elevations of the water. It was more like a series of very tall riffles, the height of each riffle, or wave, being about one foot. These riffles did not move in or out, the water was simply moving up and down, but each riffle was constant. Because of that, I was able to drag my hitched fly on the surface of the water, either as the water went up, or as it came down.

Once I finally figured out the circumstances of fishing this unique spot, I would stand at the head of the riffle in about one-foot of water. I would then cast the fly to my right and drag it across the surface of the water on the upstream surface of the riffle. By raising my rod tip slowly, I could keep my fly about one inch from the top of the riffle all the way across the runout. Fishing in that fashion was solely so that I could watch my fly carefully. My experience from fishing it higher up in the river-had convinced me that I needed to keep my eye on the fly to see the small visible streak it was making when crossing the top of the water.

As I carefully skittered the fly on the uphill side of that ripple, I was stunned by what happened. A very large salmon head poked through the surface of the water, grabbed my fly, turned and ran into the lake. Because he was into deeper water, I was able to easily play the salmon into submission and then beach him on the gravel shore, right next to the run out. I could never have anticipated such a fantastic scenario for catching Atlantic Salmon. It was also so unexpected, that I had not the foresight to build a holding pool. So I had to release that first salmon, but I waded back upstream to a deeper stretch of water and built a holding pool. I simply cannot imagine how many salmon I put in that holding pool over the next nine years. I'm guessing, in excess of a hundred beautiful Atlantic Salmon.

Very late in the afternoon at that very same spot, skimming the same double hook, tied onto a salmon fly that I invented, I was again pleasantly surprised by a huge head that poked through the wave and grabbed my fly. As per usual, once the salmon is hooked, I simply raise the rod in the air, check the drag adjustment and let the fish run. On this particular occasion, as the fish ran and ran and ran with no indication of fatigue, I brought the reel down to look at the backing. I mentioned that I always backed my fly reel with one hundred yards of woven linen line and that, underneath a thirty-five yard long fly line, giving me confidence that I would never lose a fish that ran too far.

As I glanced at the reel, I saw that I was getting precariously close to the bottom of the spool, so I feverishly twisted the drag as tight as it would go, and that did not even slow this fish. You might be tempted to think, "So what?" This was the second day of a five day trip. I was flown in and I had planned to fly out. I might as well have been a hundred miles from the nearest sporting-goods store with a broken leg. My father was already using my spare rod and reel, there was no other. If I clamped down on that line with my hand, and could not turn that fish, what would happen?

> 1. The fish might pull off the hook and I lose a fish with one of my double hooks; no problem, but not likely.
> 2. The leader breaks, I lose the fish and one fly. Flies are all expendable and regrettably so are fish.
> 3. A weak spot in the backing and it breaks. I lose one fish, one fly, one fly line: disaster. End of fishing trip.
> How about prayer? Not yet an option in the life of a heathen.

I bit the bullet, swore at the fish, grabbed the backing in my hand and held tight. Miracle, the fish turned and I started the long process of reeling him back toward shore. He hadn't quit yet, made several more runs, not as long as the first, and when I finally got the bottom of the fly line back on the reel, I relaxed. As I dragged him carefully up the beach I again was astounded. He was about thirty-six inches long and probably weighed eighteen pounds. Clearly the largest fish I had ever caught, the largest salmon I would ever catch. What was I to do with him since he was too large for the holding pool?

I was three quarters of a mile down river from the camp. It was almost dark. I was without a light and could not walk back to the camp through the woods which was an option in daylight. In fact, it was so dark I could not even walk along the edge of the river for fear of falling on the slippery rocks. I realized that I could only get back to camp by wading that treacherous river. Carefully feeling my way. I could see only silhouettes.

I was not about to give up my King salmon, because no one had seen him, and would not believe my story. I tied one end of a string around the tail of the salmon and the other end around a stick so I could carry him over my shoulder or drag him through the water and started my abysmal trek. I could not see into the water, only the surface of the water and the riffles. I could see the rocks along the edge of the river and nothing more. I slung the fish over my shoulder, held the fly rod in my right hand and a stout stick in my left.

I feel I must reiterate the circumstances of this journey, lest my readers feel I was a real wuss. The water is always cold. I think I registered a fifty-three degree water temperature one sunny day in the lake, in shallow water. The bottom of the river is always rocks and boulders, never sand, never even nice gravel. Where I was fishing, the run out, the rocks were smaller than fist size therefore manageable, but not comfortable. All of the rocks in Newfoundland are slippery. The rumor among the Newfies is every night in Newfoundland, the elves go into the water and soap every rock. I always felt that was a cute colloquialism but that night, I thought they started early. I literally staggered and stumbled three quarter of a mile upstream dragging that damnable, huge salmon. From that point on, I never went fishing without a light of some kind. Back at camp my father was already asleep. But Earl agreed with me, "She's a beauty, all right!" We shared a drink, a Chesterfield and went to sleep.

13

Fishing with the Colonel

I have mentioned that I thought salmon might hit a fly, or hit at a fly, out of curiosity, or even more strange, out of a playful nature. One particularly warm summer day, I had occasion to pass by what we used to call 'a steady.' This was a stretch of flat water with no riffles or eddy currents. There was a large rock protruding from the middle of the river dividing it into two halves. It was a day when I had experienced no fish action at all. More than anything else, I was practicing fly casting. I started at the head of the steady, fished carefully with several different types of flies, and experienced only a tired arm. As I sat on a boulder near water's edge, I thought I saw a dimple right near the boulder in the middle.

I adjusted my glasses and sunglasses and moved a little closer. Again, there was a disturbance on the surface of the water. I wondered what this might be. Later in my fishing life I learned this was a fish sipping small flies. There are a lot of flies in Newfoundland but I didn't put two and two together because at this point I had never seen a salmon sip a fly. On a later trip, I watched salmon sipping flies all day long. But to me, on this day, it was an unknown phenomenon.

Because it was a very dull day and I had nothing better to do, I would use the opportunity to better try one of my newly designed black Wulff flies. For non-fisherman the Wulff pattern is a large dry fly. It is not an imitator, rather it is an attractor. The original fly is designed by Lee Wulff whose name is well recognized by Atlantic Salmon fisherman the world over. He spent a lot of time fishing the rivers of Newfoundland; our River of Ponds was one of his favorites. I mentioned that we stayed at one of his original campsites our first trip. The Wuff pattern is tied with material that is almost impervious to water. It is designed to sit high on the water; it is fluffy. Because it is large and fluffy, it's like trying to fly-cast a cotton ball.

After carefully measuring my casting distance on the edge of the river, I flipped the fly out to the approximate area where I had seen the dimple. Notta. Repeat cast, repeat notta. Repetitious casting is the basic maneuver for fishing Atlantic Salmon. Number three cast, a pleasant surprise. A nice sized salmon porpoised just below my fly; it was not a take. General rule when salmon fishing after a strike or missed strike, take five. I stopped, sat down and lit a cigarette. Back to fishing, repeat the cast, several casts and then he rose again, clearly to the left hand side of the fly and I was standing on the right hand side of the fly. I struck violently, and got nothing but air. Repeat process; next time he rose on the right-hand side of the fly but he was back in the water before I could set the hook or I might have accidentally snagged him.

This game went on and on. I've only told this tale a few

times because it is usually met with ridicule. In fact, if you told me this tale I would ridicule you, so I understand. I watched that salmon progressively play with my fly in a different fashion many times that afternoon. At one point he came up directly under the fly and bounced it off his nose. A little later he came up below the fly and flopped his head down on top of the fly causing it to sink. Each time he did something different.

I said to myself, "I can't wait to tell my fishing friends about this" only to finally realize, this whole story was preposterous. No one will ever believe me. The final blow, as it were, is when he rose alongside my fly and flipped it with his tail as he went by. At that point I said to to the fish, " Buddy, you just flipped me, I'm gonna flip you." I took off the dry fly, went back up to the head of the pool and fished it with a standard dry fly until my arm was sore again, and then went home.

After my first full season of salmon fishing during which time I won all of my bets, the word got around the officers club that Carl and I were the 'tour de force' in the local salmon fishing world. The base commander made himself known to Carl and me, and of course my wife. Sandy and I were even invited to his quarters for a dinner and entertainment. After imbibing in a sufficient quantity of alcohol, we ended up playing broom hockey in his kitchen with brooms and upside down plastic cereal bowls. It turned out to be a lot of fun and this full bird colonel was really a nice guy. So nice a guy that he invited me to go fishing with him. Rough translation, "Would you take me fishing with you?"

At this point in time Carl had left the base, and this was my last summer on the base. There was no other officer who knew anything about salmon fishing. On this trip, we will take the base fixed wing plane called an L20 or a deHavilland Beaver. I suggested a 'steady' in the middle of the River of Ponds where several of us could fish comfortably. This was a Saturday with a high overcast, a lot of clouds that we could fly under. So we flew from the base to the River of Ponds, about a one hour flight and put down on the big steady. Some of the colonel's guests that day were fisherman so I didn't have to care for them, but I made sure the Colonel had the right equipment.

The day was very pleasant; not too hot, not too cool, nice breeze, but no fish. I felt badly that the Colonel had not even seen a salmon, let alone raised, hooked or caught one. I felt worse that I hadn't either. I began to fear if we did not take at least one salmon out of that pool, I would lose my credibility as a potential guide for VIPs. It was quite late in the day when I approached the colonel and said, "Colonel, I would like you to try this very unique fly called a 'Rat Faced McDougal.'

As I've mentioned before, entertainment on Ernest Harmon Air Force Base is at best sparse. Carl and I both spent a lot of time reading books about salmon fishing and about salmon flies. The name attracted us more than anything; Rat Faced McDougal. So we each tied a few. Each fly had a half inch long tail and a thick deer hair body which made it float. It had two upright wings and the head of the fly was finished with black fly head cement. The bottom of the fly was clipped flat so it would sit upright. When viewed from the front, one could visualize a very tiny mouse. So it was, as I was to later learn, an imitator. It could represent a small shrew. At that time, I had no clue what a shrew was. It was just a funny looking fly to be tried on a day when nothing else worked.

So I tied it on for the Colonel and said, "Give it a try." He was so uninformed that he thought it was a good idea. I knew better, it was a dumb thing to try, but nothing else worked. I was watching him to make sure he could get it out, because it was a hard fly to cast. He got it out all right and the first drift through the run, wham! He hooked and subsequently landed the only salmon of the day. Obviously, he was ecstatic and figured I was a pretty good guide. I simply kept my mouth shut so as to not ruin the ambience. It was late in the day and we had to get back in the air. So we did not have an opportunity to prove what a farce that Rat Faced McDougal really was. I have subsequently tried it several times and caught only a few nice trout but no more salmon. That whole incident provided a level of communication between the Almighty Base Commander, and the peon Dr. Harry W. Burdick; " Hi, colonel rat face." "Hi Dr. rat face guide," never witnessed before, nor since at Ernest Harmon Air Force Base.

14

The Fly Tying Table

The basement of our duplex was poured concrete, so it was dry. After I partitioned off two areas suitable for children's play-rooms, I felt the remaining space was safe enough for a fly tying bench or table. There was a small window on this south wall, which permitted a little light into a fairly dark basement. Under that window I placed a table of sufficient size, to allow two of us to tie flies face to face. I added two gooseneck lamps and two chairs, and Carl and I were in business. We ordered our basic fly tying equipment from L.L. Bean, Freeport, Maine. Carl ordered most of the material since he was a little better acquainted with tying classic salmon flies. When we began I really had no idea of the varieties of materials that we would need for tying these flies.

We almost always tied flies together since neither was an accomplished tyer, we could pick each other's brains. When we realized we were deficient in one material or another, we would either take that dreadful one hour trip up to Corner Brook where we found a marvelous fly shop, or call Dr. Duncan Rowe. He was a reasonable alternative since he came down to the base almost every other week and would help us by bringing the needed material. Because entertainment on the base with severely lacking, Carl and I spent many hours tying flies and smoking cigarettes together. We learned two things very quickly:

    1. Fly tying materials are highly flammable; be very careful with cigarettes.

    2. Alcohol severely impairs your mental acuity and your physical sensitivity; don't drink while tying.

Picture this in your mind if you can. I am tying a Green Highlander, a classic Atlantic Salmon fly. I have clamped my hook into the fly tying vise and started by locking the thread at the curve of the hook to my left. I spin and lock in place the tail, the butt, the tinsel ribbing, the body hackle and the body dubbing moving to the forward part of the fly. After adding each element, I should fix it with a half hitch, but that is time-consuming, so I just keep moving forward without half hitches. I reached the front end of the hook and tie in the throat feathers. These I lock in and proceed to tie on five pairs of feathers to go over the top of the fly. These are called the wings. They are perfectly matched side to side and well positioned from the bottom toward the top. Over the top of all of these beautiful feathers I tie in a golden hawk crest. I lock it all together with back to back paired half hitches with my fly tying thread.

It is a beautiful fly. I am congratulating myself on a job well done. What I have not told you about fly tying is, every time you tie in a part of the fly along the shank, the excess material sticks out toward the head end of the fly or toward the eye of the hook. This extra material has to be trimmed off. Usually it can be easily clipped with a pair of fine cutting scissors. Once you finish off the wings there is a whole bunch of extra stuff sticking out all around the eye of the hook. This has to be cut off very cleanly so that none of the extra material extends over the eye of the hook. It has to be cut off as closely as possible to the thread that locks it in place. Here scissors don't work. They are too gross or coarse. The standard treatment of this excess fly-tying material is critical.

I grasp the mass of material in my left hand lift it straight up, and with a single edged razor blade, I very carefully saw it off as close to the thread as possible. I have spent two hours tying this single fly. If one has more than one alcoholic beverage during that long period of time, you can guess what is going to happen. As I very carefully sawed the extra material with my razor blade, I cut too deep and cut the thread that holds the whole damn thing together. The whole front end of the fly looks like a miniature rag doll. I have just ruined two hours of tedious work. It only took one such incident for me to swear off alcohol while I tied flies.

Carl was single therefore he did not have to go to the BX with his wife or children or have any other family concerns. With extra time on his hands, he would simply walk up the hill to our duplex, through the garage into the kitchen, where he may or may not speak to my wife, walk through the kitchen to the basement and start tying flies. That was pretty much standard operating procedure for Carl.

I mentioned that we had a lot of strong wind being positioned fifty feet or so above the rest of the base. That was usually not a problem but on one particular winter day it was significant. The wind was blowing hard out of the southwest, forty to fifty miles an hour. Our second winter we had over two hundred inches of snow. This particular day it was snowing hard and blowing harder. We were all hunkered down because there was no place to go, and nothing to do but stay home and stay warm. The next day, when the storm was over, I went down to the basement to tie flies, and found about an inch and a half of snow covering my fly tying table. Apparently when they built the house, they did put on a sill plate but they neglected to put in the thin foam sill sealer. As I wondered where all this snow had come from, I climbed up on a chair to put my eyes at the level of the sill plate, and guess what? I could see right out to the back yard. To solve that problem temporarily, I simply went outdoors and shoveled snow up against the house to fill the space between the basement and the siding with a solid snow pack. No more snow on my fly tying table.

One of our very early trips to the south of our base was going to be a single day trip for Carl, me and our mutual friend Dr. W. Duncan Rowe.

For this trip we started before daylight and drove south of the base for almost two hours. We were headed for famed Highland Creek somewhere along the South West Coast of Newfoundland. We reached our destination in high spirits and parked our vehicle alongside the road. We picked up our heavy backpacks loaded with food, beverage and miscellaneous fishing gear, grasped our wading staff and headed up river. The river in this part of the country has been well fished and so there are trails leading up river on each side of the river. We simply had to pick the right side, which we did based on the apparent abundance of foot traffic. After walking well over an hour we found ourselves in a lovely bend of the river with the flow coming from our left towards a fairly high bank of bushes and trees and what appeared to be a stony outcropping. This offered a very long run beginning up high with the end of the riffle which turned into a nice deep, steady followed by another riffle, another steady and then ending in a broad riffle.

By this time of the day, the sun was above the treetops and it promised to be a gorgeous day. The three of us alternated our fishing time. Two of us started at the headwaters of each steady and worked our way slowly and cautiously downstream. As the lowest fisherman reached the riffles out of the steady, he sat down and the third fisherman started at the top of the first steady. And so we passed several very pleasant hours. I don't recall if any of us even had a hint of a hit, but we were off the base, and enjoying the beauty of our temporary home away from home, Newfoundland.

It was my turn at the top steady and I felt quite certain that I had just raised a salmon. So I stopped my activity, lit my Chesterfield, and waited for the salmon to settle down. I pretty well had the location of the hit pegged and was stretching out my line to hit just above that spot, when I heard that awful noise; the thump, thump, thump. I knew in an instant that our beautiful day on the river was about to be interrupted. Carl and I were the only surgeons on the base. We seldom left the base together, but when we did, we had to give specific instructions to our friend, Lieut. Ken Winden, one of the helicopter pilots. He had flown over most of the western half of Newfoundland because of his requirement to stay proficient in piloting.

Without realizing what we had chosen as a good-looking salmon run, turned out to be one of the only flat areas along that river. We all moved to one end of the beach area as the helicopter came in and made a perfect landing. Carl and I ducked as we moved into the door of the helicopter to find out if there was an appendicitis, or a broken arm back at the base. Which of us had to go back? The word was," Bad laceration, you both have to come." I pictured the worse figuring that we would be sewing up somebody the rest of the evening. I must admit, I faced the entire situation with ambivalence. If both Carl and I had to fly back in the helicopter, that meant that poor Dunc Rowe had to walk out by himself and then drive all away back to the base by himself. That's about a three and one half hour trip alone for our friend. On the other hand, I didn't have to do it. I'd be back in the base in thirty minutes, with no backache and no sore feet.

On the other side of the coin was the fact that we were really needed. So much of the medical care that we supplied on the base was ho-hum routine. For me a few broken arms, a few broken legs, quite a few simple surgeries but nothing difficult or challenging. This was going to be my opportunity to shine, to show people I had real skill and talent. So with that ambivalence, Carl and I boarded the helicopter and flew quickly back to the base. There was even the base ambulance waiting for us as we deplaned; high drama in old Newfie land.

We were transported from the airfield to the emergency room in grand fashion. We were escorted into the emergency room and introduced to the patient who was a twelve year-old girl who had a laceration on her left forearm. It couldn't have been longer than three inches, barely through the subcutaneous tissue, and only in one spot did I see any red muscle belly. Here we were, after all this commotion to retrieve us or extract us out of the wilds to put a few stitches in this little girl's arm, and to leave our buddy to get back to the base as best he could. Confronted with that same problem today I might sew it up, or I might fix it with butterflies and superglue. I truly felt guilty. I think I remember Carl saying, "I'll fix it, go home to your little girls." which I did grateful to be safe and sound at home with my family.

15

A Day at the Top of River of Ponds

Carl and I had been fishing this stretch of the River of Ponds faithfully with mixed results and felt we would like to try something different. We spoke to Herl and inquired as to our options. There was sufficient gas to run his boat up to the top of the pond. He described a place where one of the main rivers feeding the River of Ponds came in to the lake. We had never been to the top of the pond which was two or three miles away. It was readily accessible since the lake was deep and had no known rocky hazards in the middle. So we packed a lunch, all of our fishing gear and boarded the boat for a twenty minute trip up the lake.

It was late in the season, the second or third week in August, so that the salmon run had been able to fill the entire river system. I suspect that earlier in the year a trip to the top of the big lake might not produce salmon since they possibly may not have run the entire river early in the season. It's not that the salmon don't have the strength or stamina to run from the ocean to the top of the River of Ponds in a couple days, it's just that it's their custom to move up the river in stretches. At this time of the year we could expect there to be plenty of salmon at the top of the River of Ponds.

The day itself was fairly warm with minimal breeze and a very high overcast as we started out. We basically did not see the sun all day long, but it was a very bright day. The trip was uneventful and as we pulled near the runout of the river into the lake near the north end I saw what appeared to be a very broad gravel beach area with the river splitting the beach in half. The surprise to me was the fact that this was all gravel, there were no huge boulders or even big rocks in sight at the mouth of the river. The first rocks were visible about two hundred yards up the river. We beached the boat on the north side of the river, got out and stretched our legs. At this point in time, my only experience in fishing for salmon was in a river with all the attendant characteristics: current, riffles and large rocks, some protruding through the surface but most just under the surface. I surveyed the area carefully and decided to move up the river to the very end of the rapids or riffles, as I had done near our camp.

At this time in our fly tying experience, Carl and I had decided that we did not have enough time or patience to continue tying the classic salmon fly patterns. As I have mentioned, the full classic pattern took two hours for one fly and that was just too much work.

We had experimented with several patterns and I had found one that I liked quite well. It was very effective for raising salmon although not necessarily for hooking salmon. They apparently liked the appearance and frequently rose to it. Unfortunately not too often did they actually hit it, but it was the best that we had. It was tied on a number ten double salmon hook with a red tail a black floss body with silver tinsel and a moose hair wing. It was very simple in design and I could tie one in ten minutes, complete with a black lacquered head. The latter was important because the head had to be large enough to support the Portland Creek hitch, which improved our ability to hook salmon.

I walked up the river on nice gravel to the point where gravel was replaced by rocks and turned back down stream to fish the rapids. I tied my fly on with the hitch coming off the right side of the head at forty-five degrees and carefully fished the entire rapids to the mouth of the river. I saw nothing, felt nothing, heard nothing.

I have read several books on the art of Atlantic Salmon fishing and they are all consistent in their recommendations, one must repeat casts. There are many stories by noted authors Lee Wulff, Charlie Fox and others that one must repeat the same casting pattern many times before you can expect a salmon to rise to the fly. There are several stories of one of these ardent fisherman repeating a cast as many as twenty times over a fish he know to be 'in the lie'. So I turned around and trudged up the bank and started the process all over again. Again, the same result. So I decided to cross the river and fish from the other side giving the salmon a different look to my fly; same result times two.

After all this time and effort my arm was getting sore and my back was aching; I found myself a friendly rock, parked my butt, took out my friendly corncob and had a puff or two. I was gazing out on the lake which was dead calm and very beautiful. I could see beneath the surface close to me and about fifteen feet out. Beyond that, I could only see a sheen on the top of the water, which reflected the dull overhead sky. As I gazed rather inattentively out over the water, I saw something, which struck me as very odd; a distinct dimple about twenty-five feet out into the water. I looked around and indeed saw a number of different kind of flies in the air: deer flies, moose flies, a gazillion mosquitoes, tiny black flies and a larger broader wing fly like a moth or even butterfly which are very uncommon in Newfoundland.

Could it be that a fish rose to a fly? I had read where Lee Wulff had experienced trout and even Atlantic Salmon rising to the surface fly, and that was the basis of his famous invention, 'The White Wulff.' There had to be some basis for his observation and invention of his White Wulff. So I more intensely watched the surface of the lake just off the edge of the gravel bar. Yes, there were more rises or dimples on the surface of the water. No fish broke the surface of the water so I had no idea if these were native Brook trout feeding on a bonanza of dead flies on the water, or was it something more sinister; being, God only knows what. Mind you now, these dimples or rises were out in the lake where there was no current. There was no reason for Atlantic salmon to be out in dead, or non-moving water.

As I continued to focus on little dimples on the surface of the water, I detected a pattern; these dimples appeared in somewhat of a line. This could represent a moving fish, not a fish stuck on the bottom, but a fish that was moving along just under the water's surface. I got up on my feet and carefully and slowly moved out into the lake so perchance I could get a better look. Then I saw a site that's sent a tingle to my toes: there was ever so slight a wake at the surface of the water and then a dimple. These were moving feeding fish. Could these possibly be Atlantic Salmon cruising around the lake and feeding on flies? Ostensibly, salmon don't feed at all once they enter fresh water, so what in the world is going on?

I moved back on shore, reached into my vest and pulled out my dry fly box. I looked through my collection and pulled out a small Black Wulff. I don't recall reading anything about Lee Wulff tying a Black Wulff, but I thought what the heck, I'll try tying one.

At a later time, the black Wulff proved to be a bonanza, but not today. I tied on a 3X tippet and then one of my size ten Black Wulff's and moved back out into the lake to watch for a pattern. I soon spotted a progression of dimples that was moving across the lake in front of me. I estimated where the next dimple might come and deftly cast my fly to the spot anticipating anything. Instead I got nothing. The dimple pattern avoided my fly and kept on going. In keeping with what I just said about repetition in casting for salmon, I waited until another pattern arose and tried the same thing. Again, nothing. After about a dozen such failures I figured I needed to try another tact.

So I moved back to the shore, sat down and searched through my dry fly box again. This time I found a couple of funny flies I had tied just for the heck of it and to develop a little more expertise in tying on a body hackle. The fly was tied on a 3X long shank dry fly hook. The tail was made up of a few pieces of grizzly hackle; the body was a scarlet wool wrap with a full-bodied gray grizzly hackle, making the whole thing look faintly bushy. It really looked quite buggy. And, having nothing else that seemed reasonable, I tied on a 4X tippet and then the fly. I returned to my spot and waited for the next pattern to develop.

Shortly, a cruising fish passed by. Again I anticipated where the next dimple might be and flipped the fly out. To my amazement the fly simply disappeared. There was no smack, no wush, no disturbance in the water other than a dimple. Had I been closer I might have heard a sucking sound as I have subsequently heard with Trout thus taking a fly, but today nothing.

I had forewarned myself by saying, "Bill, you're fishing for a five pound salmon with a 4X tippet with a break strength of about 3.2 pounds. Don't set the hook!" Oddly enough, I listened to myself. I simply raised the rod tip and the fish's run set the hook. I quickly diminished the drag on the reel and let the fish run. I was not surprised when he tried to jump, but was very happy when I realized it was sort of a half way jump. Not a wholehearted jump where the salmon cleared the water by about three or four feet, thrashed his tail against the line which would ordinarily break a 4X tippet or pull the hook out. He simply broke the surface of the water without clearing the surface; good news! Nonetheless, I dropped my rod tip as soon as he surfaced thereby releasing all tension on the line. He did not have a tight line to smack with his tail so I didn't lose him. He continued his run. When he tired and turned, I gently reeled him back toward me. Then another run; this was repeated several times.

After six or seven minutes, I was able to shorten the line and back up onto the gravel beach with gentle pressure on the rod. As the salmon flipped and flopped, the gentle pressure on the line moved him out of the water up onto the beach. I dropped the rod, rushed to the salmon, unhooked him and carried him back out into the lake. I moved him slowly back and forth in the water so that he could again aerate his gills, regain his strength and eventually he swam out of my hands, hopefully to join in his fellow salmon and perhaps give another fisherman a big thrill. I removed the fly from the end of the line and stuck it into the wool patch on my hat to allow it to dry and remembered the old Newfie adage, "I bows toward you and nods according."

I was very fortunate to have several of this same type of fly in my dry fly box, so I tied on a new one, siliconed it and set out to repeat this wonderful episode. I was able to do this several times when I had a sudden inspiration. Back home in Plainwell, Michigan, I had joined the local chapter of Trout Unlimited. I was a very enthusiastic young trout fisherman and would not miss a chance to learn something new. One of our guest speakers was a 'dyed in the wool' dry fly trout fisherman named Art Neuman. I certainly enjoyed his speech that evening but I was more enthralled with the fact that he had his own fly fishing shop in Saginaw Michigan called, "The Wanigas Rod

Company." I'll give you thirty-seven seconds to figure out where that name came from. If you have not figured it out by the end of this little story, send me an email.

Art introduced me to many things in my new world of trout fishing. One was a new fly called the Borchers special. The Borchers fly in varying sizes from an eighteen down to a ten became my standard daytime dry fly for trout, forever. And when he announced in a sale flyer these flies would be available for twenty-five cents apiece, I couldn't resist buying a few: ten dozen. I still have a few of those wonderful flies in my dry fly box. But the most interesting thing from the standpoint of this story was that he offered a seven foot two ounce, two-piece split bamboo fly rod, handmade for about a hundred dollars. Considering that I had just blown three hundred for a three piece split bamboo rod from the William Mills Rod company, in New York City, I considered this to be a bargain and snarfed it up immediately.

So I find myself at the upper end of the top pond of the River of Ponds with salmon rising all around me in an idyllic scenario for my seven foot, two ounce split bamboo rod. I had outfitted the rod with the smallest of the Pflueger Medalist hand wind reels, a number four double taper fly line and sufficient backing to fill the reel. I would never have a better chance to catch a large fish on that delicate rod. I realized that it would be a challenge but I was up for it. If I hooked the fish and he ran me out to the end of my backing, I would only lose the fly because the 4X tippet would snap before I lost anything else. So I went for it. I tied the fly on a 4X tippet, a six foot leader and worked like the dickens to get that fly out to where the fish were rising.

The fly rod that I had been using was an eight ½ foot boron composite rod. It was practically indestructible and was stiff enough to throw that little fly about sixty feet. Compared with that rod, my seven foot split bamboo rod was almost like fishing with a wet noodle. It had little or no backbone and required a lot of arm action to get the fly out to the feeding fish. That rod was meant to be fished on a tiny trout stream with a maximum casting distance of fifteen feet. And here I was trying to fire the thing out about twenty-five to thirty feet.

I got there, finally, and the first crack out of the box, a salmon took my fly and the battle was on. I had lightened the drag as much as I figured the leader would handle and simply let the salmon run around. He would tire a little, I would reel in a little and then he would run again and then back to carefully reeling some more. The whole process took over 30 minutes but when it was over, I couldn't have been happier. A salmon that probably went four pounds on a two ounce split bamboo rod. Life was good! But the fish was so pooped, he wouldn't survive so we had to eat this one. Boo hoo and yum yum.

16

How I Got Caught

On September 1, 1963, Sandy and I entered a whole new world. I had just completed my final days of formal education. The beginning of it was a century ago, at least that's how it felt to me. My mother had taken me by the hand and led me over to the kindergarten classroom in Berrien Springs Michigan, 1934. At this point, my readers are thinking, how quaint! Or at least, how old-fashioned. True. The year was 1934 and I was four, almost five. The building was in two parts, connected by a basement passage and it was the typical redbrick school house that can still occasionally be seen in very small communities. The elementary school consisted of eight rooms plus a basement. The basement passageway led to the high school with an entry through the gymnasium. The second building held the junior and senior high schools, basically two floors and a basement.

For thirteen years that school building, my father's Red and White grocery store, and our cement block home at 421 South Main St. made up my whole world. My brain is fluttering as I recall the mental pictures of those days. For the most part they were pleasant days. I am now, as I did for many, many years, covering over the images that I still can recall, that were so damaging, from which I, and subsequently my wife, and my children have suffered. But that is another story.

Those 13 years were followed by four years at DePauw University and a BA degree. Next were four years in the University of Michigan School of Medicine, followed by one year of internship and finally four years, of residency training in orthopedic surgery. That is twenty-six years of education, and I was thirty-two years old when we started our new life.

My religious training had been in the first Methodist Church of Berrien, Springs where, if the gospel message had been given, I didn't hear it. Jesus was some sort of a religious person who was the object of many Sunday school lessons. That was the total extent of my religious upbringing. Without a significant background, I hardly had time to pursue a religious experience or education as I was overwhelmed by the obligation of being a full-time student, or in the summer, a full-time laborer.

My next memory of religious activity was in Plainwelll. Sandy, my sweet and loving wife, tried to tell me something. It went something like this.

"Bill, guess what?"

When the conversation starts like that I've learned that I had better be prepared for something different. It was different all right.

"You know that looking little church just down the street?"

"You mean the Baptist Church that has a neon sign on the

front that says, 'Christ Died For Your Sins?'

"Yes, well I got saved."

At that point I experienced a working definition for the word ambivalence. The first knee jerk reaction that I felt was stark fear; what did that mean, really?

The next thought, "She really sounds happy. That's probably a good thing." The third inkling for me came in the form of, " What does that mean to me? What do I need to do?" But mostly, "What am I going to have to give up?"

I felt caught, trapped, hopeless, helpless, doomed to whatever it was that laid just around the corner. I needed time to cogitate. " That's nice, I'm happy for you." Translation, "Don't bug me!"

After two years of conversations, emotional battles, within myself and between my wife and me, I finally made the big decision. Sandy's attempts to 'not bug me' included evangelistic dinner parties in our home, notes on my shaving mirror with verses written on them, Bible studies in our home with Kalamazoo doctors who were Christians, and going to church with the family to be a 'good Dad.'

Here is my story. After I left active duty at Ernest Harmon Air Force Base, Stephenville, Newfoundland, I maintained contacts with Earl Patey, my Newfie guide, and with Duncan Rowe, my orthopedic buddy in Newfoundland. My replacement on the Air Force Base was an orthopedic resident from Grand Rapids Michigan who I met before I departed. He gave me an additional contact on the base so was it reasonable for me to return to Newfoundland for a week of fishing with my father, which I did for about eight years. On each of those trips it was my father who probably enjoyed that fishing trip more than I could ever imagine; it was physically very demanding for him but he never complained.

I had ascertained from my mother and my sister, both of whom lived in Berrien Springs, that my father was becoming increasingly a problem with his drinking and anger. I had not received Jesus as my Savior, but I knew a lot about Him having sat in many church services with Sandy and the girls. I had heard what He could do in the life of an individual. Since I am a black and white thinker without a lot of imagination, I figured that if I could get my father saved, we might get him turned from his severe addiction to alcohol.

I had been attending First Baptist Church of Plainwell for about two years. They were meeting in the local high school for a period of about a year and a half while a new church was being built. I had become well acquainted with the local pastor, Gordon Blossom and of course had heard about the Romans Road to salvation. If I could just persuade Gordon Blossom to go fishing for Atlantic Salmon with my father and me, we might have a shot at getting 'old Andy' saved. So I arranged for the three of us to make the next trip up to Newfoundland, together. It took a lot of planning and a lot of money since I had to the foot the bill for the entire trip for all of us.

God is gracious and arranged for the whole thing to happen. In the first week in July in 1966 I found myself with Gordon Blossom and my father at our campsite at the upper end of the River of Ponds. I really don't know if Gordon Blossom had ever fished before in his life. But he was a willing, if not necessarily talented, student and I taught him the basics of fly fishing. I had him totally equipped with fishing paraphernalia for the trip. I recall he actually caught a few salmon and was absolutely ecstatic about his experience.

As a sideline, that was okay but that was not why I invited him to join us in Newfoundland. I expected him to talk my father into receiving Jesus as his Savior. I know he spent time talking with my father but I sure didn't see any consequences reflected in my father's behavior. My father drank just as much whiskey as he always did but it was more covert than usual, being a little embarrassed about drinking in front of a preacher.

As was my habit on some of these trips, at midmorning on a sunny and fairly warm day, I walked around the corner of the lake to a gravel beach were I proceeded to take my annual River of Ponds bath. The water had warmed up to about sixty-three degrees, but out of the wind, in the sun and in a shallow portion of water, it had warmed a trifle more. I was able to bathe quite comfortably and as I walked up on the beach and started drying myself off, I had a sudden thought; perhaps God was speaking to me.

As I now recognize, God used the occasion to speak to me and although these are probably not His exact words, this is my interpretation. "Bill, you dumb bunny. What do you think you're doing? You brought your father up into the back woods of Newfoundland, exposed him to your pastor hoping that your dad might get saved. When you have not even received Christ as your own personal Savior. You hypocrite!" Well, I heard

God, or me, whoever it was that spoke, and did exactly what I'd learned I must do. I spoke to God and asked Jesus to come into my heart. He did and He saved me.

I went back to the camp and told Gordon about my decision and of course he was overjoyed. All along Gordon had a different agenda than did I. I brought him to Newfoundland to get my father saved, and he came along to get me saved. I didn't know it at the time, but he won. It wasn't that I lost, really, because both my mother and father received Jesus as Savior that same year, as did my sister and her husband. 1966 was a good year for the Burdick family. I was determined to follow Him the very best I could.

Back home the pastors's wife and Sandy were praying for my soul. When we returned, and walked into our kitchen to unpack, Gordon Blossom walked past Sandy and winked. She got the message. God won.

With this as a background, I was very concerned about the spiritual condition of my new found friend and fishing buddy, Doug Wendzel. I knew that he was a fairly regular attendant at the local Presbyterian Church in Richland, but I felt I needed to find out if he knew Jesus as his personal Savior. Never having faced a friend with that predicament it was with fear and trepidation that I spoke to Doug about this matter. I shouldn't have been worried at all. In no uncertain terms he let me know that he was not interested in being 'saved.' As a result of several of our get together's between Sandy and I and Doug and his wife, Marie, I realized that she was a born again Christian. But how to get to Doug!

At that time in our lives we were attending Westwood Baptist church and had made the acquaintance of Don and Sandy Burns, and their two children, Betsy and David. Some of you who may read this epistle may recall the wonderful times that we used to have at Westwood Baptist church, during the service and especially after church in our social gatherings. Don and Sandy Burns had, as one of their friends from out of town, a young, handsome, charismatic evangelist by the name of David Hill.

When David was in town, Don and Sandy frequently invited friends from the neighborhood and our church to join them for an evening in their home. He encouraged us to bring unbelievers with us. That was the perfect scenario. Doug, even though handicapped and confined to a wheelchair, was a gregarious person and readily accepted my invitation to join us at the Burns home to meet with David Hill.

The evening had gone seemingly well for all parties. I am reminded of a little saying of the time, 'You clean up real good,' That covers the evening in a nutshell. Everyone was well-dressed and well behaved. They were more than kind to Doug recognizing his handicap state, and everybody quickly realized my concern for his soul. David Hill spoke in his usual inimitable way. Doug was fascinated and asked to speak to David personally; he had a few questions. David had given a clear gospel call to salvation. Doug's response was beyond my wildest expectations.

David was very kind and spoke with Doug for some period of time answering all of his questions with excellent answers.

David finally said, "Would you like to receive Christ as your personal savior?"

Doug equivocated, stumbled, fumbled, made excuses and on and on. All the time I'm thinking, " Doug, you dumb bunny, just make the decision. Say the words. Do it!" David was just softly talking to Doug, gently guiding him and finally he asked, " Would you like to receive Jesus right now?"

"Yes, I would," was Doug's response. David prayed with Doug as we all stood around, amazed and most of us crying.

The evening progressed satisfactorily as we all were joyful at the outcome. Sandy and I stayed after Doug and Marie and most of the other guests left. We were talking with David. I was flabbergasted, as David recounted his thoughts of that experience. I assumed that leading people to Jesus was an every day event for David. After hearing him personally talk with us about what had just happened for him and Doug, I realized that David Hill was a marvelous speaker, an excellent evangelist, and knew the Bible inside and out. But I honestly think this was the first time he ever personally led a person to Jesus; he was so excited he couldn't stop talking. All in all, it was one of the best evenings I have ever spent in my whole life.

17

What About Bob?

Early in the spring of 1963, Sandy and I and our three little daughters were living in our third rental in Grand Rapids where I was finishing my residency in orthopedic surgery. I realized that my two and one half years spent practicing orthopedic surgery in the Air Force might earn me credit toward my residency training. I contacted the American Board of Orthopedic Surgery and inquired. "Surely," they said.

Only to find that two and one half years was worth no more than four months of credit. "Oh, well," says I, "It's better than a stick in the eye! I'll take it." That projected me to be done with my residency and ready to start practice as of September 1, 1963. "Now, I wonder if anybody wants me as a partner?"

I had inquired of several of the orthopedic surgeons who were practicing in Grand Rapids as to the availability of a place in their practice for me. At this point in life, I was quite impressed with my affability and my surgical skills. I had never doubted the fact that I was a highly desirable commodity in the world of orthopedic surgeons. You can imagine what a severe blow to my ego was the fact that no one wanted me. The word on the street, is far as I could tell was, "Go west young man, there is no place here for you."

For the first time in my life I had doubts about me, my person, my surgical skills and my personal worth. This was long before I knew Jesus as my Savior, so I felt just as many of my readers have or will feel at some time in their life. It was nothing like, " God, where are you?" I couldn't say that because I wasn't sure there was a God. When I went into the Air Force, my dog tag said agnostic, which basically means, "I don't know!"

You can imagine how badly I felt at that point. Married, with a lovely wife and three adorable little girls, with no money and no job prospects.

The voice on the other end of the line said, "Hey Bill, I hear you're looking for a job. I'm kind of busy and I think I can use a partner."

I was speechless. In fact I was so stupefied that I didn't even think to ask, " Who is this?"

Before I had a chance to open my mouth and embarrass myself, the voice said, "This is Jack, your fraternity brother from Phi Chi."

Jack Kihm from Kalamazoo, son of Otto Kihm, the tire magnate of Kalamazoo. I was so excited I didn't even ask if he was going to pay me, let alone how much. He offered me fifteen hundred dollars a month for one year and then the possibility of a partnership.

As I was leaving the house in Grand Rapids, for my annual fishing trip with my father, back to Newfoundland, I said to

Sandy, "Why don't you drive down to Kalamazoo and find us a place to live." She was more than happy to do that. Imagine my surprise upon my return from Newfoundland, a week later, when she told me that she had found the most beautiful place in the world. " Where is it? "

"In Plainwell."

" Where is Plainwell?" She held up her right hand and placed the index finger and thumb in proximity, I would guess about a quarter of an inch apart. "It's only this far from Kalamazoo and it's only thirty one thousand dollars." We had to borrow three hundred dollars from Dr. Marshall Patullo just to move, and five thousand dollars from Aunt Rosemary and Uncle Lee Kosten (Sandy's favorite aunt and uncle) for the down payment.

As we were settling in our new home on September 1, 1963, I received another phone call. " Are you Burdick?"

" Yes, sir, I am."

" I have a kid with a broken arm. You want to take care of him?"

" You bet! Thanks."

Brief pause while I went to the bathroom, just before I almost wet my pants with excitement. "Sandy, would you please call the two emergency rooms and find out where there is a kid with a broken arm and the name of the doctor who just called me?" Sandy has been pulling my chestnuts out of the fire ever since.

We had been married for eight years and had lived in Ann Arbor, Benton Harbor, three different places in Grand Rapids and two and a half years in Newfoundland. We really wanted to settle down and get acquainted in our new home town, Plainwell, MI., 49080. How do we become assimilated into our new community given that I work out of town and am seldom am I in town? Some sort of community activity of course. Beth is already in school and we will probably meet other young parents there. What else is available? A church, of course. What church? I was raised in a Methodist Church and Sandy's parents were once-in-awhile Congregationalists. So I told Sandy where the Methodist church was located, and said please go and make friends. She did.

" Honey, I want to invite some people over to our house so you can get to know them." A short time later we hosted the Bailey's and the Sell's. Bob and Charlene Bailey had a lovely daughter, Cindy, who was going to be involved in a beauty pageant at the high school. That was important because in those days Sandy was involved in a home business selling makeup. So she immediately volunteered to help Charlene with Cindy's makeup for the pageant.

That was our introduction to the Bailey's especially for the purpose of this writing, big Bob Bailey. The funny part was, Bob always considered himself to be a big, rough and tough guy. He was about five foot ten and couldn't have weighed more than one hundred eighty-five pounds, maybe two hundred with his tool belt on. He swaggered around, he was a little bowlegged and when he stopped to talk he always spread his feet so he had a wide base stance, one of importance or authority.

He wanted his persona to be big bad Bob Bailey. In reality, he was a nice pussycat. He was however, strong and tough. He worked for Consumer's Energy as a lineman. This was back in the days before cherry pickers. When there was a problem at the top of a telephone pole, the lineman used an extension ladder or put on spurs and climbed the pole. If you are under forty years of age I doubt you've ever seen anybody climb a telephone pole with spurs and a belt. I watched Bailey and was amazed how fast he could go up and down a pole. But he did it every day for years and years. That was not nearly as amazing as watching his buddy Spike do the same thing considering that Spike weighed three hundred pounds.

Bob probably knew as much as anyone around here about electricity and wiring. I know he worked evenings and weekends helping people do all sorts of things with wires. There was probably not a single thing he could not do with electricity and wires. And he knew everyone in town and their stories, which he often told me.

I secretly felt that Bob probably suffered from dyslexia. He was very smart and very capable but spelling and the like were a challenge for him. On one of the many road trips we made with Bob, Charlene and our family, we were playing a game called Hinky Pinky. The goal was to have two or more words with the same number of syllables that rhymed. The question would be 'Hink Pink: a purple like bovine,' The answer was, 'blue moo. ' So you would give some words of information and then say Hink-Pink or Hinky-Pinky or have 3 syllables Hinkety-Pinkety. My kids are very bright and they stretched our ingenuity with their word combinations. For example: guess what is Hinky-Pinky and is: "Hi, gelatin."

Meanwhile, Bob was unusually quiet and I assumed he didn't care for the game. Well into the game, Bob finally spoke up and said, "I've got a Hinky-Pinky, washing machine."

After about five minutes of guessing the kids finally said, "We give up, Mr. Bailey. What is it?"

Bob answered with a big grin of satisfaction on his face, "Speed Queen." You may have to think a moment about that one. The kids gave him the old raspberry, but I just kept quiet and said to myself, "Bob really functions well with his degree of dyslexia."

The answer to the Hinky Pinky question is: 'Hello, Jell-O'. Get it?

Bob never spoke about himself or about his accomplishments. I learned later that he was in the military, but hardly ever spoke of that. I also learned he was all state running back for Plainwell High School. I have come to appreciate Bob as a very talented and kindhearted person. When we put our swimming pool in at 439 West Bridge St., I realized that I would have to put a fence around it. Having just spent in excess of $20,000 for the pool I was definitely in the mood to save a buck as I considered what kind of fence to put in. The fence would have to be four hundred and fifty feet long; it could cost me more for the fence than for the pool. What could I do? I shared my conundrum with 'Old Bailey.'

"Well, Burdick, why don't you use telephone poles?"

"How could I possibly do that?" He proceeded to tell me exactly how to do it; something I never would have considered in a hundred years.

He first of all explained to me that there was a graveyard for old broken telephone poles which at that time were all made out of cedar. Cedar weathers well and does not rot. The local graveyard for old cedar poles was behind what is now our Industrial Park. Those poles had been laying there for years and nobody had any good use for them I was told by Bob Bailey and he had been working for Consumers Energy for so many years I figured he almost owned the company. Then he explained to me how I could cut up those poles, haul them away and have them made into boards.

I thought, "I just heard a direct line from God." He also told me about an old guy, Lyle, who had a logging mill north of Paw Paw, Michigan.

I called Lyle and he agreed to cut my cedar logs into one inch thick boards. Sounded like a really good deal to me and maybe even a lot of fun. Big problem! How does a small town guy who is a board certified orthopedic surgeon get all this done? I talked to a lot of people including one of my partners, Bill Kube, who would likely be able to do exactly what I had proposed. I can't say what ideas came from whom, but this was my game plan.

I needed a chainsaw to cut the telephone poles; they were at least 30 feet long. I have never used a chainsaw but Gordon Blossom who by this time was my pastor at the local Baptist Church, had an eighteen inch chain saw that he would be happy to sell me, subsequent to which I learned never to trust a Baptist preacher. Actually, it was a good chainsaw. It's just that I didn't know anything about chainsaws; when they get dull, they cut crooked.

I rented a trailer fit for hauling cedar logs, drove it over to the log pile, fired up my trusty chainsaw and proceeded to cut the logs into pieces about seven feet long. There was no such thing as a straight cut. Every cut was slanted. I cut the logs, loaded them on the trailer, hauled them over to Lyle and he cut them into one inch thick boards.

Think with me a moment about the times you have driven along a country road with a row of telephone poles on the side of the road. What did you see in addition to the telephone poles? A whole bunch of signs that had been affixed to the telephone pole with tacks or large nails. When the sign was damaged or worn and pulled off the telephone pole, what do you think happen to the nails that held the sign on the pole? Correct! They were all left in the pole. What do you think nails do to the blade of a chainsaw? Right! They quickly dull the blades. So when Lyle called me and said my first load of boards was ready, he told me the bad news. The price of cutting the boards had just gone up because after every batch of boards he had to sharpen every tooth of his great big saw blade. The cost of the board fence rose abruptly.

I was cutting up my last batch of cedar telephone poles, had them loaded on the trailer and was about to drive off when an official Consumers Energy truck drove up.

"What are you doing?"

"I was just cutting some pieces off these damaged poles."

"This is private property. Who gave you permission to take these poles?"

"Why, my friend Bob Bailey told me it was perfectly okay to take some of these damaged poles."

"Just who is Bob Bailey?"

The severity of the crime just hit home. Bob Bailey was simply a lineman for Consumers Energy. He was not a supervisor or any other official of the company. I could visualize a lawsuit and the dollar bills flying right out of my pocket. I could see the wheels turning in this guy's head.

In reality, I think he was thinking to himself, we just got rid of a lot of crap, and saved a few bucks.

But he had to save face so he simply said, "Don't take any more."

"Thank you, Jesus!" I was one of those weird Baptists by this time.

Another adventure shared with old Bob Bailey was on the Pere Marquette River. It was in the fall of the year and the weather was still fairly decent. I knew that salmon ran from Lake Michigan all the way up to at least my cabin on the Pere Marquette River. I thought it might be fun to try and catch a salmon on a spinner in this river. I knew I could not catch or hold a salmon in my stretch of the river, which was the middle branch of the Pere Marquette River. It was too deep and narrow to reasonably catch a twenty pound salmon.

I knew a stretch of river downstream where there were good rapids that were shallow where we could see salmon and probably catch them if they would hit a spinner. So I invited Bob to accompany me up north to my cabin where we spent the night. After breakfast we loaded up and went down to this particular stretch of the main stream. It was an overcast day and fairly warm when we got into the river in our waders with our spinning rods and Mepps spinners. We wandered up and down the river seeing a few salmon here and there but they absolutely refused to take a spinner. I certainly didn't have my wits about me when I planned this trip, even though I had equipped both of us with waders and spinning rods that would certainly hold the salmon if we caught one. Trying to net a salmon with a small trout net would've been hilarious. Nonetheless I had an idea. From just having read about my fence around the pool you realize that not all my ideas are great, in fact some of them are ludicrous.

We were in a very long stretch of shallow rapids with a gravel bottom; the water could not have been deeper than a foot and a half at the most. I spotted a ragtag salmon across the river from me. The reason I said ragtag is that once the salmon enter the stream, their physical characteristics start to change. When in Lake Michigan they are quite light or almost silver in color. As the spawning season approaches, their color deepens and becomes orange and in some places very dark. After they have been in the river a while they develop light patches particularly in the tail area and on the belly; they actually look like they are rotting. If we waited a few more weeks they would be rotting. I have tried eating salmon after they have been in the river a while and they even taste like they're rotting. So why I wanted to catch the salmon is really beyond me. It was just a challenge because even if I were successful I would not have eaten that rotten salmon.

Having spotted this salmon slowly moving upstream, I slipped in below him and start making noise. He responded well and started moving upstream at a very casual pace. I had a plan. Upstream from me standing in the stream similarly baffled as he tried to figure out how to catch one of these fish stood Bob Bailey.

I hollered at Bob, "Quick, look Bob, there is a salmon coming your way. Turn around."

Bob did so and was looking right at me.

"He's on your right side, put your net straight down into the water and move it as I direct you." He was looking down stream at me and clearly could not see the salmon. At that time I thought it was because of the sheen on the water. There wasn't a bright sun overhead but nonetheless there was sheen and in certain positions you could not see into the water. Only later did I realize what Bob's real problem was. He had glaucoma which was undiagnosed and untreated. He was losing his peripheral vision. Only later when he also developed macular degeneration did I realize how severely he was handicapped with his poor vision.

His hearing was good and he followed my directions perfectly. "To the right, now back to the left, back to the right, he's almost there— he's there, scoop him up."

Bob executed the maneuver perfectly and scooped the salmon right into my beautiful handcrafted trout landing net.

Only to realize that the meshing in the net was just like that darn salmon, it was rotten!

The salmon went right through the net and kept on going upstream. I felt so sorry for Bob, because he said, "What did I do wrong?" I tried to assure him he had done everything perfectly. He had followed my directions to the letter, performed admirably. The whole thing was MY BAD! I hadn't used that net in years and had forgotten the mesh was not nylon. It was a cloth mesh net, hanging in my closet for years. I hadn't tested it before hand. I just now realized that I have developed a new adage. If it's old, and has been sitting around a while, it needs to be tested before usage. That applies to us old folks as well as old equipment.

Many years later after all of my trout fishing adventures had ended, and Doug Wendzel had died, I had resorted to bluegill fishing. This is really wrong wording, better yet wrong concept. I had resorted to, makes it sound as though I were on my deathbed and I had no other options. Actually my interests had changed to fishing for Blue Gill, Perch and Walleyed Pike. It was certainly different from fly fishing for trout, but nonetheless challenging because walleye were just unpredictable and bluegills were peculiar, picky and somewhat cantankerous. Perch fishing in the early part of the year: totally unpredictable. They travel in and around bluegills and are caught with reasonable frequency but in the fall, when they tend to school, perch fishing is feast or famine.

Bob Bailey's fortunes changed considerably for the worse over the next few years. With age, his diabetes had worsened, he suffered a stroke and as I mentioned, his eyesight worsened because of a combination of glaucoma and macular degeneration. His balance was atrocious. He staggered a lot and had to use a cane. But with all these problems his mind was still sharp.

About eight years before, while at one of our Plainwell social functions, I found Bailey eating a sandwich and sipping some punch. He had totally given up drinking beer or any hard liquor. We were simply chatting away when he asked me if he had ever taken me fishing on Warner Lake. My response was that I had never heard of Warner Lake but as I listened to him talk, I sensed there was something special about Warner Lake. So I mentioned that I'd like to try it but I might have trouble getting my boat into Warner Lake since it was a private access. What he said was not to worry; he had a boat on Warner Lake. Could I row a boat? "Are you kidding? I could row a boat before I could ride a bike!" That was a little stretch, but for the several years that I went fishing with Dick Chamberlain, my father and Walt Eidson on Round Lake, Michigan, if I wanted to fish I had to row the boat. And that lake was almost a mile across. So from age ten on I had done a lot of boat rowing.

In those days we did not have nice slick bottom aluminum boats. We had wooden rowboats that were more like rowing a barge than a boat. Rowing one of those boats required a lot of strength and some savvy. What I rowed was a rental boat, as I described above, more like a barge then a boat. On the other hand, my father had what I considered a real classy boat. It was hand made by Hubert Meade, nicknamed "Oily" because he owned and operated a fuel oil delivery truck.

As I reminisce about the 'good old days,' a number of thoughts come to mind. I have just finished reading a book about Asperger's disease written by John Elder Robison, 'Look Me In The Eyes.' As he was growing up, as an Asperger person, he had a tendency to give a name to all his friends and acquaintances, which was a descriptive phrase, such as mama bear, Cubby and a few others. Later in life, as he discovered that this malady had been described by a person named Asperger, he also learned that those people all had a tendency to use nicknames. As I look back on my father and his tendency to do the same, I'm beginning to wonder, could I be a latent Asperger's? Dear reader, I invite your commentary.

As we talked that day, I could readily see that Bob Bailey needed to go fishing. He had to retire from Consumers because of his many medical problems. He could no longer fish alone and knew no one who could or would take him fishing. I was still young enough and fit enough to do whatever had to be done to go fishing, so I knew I could take care of old Bailey. So I said ,"Yes, I'll be happy to take you fishing, Bob." When you read my stories about fishing with Doug, you will realize that Doug trained me to be a somewhat skilled caregiver. So with all the confidence in the world I agreed to take Bob Bailey fishing on Warner Lake. At several points that first day out, I wondered if I could ever have enough experience to take Bob Bailey fishing on Warner Lake. I will try and relay some of our experiences, but all the words in the world cannot describe our efforts, problems and excesses on Warner Lake.

Warner Lake is probably the most beautiful lake I have ever seen. It is situated north and east of Lake Doster. It is between thirty-five and fifty acres in size and at the south corner of the lake, it is seventy feet deep. So it is a spring fed lake. There is a Girl Scout camp situated on the southeast corner of the Lake but none of the buildings are visible. Only a boating and swimming area are visible on the lake itself. There are a few rowboats and paddle-boats that occupy the lake for a brief period of time, about eight weeks in the summer and therefore are not a problem to fishermen. Fairly close to the Girl Scout camp is a cottage owned by the Doster family. They have two docks, quite a few small boats and a stairway that runs from the lake up to their cottage. They are basically non-fisherman. On the south end of the lake there are two cottages I've never seen . They each have a couple boats, but similarly they are not fishing people. On the west end of the lake there is a single house trailer with a small pontoon boat.

The access to the lake for Bob Bailey and me and the Doster family was the barnyard and home owned and inhabited by Lyle and Marie Champion. Bob Bailey had access to the lake because he was a friend of Lyle. That was good enough for me. Later, after Lyle died, I learned that Marie loved to eat bluegill, but nobody ever gave her any. Every time I went fishing, I made sure I had some bluegill from my freezer to give to Marie. I was in her good graces for several years until her infirmity required much care from her family. They felt that my presence was too big a stress for their mother; she worried about me alone on the lake. The fact that I fed her a lot of bluegill didn't matter. I no longer had access to Warner Lake. Boo -Hoo!

For some time after Bob and I had talked I heard nothing from him, so I thought it was all talk without any plan. Much to my surprise, one day I got a phone call. " Burdick? This is Bob. Time to go fishing."

So we had some discussion about what I should bring and I wasn't at all sure what I would need, let alone what kind of tackle Bob Bailey had. Nonetheless I gathered some gear together, drove over and picked Bob up and headed out to Warner Lake. I had no idea where I was going and I wasn't all that sure the Bailey could see well enough to get us there but he never missed a turn.

We pulled up in front of the house and Bob said, "Go knock on the door and tell whoever comes to the door that you're taking Bob Bailey fishing. That'll get us in." So I did that and a woman who reminded me of Ma Kettle came to the door. She smiled very sweetly and said, "How is old Bob?" She came out the door, waved to Bob and he waved back. We were in!

We drove past the house to a cattle gate. I got out, swung the gate open, drove through and put the gate back in place. That gate was critical, as I was to learn. Dr. Millard Doster kept sheep back there in the pasture. If the gate was open, the sheep would wander out and get run over on the road. Such an event would certainly seal my fate, so I was always very careful to make sure the gate was firmly chained shut. We followed a two track around the bend, down a hill, up a hill, around another bend to end up at the top of the Doster stairway. Bailey could matriculate the stairway because of a sturdy rail. But once he got down to the dock that was another story. He staggered around that dock like a drunken sailor.

I found Bailey's boat. It was a fairly deep V bottom boat with a pointed bow and a stern with a wooden plate on it to which one might affix a motor. Never in my wildest imagination would I ever try to put a motor on that boat. I tipped it over and dragged it to the water and put it in. It didn't leak quite as much as I had anticipated. There was a small seat in the bow, a seat in the middle on which Bailey would place his rear fisterus (Grandpa word) and row. There was a narrow seat in the back of the boat with just enough leg room to allow me to face the stern of the boat. The oar locks were very old and had no plastic liners so Bailey's oars rattled, they were so loose. The oars were different lengths because Bob or Charlene or Cindy had found them as a bargain at a garage sale. Never mind. Bailey told me he was going to row. Unbelievable! This guy could hardly see, could hardly walk and he insists on rowing the boat. And I didn't have a life preserver nor did he. God be with us!

As we cast off Bailey started rowing. He said to me, "Burdick, you'll have to look around and make sure I'm going in the right direction."

I'm thinking to myself, "How would I know what the right direction is. I've never seen this lake before." So he directed me to a point right directly across the lake that I could figure out, so we probably would get there.

But first we had to rig our poles so we could catch fish. I had two small, ultra-light spinning rods, with six pound monofilament line, one or two split shot about a foot above my hook. Then I took a close look at Bailey's rod. He has two but only one was set up. As I describe his rod and set up, only a fisherman will understand what I'm saying and appreciate my astonishment. You non-fisherman just bear with me as I struggle to describe his 'apparatus.'

His rod was about seven feet long made of white fiberglass and was jointed; two pieces. In the place of the spin cast reel he had an old automatic fly reel. The last time I saw one of those was in 1948. My father used them all the time. I hated them and never used one. A trout fly fishing purist like me would not be caught dead using an old automatic reel.

Instead of a fly line, Bailey had on the reel an old black, braided cotton casting line. He couldn't see that line any better than he could see a monofilament line. After that trip, I pulled all of his rotten line off the reel, and put on one of my highly visible orange fly lines. My large caliber orange fishing line was a great improvement for him.

At the distal or business end of his line he had tied on a piece of huge cat gut about thirty pound test. To that he then affixed a series of side rotating spinners. He must have had three of them in line. At the end of the spinners was a snap swivel to which he attached a huge hook. So much for finesse.

That pretty well described where we started. "How about sinkers on your line, Bob?"

"Don't need em. Those spinners will get the worm deep enough."

Rough translation, "I don't really know how deep this worm is going to go and I don't know where the fish are as far as depth and I don't care cause I'm gonna catch fish anyway."

Well, he was right. He caught fish but I had no idea how deep the fish were lying or how deep he was fishing. He just caught fish!

Next item for consideration was bait. When bait fishing for trout I always use a piece of a crawler. If that were good enough for trout, it's good enough for bluegills. So I always used about three quarters of an inch of a crawler, hooked twice with a little tail dragging along.

"What are you using for bait, Bailey?"

"Worms, Burdick! Red worms."

I had to pick up my feet, turn around on my seat and grab his worm can to see what he was really talking about. I'd seen his tackle so I knew that he had a great big hook, about a size six bass hook. If he were really using red worms, they were hardly fatter than the shank of the hook.

Sure enough, he had a half of a can of the skinniest red worms I have ever seen. "Let me help you bait your hook Bob."

"No thanks Burdick, I got it."

At this point I realized to him it was a matter of pride and I certainly did not want to humiliate old Bob Bailey. So I left

Bob to his own devices hoping he would get a worm on his hook before we were done fishing that day and baited my own hook.

Again, I ask, " How deep do we fish Bob?"

"Just throw it out, Burdick, and we'll see what happens. If you get a hit, I just don't know what to tell you."

It turns out that that phrase, " I just don't know what to tell you" was an idiom with great impact.

I didn't throw the worm out, but after I had attached my three quarters inch long piece of crawler to my long shank number eight Limerick hook, with one medium-size sinker, I simply lowered it into the water and let it run until it hit the bottom. I then reeled in two turns and went along with the drift. Bailey's method of fishing, which I thought was a little strange, was to keep the boat moving. When I was a kid, my dad would row out to a certain spot in the lake, throw out the anchor so that we were stopped dead and then fished right off the bottom. I learned from my father, that this was the gospel in bluegill fishing. Only later in life, when I was fishing on Lake Doster by myself, did I realize the benefit of a moving bait.

By the time Bailey had rowed the boat across to the point, we both had our hooks baited and we were in the process of fishing for bluegills. Bailey did indeed row the boat and he knew exactly how to do it properly. We were barely crawling along, but the point was, we were moving, and that proved to be a challenge for the hungry bluegill.

This seems to be a proper point to digress and mention that all fresh water fish are carnivorous. No game fish that I know is herbivorous. They all like meat; a piece of meat that offers a challenge like, " I'm going to get away if you don't bite me quickly." A feeding fish sees life and food in that precise manner. A moving worm is a challenge to a hungry fish and he usually vigorously attacks it. So I was not surprised when I had a quick hit. The surprise was the fight in this fish, until I got it up to surface and realized that this was a nine inch bluegill. In my wildest dreams only had I imagined fish this size. And thereafter, a nine inch bluegill and or sunfish was almost the rule on Warner Lake.

So here I was, the hero for taking handicapped old Bob Bailey fishing on Warner Lake, which I thought surely was going to be a wild goose chase, when in fact it turned out to be Nirvana for an eager beaver fisherman like me.

In the meantime, Bob had managed to load his hook up with a gob of worms. I can't for the life of me figure out how he got them on the hook; he had to feel his way, as he surely couldn't see to do it. So he put his rod down on his left side so that the reel was on the bottom of the boat and the rod stuck up and out on the left side of the boat. The rod was long enough so I could easily see the tip as it stuck out beyond the end of the boat.

" You got a hit, Bob!"

" By golly, you're right." He gingerly picked up the rod with his left hand and then snapped it up so hard to set the hook I thought it would break the rod.

"It's a good one, Burdick." I then watched a master bring in that fish with his automatic reel and super-soft spinning rod. I realized that I had the privilege of fishing with a master fisherman who had a lot of physical disabilities, but mentally was sharp as a tack. His speech had been affected by his stroke, and I think that disability had fooled a lot of people. Old Bailey was still a wise old geezer.

I learned later that even though the spinning rod was white fiberglass and contrasted well with the dark water, that even the orange line which I had put on his rod had not helped him to see his rod when it moved with a hit. The boat and the seats were all aluminum and so when his rod rattled he knew he had a hit. He could not see the rod move or jump, but he could hear it. Consequently, he had a lot of gut hooked fish. That provided a challenge for me, getting the hook out of the fishes' gut, because old Bob couldn't see to do it. That was a small price to pay for the fun that we had together over the next few years. Many were the days when we hauled out thirty, forty, and even fifty sooper-dooper big blue gills. Thank you, Bob. I miss you.

18

Doug and I

I think I should begin by telling you the story of how Doug and I met. As you know I had long been interested in fishing for trout. I had heard of an organization called Trout Unlimited. It was a local organization that was part of the international group called Trout Unlimited. One of my patient's husband belonged to that group. So I found out when it met and arranged to be there at the next monthly meeting.

There I met Kate's husband Chuck Maltby and his friend Doug Wendzel. Chuck was a very personable individual who I took to immediately. On the other hand I found Doug to be somewhat strange. He was short, had very short hair, a fairly prominent nose, squinty eyes, and gripped a cigar in his teeth. Although the cigar was not lit, it did smell. Later I was to learn that he never did light a cigar; he simply carried it around in his teeth and chewed it down to a nub and then spit it out. I never did understand why. It always seemed to be a little peculiar but then that was a hallmark of Doug Wendzel, a little different.

I was later to learn that he had a similar habit with pipes. From that time on every time I was with Doug, he had in his hand or in his mouth or a pocket, a very short stubby curved stemmed pipe that stunk. His technique of smoking the pipe was to light it, chew the bit, but never inhale the smoke. I really enjoyed the smell of the pipe and it was not long after that I took up the habit of smoking a pipe, just for the fellowship, of course. However, I did not care for the type of pipe that he used so that I experimented until I found a pipe that I enjoyed; it was a corncob pipe.

Although our interaction was limited to our monthly meeting of Trout Unlimited, I did learn a lot about Doug and Chuck and their twenty-five year long friendship. I would be remiss if I did not mention that it struck a certain longing in my heart; a friendship of twenty-five years which seemed like a lifetime to me. Here were a couple of guys whose families were familiar with one another, who spent time together not only fishing but socially in between fishing times. They really appeared to genuinely care about one another. I longed to have a friend like that.

Over a period of several months I got to know both of them fairly well. We shared stories of battles with mighty Leviathan in which we, the fisherman, were usually triumphant. I learned that both of them were basically worm fishermen although that was quite disgusting to me since I was a purist fly fisherman. However, I could see some value in doing battle with trout with the worm instead of a fly, especially if you're hungry for trout to eat.

Besides, I had never really learned the art of stream fishing with worms for brown trout. I now say that because I realize there is an art form in worm fishing for brown trout. One does not simply drop a worm laden hook into the stream and have the fish gobble it up. Brown trout are very discerning and very difficult to coax into biting a worm especially one with a hook in it. However at that time I was very contemptuous of worm fishermen. Only later in life did I recognize how much fun it was to coax a trout into taking a worm in a stream that was gin clear, with no rain and no clouds in the sky. It was every bit as much an art form as dropping a dainty number twelve Adams dry fly on top of a rising trout.

Later, Doug would regale me with his many stories of trout fishing with a worm. I was particularly impressed with his stories about fishing for trout with the worm after a rainstorm. He told me that he would wake up in the middle of the night to hear thunder outside the house. At that point he could not get back to sleep but waited until the clock showed it was about one hour before sunrise. Then he would get into his car which was always loaded with one or two fishing rods, a fishing vest, a pair of waders or hip boots and a can of worms. And of course a creel.

The fishing rods of necessity had to be spinning rods. He would carry in his vest a collection of sinkers, a number of which he would fix to his line dependent on the flow of the current in the stream he was fishing. When worm fishing, it is imperative that the bait is on or near the bottom of the stream. However, if the line is too heavily weighted it will stop. It is very necessary that the worm floats down the stream at the rate of the stream-flow near the bottom so that the trout, always looking at the bottom, will see the worm and suck it up.

So Doug would drive his trusty International Harvester Scout to a nearby stream with which he was very familiar, don his waders and step into water, by then, muddy water, and drop a crawler into the stream, hopefully to the bottom.

I have subsequently learned when fishing worms one always fishes up stream. The reason for that is very simple; water in the stream by definition flows down hill or down stream. Food that the fish will eat also flows downstream therefore the trout is always facing upstream so he can see everything that comes down the stream; that includes eager fisherman, at which point, the trout will seek cover and will not bite. They are spooked.

So when one approaches a trout stream to fish in any manner he must do so with great stealth. A heavy tread on the bank will send vibrations into the surrounding land and water and alert the wary trout. A heavy tread will spook fish. Similarly when entering the water one enters very carefully so he makes no splash and when his feet hit the bottom of the stream there is no vibration.

The fisherman faces upstream and casts or throws his bait upstream from where he is standing. Since the stream is moving down toward the fisherman, he must take up slack line so he has reasonable control of the worm at the end of the line. If you reel too fast, you'll pull the worm downstream in an unnatural manner and will spook fish. If you fail to keep the loose line on the reel, when the fish strikes you will have too much slack line and can't set the hook.

It takes quite a bit of practice to assure that:

1. You are throwing the worm in the right spot.

2. You have judged the speed of the stream correctly to have the right amount of weight on the line.

3. You reel in an appropriate amount of slack line so when you feel the hit, you are ready to set the hook.

Setting the hook for a feeding trout can be very difficult. Ordinarily the trout does not simply grab the worm, suck it down and hook himself. In the usual setting the trout is somewhat cautious and when moving up to the worm, you could almost imagine, after a number of years of experience, what is going on. He mouths or nibbles the worm and you can feel a jiggle at the end of the line. If you set the hook at this point you will probably miss that fish. After a sufficient amount of fishing one gets the idea that you can tell when he has actually ingested the worm; the jiggling either slows down or stops. At that point you set the hook. That means you lift the tip of your spinning rod up, take in the last bit of slack, snap the rod straight up so as to set the hook in the roof of the trout's mouth where it is very solid.

At the point where you have the trout hooked, it is important to keep him away from snags which can be anywhere; in the middle of the stream, on the edge of the stream or some overhanging tree or branch. It is important to keep a constant pressure on the fish by pulling the rod with a reasonable bow in it and a tight line. Only with a tight line does one have a modicum of control over the trout.

To land a trout, one must bring the fish to the net. It is important to realize what I just said, bring the fish to the net. There is a tremendous temptation to reach out, or better said, lunge out with the landing net and try to snag the trout. This may work but I am a living witness to tell you that move is fraught with hazard.

A number of factors must be considered when trying to net or land a fish. The fish is alive and is a lot quicker than you think. The current is usually flowing at a pretty good clip, which means frequently faster than you think. The landing net has a bag that hangs into the water. When lunging forward it is not uncommon for the bag to snag on an unseen root or twig in the water. The best way, in my experience, to net a fish is to place the landing net under the surface of the water by six inches or so. Then allow the fish, which is hanging from the end of your line, to drop down in the current on top of the net and simply raise the net up. I have two stories, actually many stories, about missing while trying to net a fish. Some happened because of my ignorance and enthusiasm but the most classic case happened because of poor planning.

Most of what I have just related to you, is true and Doug basically taught me the concepts involved in worm fishing. Once I caught on to this concept, how to deceive a Brown trout with a worm, I practiced and embellished my techniques to the point where I became a seasoned wormer. Since the concept is to deceive the trout in order for him to bite the worm with a sharp hook in the middle of it, I will digress to speak a little on general deception by a seasoned fisherman, liar and deceiver. Actually, all fishing is a form of deception. The most obvious application of deception is that which the fisherman uses on his very wary opponent, Pisces.

Unfortunately there are some innocent bystanders involved in and around the fisherman's life. Most obvious, of course, is one's spouse, followed closely by his children, his friends, his business associates and unfortunately, only late in life does he realize the greatest victim of deception is himself. On the surface, deceiving fish seems to be a victimless crime. It is not so! The fisherman's trail is littered with debris: broken rods, damaged reels, torn landing nets, shirts, pants, and waders. The lost items are almost too numerous to be recalled or to be mentioned, but I'll try a few: sunglasses, regular glasses, hats, gloves, flies, leaders, hooks, sinkers, patience, temper and time.

Deception is a way of life for the skilled trout fisherman. Who do we deceive? The ultimate goal is to deceive the trout, but to get there we have to deceive people. We, who are fortunate enough to be married, use a certain amount of deception in order to get away from our household duties and chores in order to get to the trout stream.

"It's going to rain tonight and the trout will be on the feed tomorrow morning."

"This is the only day I have to go fishing this week."

"I'll take the garbage out on my way out."

"I've been sitting in the office too much and I need the exercise."

"We will go out for dinner Saturday."

"I'll paint the outhouse Monday night."

"My boss will really be impressed if I can serve him a nice trout dinner next week."

"It's the opening of trout season, honey."

"The season closes Saturday you know."

"I promised Doug that we would fish this Wednesday and Thursday."

And so the excuses go on and on. That is only when dealing with our wives. There are others who we must deceive. Our bosses, our children, our friends, the pastor and God only knows who else we have deceived in order to pursue the hunt for the mighty trout.

Each of us thinks that he is God's gift to the fishing community, that each of our experiences is unique, never before experienced by other fisherman. The only reason that a fisherman listens to the tale of another fisherman is so that he can 'one up' him in the story that he is waiting to tell. The simple truth is there is very little new in the fishing world. Most of us have heard many strange and mystifying stories and have participated in a few ourselves. So who are we really fooling? No one! So if anyone reading these words is surprised in the least, then I truly am surprised.

But we the steadfast, dedicated trout fisherman have in mind the ultimate recipient of our deception, the wise and wary, almost sacred German Brown Trout. There are any number of things that we must consider in our ongoing battle to deceive the ultimate foe.

Let us first of all consider our foe, the German Brown Trout. I personally do not believe the trout were brought over by a few unruly Hessians to fill the entire North American continent. However that could be the case, I don't really know nor care. All I know is that they have readily adapted to the waters of North America and elsewhere, reproduced plentifully and are a very wary, worthy opponent to all of us who espouse our undying love of trout, especially German Brown Trout.

A simple note here is sufficient for the time. We also have an abundance of rainbow trout in North America and we do have a trout that is known to be native called the Eastern Brook Trout. We seldom deal with or talk about the Brook Trout because they inhabit very cold water. Trout fisherman in the United States seldom encounter the lively little Brook Trout. In Michigan they are limited to a very few, very cold, usually spring fed streams located mostly in the Upper Peninsula.

I have to surmise that the goal of every fish that I have ever encountered is to eat and avoid being eaten. That being said it is probably a summary statement of the life of a trout. To that end most fish are quite wary and especially so trout.

I remember well the first day that I viewed my stretch of the middle branch of the Pere Marquette River. It was a very cool autumn day with most of the leaves fallen from the trees. Of course there were multiple pine trees that retained their color but that was virtually the only color visible to me as I gazed into this stretch of prime trout water. I remember saying to myself as I viewed that water which appeared to be gray and lifeless, "What the hell have I done?"

And that was in response to the fact that James Roger Glessner and I had just purchased twenty-seven acres of this prime water, and some swamp, for ten thousand dollars. That was shortly after I had to borrow three hundred dollars just to move to Plainwell in 1963. I wondered if my wife would ever forgive me. But as I looked into that gray very cold water I could not see any evidence of trout ever having lived in that stream. At that point I could not possibly conceive the fact that sometime in the not too distant future this cold lifeless stream would produce thirty trout in one evening.

As I was to learn by reading books and by experiencing fishing on my own, trout are rarely visible in a stream. They are always wary and always hiding. Things that I know can bother trout are some of the following: loud noises that can cause vibrations on land and in the water, flashing lights, moving shadows, surface disturbances, highly visible lines, and food in the water in that does not follow the pattern of the moving water. Things that excite the fish are sometimes curious, obvious foodstuffs that appear to be fleeing the trout: tadpoles, minnows, small water insects, struggling small fish, small lamprey eels, small salamanders and finally small shrew.

Back to deceiving the feeding trout. When one is fishing with worms for trout, one must employ several deceiving techniques. Spinning line is monofilament nylon. It comes in multiple sizes, that is diameters, and is commonly referred to by the weight the line will support; a six pound line. Hopefully that line will support a six-pound weight at a dead hang. If you have a six pound weight on the end of a line you're holding and attempting to jiggle it, the line will break. As long as it's a steady pull, not a jerk, a six-pound line will support six pounds.

And so on up and down the register. I have heard of fishing with a one-pound line but I think I would prefer fishing with a spider web. I would sometimes use a two pound line when ice fishing or as a tippet on a fly line. The run-of-the-mill worm fishermen prefer a line of about six pounds. A purist might go down to a four-pound line but also may go hungry. A six-pound line is probably not invisible to the trout but is less visible than the lines I used when I was fishing Lemon Creek in Berrien Springs.

The food we use when bait fishing for trout is usually a worm or more properly speaking a piece of crawler. For bluegills, I use about a one-inch piece of crawler, hook it twice with a tail dragging. For trout, I would use a slightly longer piece; perhaps up to two inches long, again hook it twice with a large tail dragging in the water.

The technique used in the trout stream has to be observed. One has to be fishing in a shallow stretch of water, where he can watch material drifting downstream. The material needs to be slightly heavier than the water so it tends to sink. But if it sinks too much because it is heavy and sticks to the bottom, it will not move with the current as should debris and food when drifting down stream. That is why Doug always carried a string of titted split shot on a piece of line tied to his vest. When the stream was fairly straight and the current fast, he would put on extra weight. If the stream slowed, such as in an eddy current, he would decrease the weight. With titted sinkers, he could easily add or remove a weight. If he used plain split shot sinkers, he would need to cut the hook off, slide the sinker off, retie the hook and then add the sinker. A big waste of time. With titted sinkers one could simply pinch the tips together and the center would open up for a quick change.

One might be tempted to think that's a bunch of hooey, no fish is that spooky. Not so. I was fishing a fairly shallow stretch of sand bottom river so I could see everything very well. I had seen a fish flash out to the middle of the stream from an over-hanging bank, so I knew he was there and hungry. I carefully measured the weight with the stream flow and tossed out the crawler upstream with a single sinker. I could see the crawler drifting down at just the right speed. I saw the trout move out from the bank, position himself to take the crawler, when the crawler hung up on a tiny twig that I had not seen. Unnatural! That trout shot back under the bank and would not come out no matter how well I floated subsequent crawlers. Lesson learned!

All of this is simply to say that Doug Wendzel was a dedi-cated and skilled worm fishermen. As I write this and think about Doug putting away fish in their refrigerator or freezer, I call to mind a scene from a movie about the lawyer and skilled trout fisherman from the Upper Peninsula, Robert Traver au-thor of 'Trout Madness.' In the opening scene of this part of the movie, Robert Traver was standing in waders, opening the freezer compartment of his refrigerator and placing in two brook trout he just caught. As he opened the door, one could see nothing but stacks of brook trout, two to a package wrapped in foil. That's the minds eye picture that I have of Doug Wendzel taking care of the many trout he caught fishing exactly the way that I described.

19

Graham MacDougal

After spending considerable time with Doug Wenzel I realized that he virtually lived to fish. As he regaled me with many tales, I sensed his deep satisfaction with his fishing stories. He told me how his very good fishing friend, Chuck Maltby, had tried to get them back into the swing of fishing since his very debilitating accident. I knew Chuck and liked him very much. He was very kind, quiet, and extremely talented; I perceived his great loss of camaraderie with Doug. I say very talented because as I am writing this now, I am drinking coffee from a cup with a fishing design on it that Chuck created for our local chapter of Trout Unlimited. I have only one cup and with the loss of both Doug and Chuck, I would hate to lose or break this one. So if any of you kind souls have an opportunity to read this epistle and have in your possession or knowledge of the existence of another such cup I would very much appreciate a big 'you-hoo.'

Chuck had helped Doug get into an ATV and they tried to take it on a fishing adventure. The story I heard was Doug could not control this vehicle with hand controls alone, so he ended up running it into the river and floating down stream. I could understand how that might dampen one's enthusiasm for getting Doug back into their world of fishing.

I can almost visualize that terrifying but humorous moment in their lives. "Doug, this is an ATV, all terrain vehicle and here is how it works."

Doug, " I know all about ATV's. Just put me in and let me get going!"

Chuck, "Turn the key -- "

Doug, " I know. I know."

A long silence. The sound of the motor starting, the evidence of the machine moving and probably something like this, " Hey, this is really good. Whoops, whoa, how do you stop this thing? Help! I'm floating down the river."

Chuck. Nothing, just silence. End of the story. I know Doug didn't fall in but Chuck was scared to death that he would tip over in the water and drown. I rather think at that point Chuck figured out he was not going to be able to get Doug fishing again. And that probably broke his heart.

Enter the picture, kindly and nosy, doc Burdick. "Hey Doug, I've got an idea." And indeed I did. I had at this time become one of Doug's treating doctors. In case I forgot to mention the incident that caused Doug's fall and changed his life and the life of his family forever, I'll give a very brief summary.

Doug was a dynamo. He was about five foot six, forty two years old and was extremely active and involved in the community of Richland. His father was a professor at Kalamazoo

College. I believe he was retired at the time I knew Doug. He, his brother and father were involved in a land development and building company. At the time of his accident Doug was the main cog in that wheel. He and his brother Tom were purchasing land under the supervision of their father. Doug would build homes after the land was developed. He was also active in the Richland Village Council and a member of the volunteer fire department.

On that fateful day in July, somewhere around 1965, Doug, as a volunteer fire fighter, was climbing an aluminum ladder, without protective footwear or gloves, to cut the hot line into a burning home. As soon as his shears hit that 440 line, zap! Doug fell some twenty-five feet to the ground crushing the vertebra of D-6: instant paralysis!

I knew little of his initial care, since I was on my annual Newfoundland fishing trip with my father. Upon returning to Michigan, I learned of the tragedy and made a point to drop in to see Doug every day as I made my rounds at Borgess hospital. I was not involved in his initial care at all since he was under the maintenance of Dr. Robert Fabi, with whom I had a good relationship.

I also got to know Doug's personal doctor and very good friend, Dick Kik. I was somewhat involved indirectly in his total care from that point on. During my residency training, at Blodgett Hospital, in Grand Rapids, I had extensive experience in treating the acute injuries of both paraplegics and quadriplegic patients. Moreover since my bosses, Al Swanson and

Jim Glessner, were heavily involved in reconstructive orthopedic surgery, I had a lot of experience in this area.

So when many months later, Doug was complaining to me that he could not bring his right thigh up high enough to allow him to sit comfortably in his wheelchair, I knew immediately what his problem was. Fixing it was another whole ballgame. An x-ray revealed that Doug had a large exocytosis, or bony mass, starting from the front of his iliac crest down towards his right thigh. This is very common in post traumatic situations such as Doug had gone through. Bob Fabi and I both knew what it was but it seemed like we were living on another planet. It appeared to be some mysterious disease to everyone to whom we tried to explain. "It's a great big chunk of rock hard bone growing where it ought not to grow, and it blocks his right thigh from coming up to a sitting position. Until we get rid of it, he will never be able to sit in his wheelchair." That overly simplistic explanation stopped a lot of stupid questions.

Surgery to correct this malady was not especially difficult, but more than anything else, it was a tedious procedure. The biggest complication of the procedure was a recurrence of this ossification and even possibly a worse predicament more bone. I planned this procedure carefully having read everything available in the literature and very confidently entered the operating room only to discover it was packed with orthopedic surgical residents, most of whom had never heard of the problem let alone seen it. My basic thought was, "This is sink or swim, thank you, Lord Jesus. Amen."

Healing was not routine since there is no routine for resection of this myositis ossificans. Healing was adequate, and we were both considering trout fishing again for Doug, even though I had not figured out the whole scenario, at least I had an idea.

I was in Ed's sporting goods store, in Baldwin, Michigan, talking to Ains Borsum about my concern with my friend Doug Wendzel; how much he loved to fish and how he was no longer able to ply his trade in pursuit of the wily trout.

To whit, Ains responded, "Why don't you go see Graham MacDougal?" That simple question opened a whole new chapter in my life in my pursuit of the wary trout in conjunction with the fisherman soon to become one of my best friends, ever.

Who is Graham MacDougal, where does he live, and how can he possibly help us? Graham MacDougal is an old time Pere Marquette River guide. That probably meant a lot to Ains Borsum, but it didn't mean spit to me.

He gave me directions to the MacDougal Lodge on the mainstream of the Pere Marquette River. My hopes were raised thinking I might stumble onto a beautiful, well-situated modern fishing lodge with all the accouterments therein. My amazement began the instant I turned into the driveway, which was, due to a recent deluge, rutted out, to the point where I feared my transmission might be ripped out of my vehicle. At the bottom of the drive I was greeted by a nice green lawn at the edge of a gorgeous stretch of the Pere Marquette River. It was idyllic.

The next shock was to look left to the Lodge building. It was over a hundred year-old, two-story, white farmhouse, which was in need of some repair and a new paint job. The third shock was when I looked back toward the river and saw standing on the bank, Rip van Winkle; a very tall, very thin, and very old man leaning on a very long stick.

My thinking was, " My God, the Grim Reaper has come for me already." Pause, catch my breath, and settle down. " Ains, you got me this time, but you ain't never gonna get me again!"

"Are you the young doctor who's looking for a riverboat ride?" As he started talking, he started walking toward me, or rather started stumbling toward me. He was so bowlegged that he couldn't catch a pig in a blind alley.

Astute observer as I was at that time, I said, "I see you have a little arthritis in your knees."

" They bother me some." He could hardly walk. And this is my new river guide. "Come on over and I'll show you my boat."

I parked the car, jumped out and practically ran over to meet Graham. Partly I just want to reassure myself that although my knees hurt some, I was in a whole lot better shape than old Graham. He led me to the edge of the river and we looked down to see his 'riverboat .'

I'd just finished reading 'Washington's Six,' which is a wonderful story about the six spies who served Washington on Long Island during the Revolutionary war. I was mindful how they traveled up and down the river and across the bay in barges. That's exactly what I thought of when I saw Graham

MacDougal's riverboat; it was nothing more than a huge green barge.

It was monstrous! It was made out of three-quarter, one by six pine boards. It was rectangular, with sloping ends, about four feet wide and about sixteen feet long. It was not a boat, it was a barge, but it had a top on it. In the top were located three square holes which allowed people to stand or sit. The front and middle holes were for two fishermen and the back hole allowed Graham to stand and steer the boat; there really was no running of the boat.

The boat sat in the water which ran the boat, and Graham stood in the rear end with this long pole that I saw him holding initially. With the pole, he pushes the back of the boat one way or the other to keep it flowing where he wants it to go. There is no anchor big enough to stop this barge. So when he wants to stop he has two rings on each side of the stern of the boat. He simply rams the pole through the two rings down into the sand at the bottom of the river and that stops the boat. The flowing water was the means of locomotion on the river. There is no such thing as going back, that sucker goes only one way; down stream, lickety-wop.

Fast-forward a few days or a few weeks. I spent a lot of time calculating how we could make that boat work for fly fishing for both Doug and me; or one of us at a time. I say that to help you realize what we were facing with Graham guiding the boat. I'm not sure Graham ever guided that boat for a fly fishermen. I have no doubt that he guided it many times over many years for fisherman but I would have to guess they were all wormers.

I had spent a lot of time with Doug convincing him that fly fishing for trout was in the future for both of us. After all, that is a gentleman's way to fish for trout, right? So we arrived at Graham McDougal's Pere Marquette River Lodge fairly early one weekday morning and loaded up the boat with all the accoutrements that Doug required. I'll give a detailed account of our daily trip down the river at a later time after we had settled into a more predictable routine.

For that day with Graham MacDougal, I used a motorcycle tie down to strap a lawn chair in the bottom of the front well into which we unceremoniously dumped Doug. After assuring ourselves that Doug probably would not fall out of the boat, we cast off.

Mac polled us over to the short side of the river and threw out one of his dragging chains. I said that we didn't have an anchor on the boat, but all the boats that drift rivers in order to fly fish for trout, have an assortment of dragging chains to help control the speed of the boat. We moved down a stretch of the river I had never seen before. It is a beautiful river and is hard to concentrate on fishing when surrounded by so much beauty.

Several things became immediately obvious to me even though Doug may or may not have been aware of these circumstances. The guy in the front of the boat has to fish in front of the boat. He cannot fish straight sideways, because that's where the guy in the middle of boat is fishing. After numerous arguments about who was responsible for tangling the lines, we finally reached a truce and an understanding.

"Doug, you fish at a forty-five degree angle forward, no backward fishing in spite of how good the lie appears."

"Bill, fish short lines so you don't inadvertently snag the bow in Doug's line."

And so forth and so on. I quickly learned that Doug is a right-handed fisherman. His paralysis prevents him from twisting to the right. So he can only fish the left side of the river. Boo-hoo. I get tired of fishing only the right side of the river, so we get tangled again. That's just for starters.

I couldn't really see what Mac was doing in the rear of the boat, but I was amazed how well he kicked that boat around and kept us out of the brush and off the rocks. He was really good at running a boat, but unfortunately he had a different mindset as to why we were running the boat, and where we're running it. That I figured out when we approached a large long deep hole. He maneuvered the boat onto the edge on the short side of the hole, jammed his pole into the sand and said,

"Fish."

He was used to wormers throwing a gob of worms on to the bottom of the hole and riding it through the entire run.

At this point, I have vague recollections of having done this before. When I was a little kid, my dad would take me fishing on Dowagiac Creek, in his little plywood boat with a 1.2hp motor. He would plant us in the middle of the river, throw out an anchor and say, "Fish!"

With a big crooked fly rod, a fly line with a good-sized hook, weighted with sinkers, I would drop it down to the bottom of the creek. Then I would wait for some dumb trout or sucker to come along and chew on the worm. I know we did get some trout, but I was bored out of my gourd. That's where I learned about ambivalence even though I couldn't spell it and didn't know what it meant. I loved to go fishing with my dad but hated to sit in the boat for hours on end with no hope of catching a fish. That's where my mind went as I was trying to figure out how to fish a deep hole with a dry fly. Nymphs and streamers were not part of my thought process at this time in my life.

I don't remember if Doug or I caught a trout that day; based on my later experiences I'm sure we caught at least a few rainbow trout. I'm sure we didn't catch a significant sized brown, but that didn't really matter. The experiment had worked.

As it turned out, my gamble had panned out and Doug and I learned a whole lot about fishing that day: fishing together, fly fishing together and a lot about boat etiquette. It didn't stop our arguing or occasional fits of rage or anger, but it taught us a lot about how to get along with one another. That was the most important lesson as we were starting out a lifetime of fishing adventures together; twenty-five years of boat fly fishing for trout.

20

The Wood Pile

The boat idea worked. Somehow I didn't feel that running the river with Graham MacDougal had a significant future for us, the intrepid fly fishermen. Fishing that day out of Graham's barge was a severe challenge to me. Even though I could stand and turn around and fish three hundred and sixty degrees, the boat's positions, speed and course were not predictable enough to provide confident fly fishing. How long would Graham be able to transport us downriver in his 'fancy' barge. Suppose he were ill on the day we wanted to fish, or worse yet suppose he grew ill or had a coronary and died while transporting us downriver. Would I be able to stop that huge barge anywhere short of Lake Michigan, and if he died how do we dispose of the body with a reasonable story? No, we had to look else-where.

We would have to have a different portable venue for our activity. So a great number of tasks begin to show up under my calvarium during my frequent journeys up and down the high-way from my home to my cabin. What kind of boat would be the best, where do I look for a boat, what do I look for in a boat, what is our home base, my cabin or Doug's, and can we make the trip in one day? If not, would we stay at my place or at Doug's? What part or parts of the river are suitable for our type of fishing? And as a matter-of-fact, what is our type of fishing? The questions were endless and the answers became quite imaginative. For my inquisitive mind, I had just uncovered a plethora of challenges.

After attending numerous boat shows, speaking with many boat owners and several fishing guides, who ran boats, I found that none of them had any idea of the problems that I faced. Each one had a solution but it was different from the last one and none was applicable to our circumstance. Decision time. I chose a fourteen foot long pram. That is a flat bottom, square ended boat that weighed only sixty-eight pounds. As a later story will attest, that was a very important and wise decision. The trailer that accompanied the boat was adequate. I fitted the boat with wooden oars because they float. I attached an anchor winch, an anchor rope, pulleys and a collection of chain anchors to control the speed of the boat.

We quickly learned that we could not make a trip for a day's fishing from either my home or Doug's. We each had a cabin near Baldwin; mine was three miles south, and Doug's was four miles northeast. He could not function in his cabin with a wheelchair so we started in my cabin after I widened the door frame for the toilet. Later, his cabin buddy, Milo Holroyd, modified their cabin so Doug could easily move around in his own cabin. After that, we never returned to my cabin, as long as Doug and I fished together.

What part of the river should we fish today? We would try different stretches of the river for a days' fish until we learned the approximate distance and time involved in each stretch. A number of factors entered into our daily decision as to where to fish. We needed to have the car and trailer spotted; that is have someone pick up Doug's car with the trailer attached and move it from where we planned to get into the river—to the spot where we planned to get out of the river. With time and the help of some very kind persons, that did not any longer provide a problem, with a couple of notable exceptions. The stretch of the river chosen for the day also depended on the time of the year, the time of the day that we could start, or the time of day we needed to finish our journey. So every day was a new adventure and some of them were harrowing.

It's near nighty-night time for me this evening so I will relate one of our night tales from the river. Doug and I had been fishing together for some period of time when we stumbled into this circumstance. We had put in at the thirty-seven bridge, which is right adjacent to Ivan's canoe rental business. At that time, Ivan Kokendoefer and his wife, Irene, were our spotters. Irene was a very attractive woman even though she was well into her 60s, and extremely pleasant. We dealt with her often. Ivan was a tough old Dutchman who was considerably past his prime but was still very strong and capable. I remember seeing a portrait someone had done for him, as a younger man. He had black hair and a very small gentlemanly like mustache, much like Nick Charles from the Thin Man movie series. I would have to say he was ruggedly handsome, and was a good match for his very attractive blonde wife. However, they both cheated, she dyed her hair blonde instead of gray, and he used an eyebrow pencil for his perfect mustache.

Our take out point was the sportsman club downriver from Ivan's canoe rental. Ivan and Irene delivered the scout with the trailer as best they could given the circumstances. I was not aware of the circumstances until I neared the landing site. We had a productive day, boating a couple dozen fingerling rainbows all of which we released, and a few nice edible brown's, which we did not release. It was dusk as we approach the landing, as a matter fact it was almost dark. I had a terrible time picking out the landing site and little wonder as I actually beached the boat. I recognized the beaching area which was very low with a little bit of sand and then a rather flat bank. I simply couldn't find my way around. I didn't see Doug's truck or the trailer. There was some big obstruction right near the edge of the water. As I got out my flashlight and walked around I thought I was going to have a heart attack. It was a hot night and I was already sweating just walking. What I discovered was almost unbelievable.

The DNR was setting up to perform river improvement for a mile or two up-and-down from this landing spot. It had provided them easy access for a truck to drive down and dump a whole bunch of eight foot long pine logs, which were going to be used to build bunkers and deflectors in the water. The two track that I usually used to back the trailer down to the edge of the water had been filled to a height of six feet with these logs as far as I could see up and down stream. The pile of logs was situated that I could not go around either above them or below them. I had to move the pile to allow egress of Doug's wheelchair. I slowly and laboriously moved the logs one by one until I had a path wide enough to roll Doug's wheelchair through. I was finally able to do that and placed him safely into the confines of his International Harvester. I then proceeded to unload the contents of the boat into the back of the truck, detach all of the anchors from the boat, carry them to the back of the truck and load them. Since when empty, the boat only weighed about seventy pounds, I was able to hoist it up over the log pile and thence onto the trailer.

The whole process took me approximately two hours of severe hard labor. I was soaking wet with sweat, dirty as a pig, and I'd long since run out of water; one doesn't drink river water, it is loaded with bad bugs. The drive back to Doug's cabin was only twenty minutes, but I didn't remember any of it because I was asleep before we left sportsman club.

21

Doug and Our Routine

I recently read 'The Checklist' that was written by a gentleman who is a physician whose name was Atul Gawande. I don't recall how I came into possession of the book, but its emphasis was on checklists and how important they are in our everyday life. As I read, I realized I have been living a life facilitated, or encumbered, by checklists. All of you who have fished with me, anywhere, realize that I always have a list, a checklist. I hate making mistakes. I hate forgetting things. So as I have aged, I find that a pen and a piece of paper facilitate good end results.

As I look back on my life, I think I have always been aware of the importance of order, and therefore lists. When I drove the delivery truck for Andy's Grocery, I made a mental list of my route. In those days, that was important since we were involved in the 'Great War.' Gas was rationed and our tires were almost bald; we did not want any extra wear on them. Ergo, I learned about lists, although they weren't written, they were in my head. As I sit here and dictate this story, I realize how important that whole process turned out to be in my life. Making lists and memorizing them became my very life style.

Upon my return from my month long trip out West with Dick Chamberlin, which was my high school graduation present, I learned I had no old job. My father had sold his store.

The next application of memory and checklist appeared while I was in the employ of Jack Dean and his dairy, Dean's Dairy of Berrien Springs. Again, I must thank my father for finding me this job as a truck driver for the wholesale ice cream business being developed by Dean's dairy. I would be driving a 1937 Studebaker truck with a freezer box on the back. It was packed full of ice cream goodies that I was to deliver. That whole route was my business.

John Kingsafer, my boss, had driven all over Berrien County and set up places for me to deliver the ice cream. The ice cream was packed in pints with several flavors and quarts of vanilla only. There were two and one-half-gallon containers and many other things such as popsicles, ice cream bars, ice cream drumsticks, and a few other items. I carried all this material around and made approximately fifteen to twenty stops on each of my two routes. I carried a sales pad and made a note of every item that I sold to every store, thus I could balance my own accounts at the end of the day and would know what to order for future trips. For the total of fifteen stops and the potential of ten or more items for each stop, it was important that I keep records.

You could probably write this next line. After the last stop of the day, about thirty miles from home, I realized I no longer had my pad on which was safely stored my days sales and receipts. I had left it and had no idea where. What to do? It was too late in the day to retrace my steps to every store that I had visited. That would tell all my customers that they have an idiot delivering their ice cream.

I pulled the truck off the road into a quiet area and gathered my wits. I realized that with care, I could reconstruct the entire days sales. I did that and checked it by the amount of money I had collected to make sure I had not missed anything. I had never ever considered anything like that in my life. Imagine my utter jubilation as I did this crosschecking and found out I was right. I had an almost a pictorial memory.

Throughout the six summers I worked for Dean's Dairy, I had this happen several times, each time being completely satisfied that I had mastered the problem. I had the capacity for a pictoral mental checklist. I then realized why I had always done so well in school, a very good memory. That memory game had been my checklist. From that point on, I became a believer in 'the check list.'

When Doug and I had made the decision that we would endeavor to become fishing buddies and needed to make some decisions and plans, I started my formal process of making lists. I was thinking like a genuine, mature, dumb list maker. How about you? What is the first thing you did this morning? That is after you went to the bathroom and had a cup of whatever. You ask yourself, what am I going to do today or what do I have to do today in order to stay happily married?

You make a mental list. And when you get old and don't have a lot to do except sit around, you start writing down your ideas for today, because you are old and can't remember any list for a whole day. Those of you old geezers who have accompanied me to the wilds of Canada have seen my extensive list. Those of you who have not seen my list, or haven't gotten the idea and formulated your own list, have arrived at Wintering Lake without some of your valuable stuff. And you grandkids, how did you figure you got all those goodies at Jay's resort without GPa's checklist. Just remember the world consists of two types of people, those who make lists and those who wish they had made a list.

In all fairness, the process for making lists for our fishing trip was trial and error. I certainly would like to tell you that I simply sat down and made up a series of lists for each and every occasion but George and I have to be honest. Every step toward planning each trip was frustrating and challenging. Throughout the twenty-five years of fishing together the lists had to be modified frequently, and we were still trying to perfect the process when we finally had to quit fishing when Doug died.

The first consideration was the vehicle we would use. Doug owned an International Harvester Scout, which he had fitted with hand controls. Driving this vehicle up and back provided Doug with a source of comfort and a sense of satisfaction. He was contributing to the success of the fishing trip. After suffering the pain and humiliation of the fall and its subsequent consequences, for someone who has been virtually a dynamo, to lose so much capacity is to lose a large portion of his self worth. Even though I had spent many hours with Doug fishing and otherwise, I could never put myself in his shoes and understand the amount of pain and humiliation that he suffered for the rest of his life.

"How could he drive that vehicle?" How he chose this vehicle as his means of locomotion I never did understand, but I know he considered many different types of vehicles before purchasing this International Harvester Scout. It had a very short wheelbase with a relatively large engine. It was four on the floor with perhaps a few extra gears because it was powerful and would not get stuck.

The function of that vehicle was always Doug's concern. Every once in a while I would help gas up the vehicle, check the oil, wash the windshield and drive the vehicle around so that he could get in. But the vehicle was his concern, and he did take excellent care of it and of us in it.

Doug was a fantastic woodworker; evidence the number of carved ducks and other wood workings I have in my possession. But he could hardly tie a knot let alone tie a fly. So I always carried flies for the both of us, and at any one time I would probably have enough flies for each of us to last two seasons.

We each had our own list for our personal preferences when it came time to actually cast the rod and they were quite different as they should've been.

Back to the routine that we established for minimal waste of time and maximum fishing for the available time. I would finish my work at the hospital or my office on Tuesday, call Doug and tell him I was leaving for home and he would plan his trip accordingly. He would arrive at my house, I would throw my gear into his vehicle and we would drive up north. We were fishing out of Baldwin, Michigan, where we each had a cabin about twenty minutes apart. I was on the middle branch of the Pere Marquette River and Doug was on the Baldwin River.

When we first started fishing, we drove up Highway 37 which we picked up north of Grand Rapids. We would be driving close to my cabin where we would pick up my boat. Early in our fishing ventures we would fish one of two sections of the upper P.M. and use Ivan and Irene Kokendoerfer to spot us. Later, we fished the main river almost exclusively. So we would drive to MacDougal's' Lodge and Irene MacDougal and her sister-in law would spot for us.

We would always arrive late afternoon or early evening on the day that we actually fished; Tuesday evening. So once in the river I would casually guide us down, or if we had limited amount of time to fish, I would turn the boat around and row as fast as I could to our designated spot where we would start fishing.

At the end of the run we would come to our landing area and beach the boat. I would drive the vehicle around, Doug would slide out of the boat into the wheel chair using a sliding board and then lift himself into the truck. I would unload the contents of the boat into the truck and then load the boat onto the trailer. We would then proceed home, which became Doug's cottage, and I would simply reverse the whole process. So I helped Doug into his wheelchair, and pushed him into the cottage and proceed to unload the car after I parked the boat.

Once inside the cottage I would turn on all the switches so we had heat light and music and some hot water. After Doug had cathed, and I cleaned up whatever needed to be cleaned, we would sit down to play cribbage. I didn't like to play cribbage particularly, but it was a good game for the two of us. I would keep a running total and fortunately for me Doug was very forgiving. At the time we finally had to quit playing cards I owed Doug one hundred forty-seven dollars. So I had to charge him guide fees to even it out.

We had our little snack which was for me the remaining half of my sandwich and a chocolate chip cookie. For Doug it was usually a stack of oreo cookies and a glass of milk. He could not eat just one cookie, or even just two cookies; it was usually a minimum of six but that gave him a lot of protein? He was seldom hungry, but on occasion he would ask for his favorite; fried bologna. So I go to the fridge, haul out bags of sliced bologna and say, "how many?" Two would be a big night. I would have to make four cuts to keep the bologna from curling up as I cooked it in butter. Actually fried bologna isn't bad but I preferred my calories in the form of a whiskey sour, which in those days was my drink du jour.

Next day is a sunny day. I get up fairly early, take the fly rods and stretch out the fly lines on bushes and trees in the backyard to allow the lines to dry. After a couple of hours, I rub the lines down with silicone and then wipe them clean. The combination of silicone, plus wiping all the dirt off the line, restores the capacity of the line to float on the water for the next day's fishing.

Eat breakfast, make and pack the lunches, hot water in the red cooler for hand washing and cold water in the green for drinking, hookup the boat, load the car and we are ready for another day of fishing.

That was pretty much our routine for all those years of fishing. I started out by making all kinds of lists, but after a number of times on the road, the list became ingrained in my brain. The check lists were there and used but they were not written down anymore.

22

The Olympics

The evening activities that I'm about to relate to you, occurred on a warm summer evening during the time of the Olympic games. I do not recall the specific date, or year but it was on a Tuesday night in keeping with Doug's and my greater plan. All of our trips down the Pere Marquette occurred on Tuesday and Wednesday evening during warm weather but only in the day time early and late in the season. We both had been looking forward to this evening's fishing. The forecast had been for a bright sunny day, a warm night with a slight breeze and no overhead moon. As I pause to reflect on what I've just said, and its impact on you, the reader, recognize it is different for me; the night time fisherman. I'm sure you've all had the experience of walking in the yard or a field or somewhere at night when there has been no street light. First of all, if there is no cloud cover, there is a significant ambient light.

That light is partially from the stars overhead which give a very faint luminosity to the background sky. The sky is not black, neither is it light, as compared to daylight but there is a certain level of luminosity, or ambient light, at all times. This light is vastly diminished by heavy cloud cover which produces the black night. The light is significantly enhanced by moonlight. The light from the moon in turn is dependent on two factors. The first factor is the degree, or extent of the moon exposed; from Crescent, to full and back to Crescent. The other factor is the position of the moon in the sky, which in turn is dependent upon the season of the year. I don't want you to think that I understand all this, because I don't. I am simply relaying what I have experienced through many years of evening fishing.

"So what?" Most of you are saying at this point and as I used to say frequently. Well, trout are quite sensitive to light, because they are exposed to attack from predators who have excellent vision in very bright light. They become the hunted rather than the hunter. Brown trout are probably the most sensitive of the trout family, to light exposure. Brown trout almost always hide in deeper water, dark bottomed water, overhanging branches, under logs and in rapids or riffles where visibility from overhead is impaired. In a trout stream, the little rainbow trout are relatively unaffected by high visibility, as is evidenced by the fact that they are everywhere and will readily hit a bait or lure any time. Some fishermen might call them dumb, whereas I tend to think of them as lunch, sometimes for me and sometimes for a ravenous brown trout, or a great blue heron.

I had spent many a pleasant evening on the middle branch of the Pere Marquette River, around where my cabin was located. If the water had been unaffected by a recent rainfall, visibility was perfect, the water was gin clear. In my early formative fishing years, I viewed this scene on the river as very pastoral. After a few fishing trips, that were fishless, I began to wonder if Jim Glessner and I had wasted a lot of money on this beautiful, but apparently sterile body of water. I find I must finish my point about the moonlight before I move on to the story that convinced me that we had indeed purchased a gold mine and not a stretch of water in a desert.

I was plying my trade, that is, dry fly fishing at night, along the edge of the swamp where I got lost on a very dark, moonless, completely cloudy night. I had been rather unsuccessful in my attempt to tease a hungry trout out from under an overlying branch when my footsteps took me up to a very shallow stretch of river. The moon was full and almost directly overhead. I could see a broad stretch of river ahead of me, because of the brightness of the moon. I spotted a medium-size trout, smack dab in the middle of the river. I could feel both of my sphincters tightening. This was the first evidence of a live trout in my river that I had seen, or experienced, all evening. I carefully shifted my feet to the left side of the stream, so I had a perfectly clear right-hand shot at this fish, sitting in the middle of the river, obviously waiting for my dry fly. The moon lit up that stretch of water to make it almost as clear as daylight. I started my cast and performed a classic figure of eight false cast above the fish preparing to drop the fly precisely seventeen inches in front of and to the right of the trout.

Of course I am being facetious. At that stage of my development as a fly fisherman, I was simply lucky not to snag on a bush behind me or to drop the fly right on the trout's head thereby spooking him. As I completed my false cast over the trout, picked the line up to make my final thrust, before that fly ever hit the water, that trout was gone. Yes, the fly hit the water in approximately the right position but made no difference because there was no trout available to glom onto the fly.

What had I done wrong? I had not fumbled, I had not coughed, and I had not slipped or stumbled in the water. What had spooked that fish? Well! So much for that pastoral scene. The moon had indeed lit that entire area to the extent that the shadow of my fly line over that fish had spooked him. Moonlight was not my friend.

My concept of night fishing had changed drastically. Brown trout always maintain cover, to minimize their visibility to overhead prey. Their lateral line provides sensitivity to pressure change, noise and sudden water motion, and their visibility sense protects them from overhead motion or attack. I have had many opportunities to test this hypothesis, and it has always proven to be so true, that I actually stopped night fishing when there was a bright overhead moon

On this particular night, although the circumstances were generally favorable for a good evening fish, we were a little late. So I spun the boat around and rowed as hard as I could for thirty minutes to put us in the right position for our anticipated wonderful evening of fishing. As I approach my goal, I turned the boat around and dropped a light drag anchor. Immediately we spotted a feeder on the right edge of the stream.

"Doug, did you see?"

"Yes, I got him," And indeed he did. He very deftly flipped the large white Wulff in front of the feeding trout and promptly, "Gulump"

"Fish on!"

It was a spectacular evening for the two of us. We caught a good number of fish, so many, in fact, that we didn't keep anything under ten inches. We neared the end of our float at about eleven o'clock at night. I maneuvered the boat to the right side of the river as we passed Peg Stearns cottage. I noticed that Peg's inside light was still on. That was unusual because Peg usually goes to bed at sundown. I simply noticed that and wondered. We passed the next two hundred yards or so of river and I beached the boat at our usual spot. My suburban and the trailer were sitting on the edge of the landing as was the usual case when Irene McDougal delivered it for us. It was her custom to take our car and trailer down to the landing shortly after we pushed off from her farmhouse. She would have her sister-in-law drive down and pick her up. It was all so very convenient for us, and not very expensive. Irene is one of the kindest women I have ever known. On several occasions, when she said she worried about us, she would drive the suburban down and sit in it until we came floating down the river. I have known very few people as considerate as Irene McDougal. The suburban was there, but Irene wasn't. That turned out to be most unfortunate.

As I gazed across the launch area, I thought there was something funny about the suburban. So I got out my flashlight to have a good look.

"Oh my goodness, I have a flat tire right front. NUTS! This means a lot of work, and I am old and tired."

At that point I had used a little different expletive rather than nuts. When I turned the light on the right rear tire, that original expletive would have fit well in a Sunday school class compared with a string that I then let out. The right rear tire was flat, as were the left front and rear. Some dastardly black-hearted villain had slashed all four valve stems. I had four flat tires that I could not fix. It was close to midnight, we were both tired, hungry and thirsty and in pain. We were out of rinse water for Doug's hands so that he couldn't do another catheterization, but his bladder was getting quite full.

What happened to us next I could only say is God's provision. I remembered that Peg's lights were on, could she possibly still be awake? Only one way to find out. I made sure Doug was as comfortable as possible, walked up the hill and back to Peg Stearns' cottage. I could see the light on and the TV was on. Oh yes! The Olympics are on and Peg is a sports enthusiast. I boldly knocked on the door hoping that she would not greet me with a shotgun or a 45, hollering all the while, "Don't shoot, it's Bill!"

She opened the door with a very cheerful greeting and said "Can you come in?"

My first thought was, "Yes, Peg, I could sure use one of your martinis." But instead, altruism won. I quickly explained our situation not knowing what to ask for in the line of assistance. Without hesitation Peg said, "Take my Lincoln and bring it back when you can."

I drove the Lincoln back to the landing, unloaded Doug and all his paraphernalia into the car and his wheelchair into the back seat. We drove back to the cabin in silence. Doug fell asleep and I fought hard to not do the same. Back at the cabin we unloaded Doug and all his stuff. Doug ate his usual 6 Orioles with milk, I had an extra large nightcap and it was lights out. No cards tonight. I hope the fish got cleaned but I couldn't remember at that point.

Next day I called my road service and they went to the spot of the ravishment, replaced all the valve stems, pumped up the tires and we were good to go. We returned the Lincoln Continental to Peg with many, many thanks and a goodly pile of nicely cleaned brown trout. It appears that I had remembered to clean the trout.

Fly fishing on Pere Marquette

Bill mentoring a young man

Erik and Grandpa

Bill Stoub and Bill with a steelhead

Fish on!!!

My buddy Doug

Damn Pike

Dan's Steelhead

The "old guys" at Wintering — John Hamilton, Mick Kiss, Larry Moon, Skip Cook, Jim Keller, Richard Lee, and Bill Stoub

The Bear Lookers — Dave Leuker, Mick Kiss, Larry Moon, John Hamilton, Bill Burdick, Richard Lee, and Bill Stoub

Andy's Red and White Market - 1941

My old friend Roger Alliman who helped with this book.

The grandboys growing up — Preston Comfort, Andrew Kuiper, Heath Kupecky, Jeremy Kuiper, Seth Anderson, Austen Comfort, Erik Anderson, Joel Anderson, Ryan Anderson, and Parker Comfort.

Most of the Burdick clan.

23

Harry's Horrible Hopper

Tying flies for the express purpose of imitating something that looked like food to a fish has always fascinated me. So shortly after Sandy and I were married, I changed my focus from chasing girls, Sandy Cook, to chasing bluegills. When we lived in our small apartment in Ann Arbor, we had an egg man who came to our door periodically to supply us with fresh eggs. Somehow I learned of his interest in fishing and before you know it he was helping me to tie some flies with chicken feathers and buttons so that I could fish for bluegill through the ice with this homemade contraption. I have no recollection of ever using one of the flies or even catching a fish with one of these flies, but I know the whole concept of tying flies fascinated me. Through the years I learned more and more about fly tying and therefore accrued more and more equipment and material, not to mention some degree of experience. Art Newman's unusual offer of Borchers special for twenty-five cents apiece convinced me of two things. One, I was not that good of a fly tyer, and two, I would be well advised to spend my effort in tying flies that I could not buy or that I had invented.

Flies purchased from a sporting goods store would cost a minimum of a dollar apiece, and some of the more exotic types could be up to two fifty a fly. When wading the stream, a fly snagged in a bush was not a problem. I could usually retrieve it and save myself a whole dollar. But when Doug and I were fishing from a boat, retrieving snagged flies is a whole different ballgame. Snagging flies in bushes was the rule not the exception. On a particularly bad day we could each lose in excess of a half a dozen flies. Over the course of an entire summer, that could add up to significant bucks. Being the tightwad that I am, I sought to build a better mousetrap, tie my own flies for about ten cents a pop.

In later life, I have settled for tying mostly terrestrials and in particular the grasshopper fly. I have looked up and attempted to imitate at least eight different versions of the grasshopper. I was always unhappy with either the way I tied the fly or the effect that particular grasshopper had on a feeding brown trout. So I finally decided to go to the well, that is catch a few grasshoppers and look at them. First of all I was quite surprised by the different appearances of grasshoppers, depending on when you caught them and where you caught them. That explained to me why there were so many varieties of grasshopper flies that were written up and offered to the fly tyer. I finally decided that it didn't make a hill of beans to the trout as long as there were several constants in the construction of the fly.

I present here my thinking about what should constitute a reasonably effective grasshopper fly. When tying a fly the first consideration is the hook; size, length, eye position and strength. The grasshopper is a fly that you hope will float therefore you use a light weight, fine wire bronzed hook. The grasshopper is long so the length of the hook will be from a 3X to a 6X long dry fly, straight eye.

When tying a fly one starts from the bend of the hook and proceeds forward to the eye of the hook where you tie off the fly. The inside of the grasshopper's thigh is colored bright red. For that reason I tie on some bright red material in the position of the tail which can be a piece of red yarn or some fluffy feathers dyed red.

I am then ready to tie the body of the grasshopper. Everything that is going to comprise the body has to be tied on at the butt end of the fly at the same time even though the material will be wrapped on separately. First I tie on a short black and white grizzly hackle, which when wound around the body will represent body hair. Next is the substance that will cause the fly to float and that is polyethylene yarn, bright yellow, dull yellow or dull green. I don't really think it makes a lot of difference but I prefer dull yellow. The yarn is then wrapped from the butt of the fly forward till you reach the head area and then tied off by three wraps of the fly tying thread coupled with two half hitches. The hackle is then wrapped from backwards to the forward end about an eighth inch apart and again tied off at the head end.

Next comes the material for the wing of the grasshopper. The most common material for the store bought grasshopper wing is a piece of bustard turkey feather. That's just a fancy way to say, "I don't want to fool around with this crap," so I simply tie in eight to twelve pieces of deer hair. Deer hair is hollow and therefore it floats and that's a big plus for a floating grasshopper fly. After I tie off this deer hair, I trim the forward end to make a sort of head to the fly. The final part of this fly is to imitate a pair of legs. For this I pick two pieces of peacock herl and tie a knot at one end of each piece to represent a joint. I leave a half an inch out from the joint and tie the legs to the fly at the front so the legs hang down the entire length of the body of the fly. Once the legs are in place I tie the entire fly off, cement the head and I have a reasonable imitation of a Michigan grasshopper fly.

I have just taken about twenty times longer to describe the tying of the fly then it takes for me to tie the fly. When I had two good hands with good fingers and two good eyes I could tie one of these flies in about eight minutes.

The purpose of this dissertation is to introduce my readers to the first ever field test of Harry's Horrible Hopper. The opportunity for this field test arose on about the second week of August in one particularly dry summer. Doug and I had traveled up to his cabin at Baldwin and had a very pleasant experience on the main stream of the Pere Marquette the preceding evening. As we sat around our breakfast table discussing life in general and our prospects for a float on a beautiful stretch of river with little wind and a lot of sun, I produced one of my newly invented grasshopper fly's.

Doug looked at it and said, "Not bad. If it works out, I'll have Chuck tie me a few." That struck me like a double-edged sword. Was the way I tied it not good enough? On the other hand if he was willing to have his good friend Chuck tie up a few, it meant that this looked like a reasonably good fly." Yeah, I'll try it."

So we put in at the sportsman club which would be halfway down that stretch of the river and allowed us to get out in time to drive home that night. The day was absolutely gorgeous. There was just a wisp of a breeze from the west so that dry fly fishing would not be impaired at all. The sun was bright overhead without a cloud in the sky. The temperature was in the high eighties and we were both in T-shirts and high spirits. Doug selected one of my new flies, for I had supplied him with probably a half a dozen figuring that this might be a tough day on the river and losing a few would not be unreasonable.

I, too, had tied on one of Harry's Horrible Hopper on one rod and Gold Ribbed Hare's ear nymph on the other in case I had to go underwater to catch a brown trout. As it turned out I never picked up my wet fly rod the entire day and I had little time to even pick up my grasshopper rod because the action was so ferocious.

I had barely gotten into the boat and pushed off when I heard Doug holler, "Fish on!" I quickly dropped the anchor and watched Doug play the first fish of the day. I was not at all disappointed to see him pull in a six inch rainbow, because I knew at that point the fly might work. Doug unhooked the fish and returned him to the river and as I was pulling up the anchor he flashed his fly line a couple of times to dry the fly out and dropped it in a run. Bingo! Another fish, another rainbow, but this time seven inches. I simply held the boat with the oars while Doug unhooked his second rainbow, dried his line overhead and dropped his fly in a third time. Again in a nice run and again bingo. This time it was a ten inch brown. This trip was basically for Doug, three casts and three fish. Incredible! Neither of us had ever had a day begin like this one. Doug was in his element. He was casting with his right hand, his left hand, downstream, upstream, across stream, under bushes, under limbs, under logs, he could do no wrong. He was hot. He was having so much fun that I didn't even want to fish. I was having so much fun, watching him have fun, that catching fish was of secondary interest to me that day.

I am sure that this was one of Doug's finest days of fly fishing ever. He put that hopper wherever he wanted it to go and the fish responded accordingly. I watched him sneak that fly under overhanging bushes and logs like I've never seen him do before. First of all, he was not having a lot of pain that day and was free to move in his chair and fish either right or left-handed. Second of all it was a bright day and he could see clearly what he was doing. And what he was doing, he was doing exceedingly well. All of the practice time he spent in his backyard was paying off in spades.

At one point I stopped and said, "Let me see that fly." The legs were gone, the body hackle was gone, the tail was still there but the body yarn was starting to fray. Some of the deer hair wing was missing. I offered to change flies for him.

"Not a chance," he replied, "they might stop hitting it." And the day continued on. I managed to lose two hoppers in bushes, and I think I caught a few fish but I don't even remember for sure. I maneuvered the boat downstream as usual, and even while I was swinging the boat from side to side, Doug was catching more and more fish.

When we finally reached the pullout spot, I pulled the boat up on the sandy bank and asked to see Doug's fly. All that was left of the fly was a bunch of yellow fuzz around the shank of the hook. The tail, body hackle, legs, and deer hair wings were all gone. I asked Doug how many fish he thought he caught that day.

He said, with a big grin on his face, "Probably fifty or more." I grinned back at him because that was my best guess also. Can you imagine in this day and age any one catching fifty trout in one day. The memory of that day and watching Doug 'slay trout,' is ingrained in my mind for ever.

"I guess that fly will work, do you have any more?" That was my reward for a day well spent with my buddy, Doug Wendzel.

24

The Hex Hatch

Hexagenia Limbata is the largest of the over four hundred species of mayflies in the state of Michigan. Worldwide, there are over three thousand species of mayflies and they fit into various food chains throughout the world. In Michigan, they are frequently called 'fish flies' and are seen around streams and other bodies of fresh water in June and July. I have heard the term 'fish fly' all my life never realizing the affect it would have on my life as a fly fishing enthusiast, especially in my pursuit of Salmo Trutta, the wiley Brown Trout.

My first experience in attempting to fish the 'hex Hatch,' was at the behest of George Benisek. I met George in medical school primarily because we were both 'B's' so we were fairly close to one another in a lot of labs. George was an outdoor enthusiast having spent several summers working in the Department of Natural Resources out of Denver, Colorado. He was an ardent fly fisherman and we were able to spend time talking about fishing and in particular fly-fishing. He had many times tried to convince me I should try nighttime fly-fishing with him during the Hex Hatch on a branch of the Muskegon

River. That is a big river and I wasn't particularly excited about that adventure. But George was persistent so I accompanied him to an area of flats on one of the branches of the Muskegon River.

I was able to cross the river in my waders without drowning. I stood in one spot the entire evening, throwing a single ridiculous fly so an even more ridiculous, dumb trout would take it and I would go home with a world record. I don't even recall if it would have been a world record trout or black bass, that's how uninformed I was at the time. Needless to say I did not catch a fish, nor did I even see a fish rise, or flop the entire evening. I just had a lot of exercise, and was happy to get back across that big river in the middle of the night without falling in. I'm sure I made a vow or maybe several, but I never went back there again.

Fast-forward a few years. While I was still in my residency training program in Grand Rapids, having spent my obligatory two½ years fulfilling my military obligation, I was again enticed to pursue the mighty Hexagenia Limbata. At this time in my life I had a little better understanding of fly-fishing for trout and a lot more experience in the use of a fly rod. However, I did not have the assets that would provide me a quality fly rod, so I was still stuck fishing the seven foot, nine inch fiberglass fly rod that I had spirited away from my father. It was a 'soft action' fly rod; translation, it was almost as bad as fly fishing with a wet noodle. It had no backbone, so casting a distance was virtually impossible. Setting the hook, especially at a distance, was a difficult feat. All of this to say, I was filled with enthusiasm, but not a lot of experience with an inferior rod and reel combination.

My next memorable fly fishing trip in Michigan was again with good old George Benisek. I knew nothing about the Pere Marquette River but he seemed to know his way around. He knew exactly where we had to go, what we had to do and how to do it. I am a sucker for somebody who really knows stuff. We drove to a place where his friend owned a cottage, got out of the car, donned our waders and traveled to the edge of the water. He apparently knew his way around and he appointed a spot to me and said, " Wait here until they start to rise and then fish for them."

By this time in my life, having spent two ½ years in New-foundland, I had learned how to tie flies and I make my own version of Lee Wulff's, big White Wulff, on a long shank number six dry fly hook. It was a killer fly and became my all time favorite night fly.

I was situated at the base of a very high bank on the south side of the river. He stated emphatically, "Don't try to fish until you see the fish rising."

That's like telling a kid not to eat from the bowl of ice cream you just set before him. But this idea of fishing the Hex Hatch was new to me. I was a strict neophyte so I was still willing to admit that there are some fishermen who are smarter than I. So I waited. And waited, and waited. We had started fishing at about eight-thirty at night just before the sun started setting. It was still very light and my understanding was that it had to be near dark before the Hex Hatch would occur.

Then I heard it. Splash! I strained to look up stream and then down stream and could not locate the source of the noise. It was not huge, it was just a little splish rather than what I hoped would be a big 'Spaloosh.' My interest had been piqued and I was yanked out of my lethargy.

As my gaze shifted up and down the river, I heard and saw that mysterious 'Spaloush' right across the river from me. That was a trout. That was a very large trout. 'Spaloush' Again. No! That was a huge trout and he's all mine! He was spaloushing again and again. He was in a feeding pattern and I recognized it. There were no flies visible on the water, so-called spent wing Hexagenia Limbata. That meant he was feeding on the nymph form of the fly as it as it broke out of the mud on the bottom of the stream and wiggled it's way up to the surface.

Once on the surface the nymph would burst through its shell casing, sit on the water for anywhere from a few seconds on a night like this, to a few minutes on a cooler or more humid night. The nymph would break the casing, spread its wings and then fly. This fish was hitting the fly before it was able to take off. And he was feeding regularly, which means he would hit anything that came close to him. But my fly would have to come through his feeding lane, because he wouldn't move to the right or the left. He was simply coming up feeding going back down until another insect came along. That's the way it works.

I stepped out as far as I could from the bank so I could cast my fly out. The bank behind was high and that precluded a direct shot across the river. I had to maneuver my body into a position where I could cast my fly upstream from where he was feeding. I mentioned that my fly rod was a very soft action, and add to that a big White Wulff caught a lot of air as it was being cast. Fly-fishing is totally different from bait casting which is what we do when we fish for bluegill and bass with a spinning rod. We are throwing a weight at the end of the rod and we can all understand that. When fly fishing, the basic assumption is that the fly weighs nothing; therefore you cannot throw it out like you would a hook, line and sinker. It simply doesn't work that way. Instead, when fly fishing you have to learn to throw the fly line with the power stroke backward not forward; it is backstroke power.

To successfully and easily fly fish for that huge trout, I should have had a stiff rod and a very tiny fly. Instead I'm stuck with a soft rod and a huge fly, which resists wind. My first cast was about twenty-five or thirty feet upstream and fell way short of the feeding fish. That was good because I didn't disturb him at all. I slipped a little further down stream and then a little further out into the stream until my waders were about two inches above the water's edge. I pumped the rod; that is I false casted and fed out line again and again until I felt I had the right distance and then dropped the fly on the water. I lost track of where he was feeding and I could only hope that I was in his lane. Bingo! Spaloush! My fly disappeared. I snapped the rod up as hard as I could, fearing I might even break it. No chance of breaking. That rod was so soft that it nicely slid the hook into of my trout's jaw. "Fish on!"

Having fished for Atlantic salmon for three summers in Newfoundland, I had a real good idea of when I had hooked a fish and when I had missed the fish. This was a big hook with a good barb stuck in his jaw, I knew I had a winner. Broken leader was not a consideration. You don't go fishing for big fish with a two pound leader. My tippet for this guy was ten pound, no fear.

Nonetheless, it took me almost ten minutes to drag this trout across the river and into my net. Time could become a factor with a large fish. As the fish sachets back and forth, the hook tends to wear a hole in the jaw. That possibility always exists so I don't play with a fish, but I do play a fish. Big difference. This guy stayed on and came to the net at twenty-three inches. That is probably the biggest brown I have ever landed. I staggered out of the water without falling down, made the shore and took my prize home, gutted him and froze him to show all my friends. Have I shown it to you, yet?

Another of my hex stories occurred during the early years of my possession of the Baldwin cabin. It was another very warm evening in mid-June, with very little breeze and no threat of rain. I had no idea where the moon was on this occasion, because I had not yet figured moonlight to be a problem for me. I had gone on a trail, downriver past the swamp, to an area almost to the cottage below me on the opposite side of the river.

I had every get-in and get-out area of the river calculated for the time involved in fishing it; in good weather and in bad. I had gotten into the deep, cool running water just before sundown, and was working my way slowly up stream. The water was low and clear and so I was using a very small fly; a sixteen Hendrickson and a 5X leader tippet. I had several hits from little fish and managed to miss every one of them. When the little fish are rainbow, missing them is a good thing. If you catch them, they slop up your fly and make you take time to dry it. If that doesn't work then you have to keep changing the fly, putting the old soggy fly in the wool band on your hat and replacing it with a new, perky, high riding fly.

I had steadily moved upstream with no particular complications to either my wading or my fly fishing. The small trout, both rainbow and brown, were cooperative and seemingly hungry. I had taken no fish of size, and had released all as I drew into a stretch with crossed tag alder bushes. I moved to the left side of the stream, was able to sit down on the bank to rest my back. I noted an industrious muskrat carrying a mouth full of grass back to his home and I assume children. Muskrats are very unassuming, make little noise and do not bother either the fisherman or the fish. They frequently have homes near the edge of the water which in no way affect or impede the flow of the water down the river. They are totally friendly creatures.

As I sat resting and reminiscing I realized how fortunate I was to be able to have this evening on my river and enjoy the beautiful out-of-doors that has been provided to us by God. I was in the process of honoring Him by a short prayer when my attention was drawn to a commotion upstream. I recalled the evening when I was startled by a huge head swimming down stream to 'get me.' Merely a beaver going home after a hard day of gnawing on trees. It had really startled me and I was thinking of that as I looked up stream. I saw no beaver, rather large numbers of trout rising all over the stream. I was totally unaware of the possibility of a hex Hatch on my river. But that is exactly what was going on.

As soon as I realized that, I quickly took off my tiny fly, cut back my leader and put on a business fly; a medium-sized white Wulff on a number eight long shank dry fly hook. I dislodged myself from the bank, turned up stream and flipped my fly out about five feet ahead of me, whoosh. A trout had my fly and it was not a small trout. I brought it in; about a fourteen inch brown beautifully colored and fat as a pig. I unhooked him, slipped him into my Creel, false casted my fly to dry it out a little and dropped it in again. Immediately whoosh! Another nice trout. It was not quite dark, but I had to very carefully look to see what was going on. Thousands of huge 'Fish Flies' in the air and flopping on the water; I was in the middle of a hex Hatch on my own river! I had never anticipated such could have happened, another praise the Lord.

When I finally realized my situation I decided I had to make a big decision. I felt that I could easily clean out this section of river because the trout were insane. They had reacted to this overwhelming hatch of Hexagenia Limbata, May flies. and were hell-bent on suicide at the hand of Harry W. I immediately decided to restrict my catch and took extreme measures to catch and release these crazy, but beautiful brown trout.

By the time I reached my cottage, I was exhausted, exhilarated and had caught and released in excess of thirty trout, most of which were over ten inches in length. At this point in time I had long since forgiven Jim Glessner for dragging me into this fiasco of a trout cabin. It obviously was one of the best deals of my life. "Thank you Jim Glessner, thank you, Lord, and good night."

25

My Neighbor, Howard Davidson

Part of my early ventures on the middle branch of the Pere Marquette River was just to fish the water slowly and be very observant of the river itself: the bottom, the banks and the neighbors. One very bright and sunny day I was moving along quite well, enjoying all aspects of being in the beautiful out-of-doors on the middle branch of the Pere Marquette River near Baldwin, Michigan. As I rounded a bend, I saw a well built foot bridge running from a very high bank on the right, over the stream to a small flat bank covered with well mown grass. It was extremely pastoral in appearance, very restful. High on the bank on the right was what appeared to be a very old, two-story wood frame building. Although old, it was very well built. In the center of this building were windows in two sections reaching the roof of the second story. Later I learned that it was only a one story building with a small basement beneath it. The two-story windows were all part of one great room that had a very high ceiling and a chandelier that hung all away down from the ceiling. It was a beautiful, old, fisherman's cottage.

Compared to the relatively squalid cottages that I had just passed, I found this very refreshing. I was quite sure that the owners of this lovely domicile would be quite different. As I clambered up the bank, and thence up and around to the front of the building, I could hear a booming voice inside. I could not understand the words that were being spoken but I was greatly impressed by the volume being exercised from within this cottage. The gentleman who was the possessor of that very prominent voice had obviously observed my presence because as I walked up to the front door and endeavored to knock, it was vigorously thrown open. I rather quietly introduced myself as the new neighbor from downstream. The booming voice said, "Well hi, I'm Howard, and this is my wife Dorothy." I later learned their last name was Davidson. He and his wife appeared to be in they're early 70s, and were very hospitable. They invited me into their cottage. I removed my waders, entered and was offered a cup of coffee. Of course I accepted and we became acquainted.

Howard was an industrialist and had established a company in Grand Rapids that was under his name, Howard Davidson. He had family and one of his sons had assumed operations of the business. All of this is setting the background for some of the curious episodes that followed during my many years of association with Howard and Dorothy Davidson. Almost every time that I went fishing out of my own cottage, I would drive over or walk over to visit the Davidsons and we would have friendly little chats. I have to admit there were ulterior motives in my frequent chats with Howard and Dorothy.

There were very tall windows overlooking the river that allowed a clear vision into the gin clear water of the Pere Marquette directly below their cottage. Howard had a pet brown trout living in the river under the bridge and was clearly visible from the window. He was about sixteen inches long and after hearing Howard talk about, 'his fish.' I realized had I better not make a mistake and catch his fish or I would never again be invited into his cottage for coffee and cookies. But one of my ulterior motives for visiting Howard and Dorothy in the morning when I was going to fish during that day was to get a good idea of how the fishing was going to be. If the fish was visible under the bridge and was drifting back and forth occasionally feeding on a fly, I knew I had a good chance of catching trout that day. If the fish was not out feeding, I knew I was not going to have fun.

I realized not only was Howard hard of hearing and therefore the booming bass voice, his vision was a little impaired. One of the mornings while we were chatting and drinking coffee, Dorothy looked out the front door and said to Howard, "That squirrel is on the feeder again."

Whereupon Howard swiftly rose from his chair and while mumbling something about "that damn squirrel," moved quickly toward a closet, rather clumsily opened the door and pulled out a double barrel shotgun.

"I've been waiting for that damn squirrel." And he slowly approached the front door and swung it open as he raised his shotgun. As he sighted down the barrel, I slid in behind him to see where this squirrel was feeding and watch him while he entered the squirrel graveyard. As Howard raised the gun up and took sure aim, I screamed, " Don't shoot! That's my car on the other side of bird feeder." Had he shot, I would have had about a gazillion pieces of birdshot in my brand new Oldsmobile. Yes, life around Davidsons could be exciting.

My favorite remembrance of Howard and Dorothy at the cottage started in the middle of the night. I was fast asleep in my bed inside my cottage when I started a nightmare. I was dreaming the phone was ringing and I was about to get called to the emergency room in Baldwin. I suddenly awoke and realized the Baldwin did not have a hospital or an emergency room. This was real. My phone on the wall of the cabin by the front door was ringing in the middle of the night. This could not be good. Only my wife knows this number and something awful has happened at home. I stumbled out of bed and to the phone in the dark, grabbed the phone and practically screamed, "What's wrong?"

I heard, on the other end of the line a familiar voice. No not just a voice; it was the voice of Howard Davidson in the middle of the night. This has got to be a disaster. "Hello, Bill?" I answered in the affirmative and the voice said, "This is Howard." As if I didn't know. Even as I am dictating this stoty, I can still hear his booming bass voice in my ear.

"This is Howard Junior, calling about my father. I assume you're at your cabin." At that point I became extremely terrified. In my stupor, I began to put two and two together. Howard senior had the good sense to give my phone number to his son Howard Junior down in Grand Rapids. That's how Junior had my phone number; he had to be calling for an extreme emergency.

The story began to unfold. "Mother just called and I can't make sense of anything she said. Could you please go over to the cottage and check her out?"

I responded in the affirmative, pulled on some clothing and whipped over to their cabin. I recalled that Howard was a diabetic and he had demonstrated to me on several occasions how he would give himself insulin injections. Each time he would proceed to demonstrate how he got out his little jar of insulin from the refrigerator, took out a syringe and needle, withdrew the insulin, wiped off his skin and injected. As you read this you must think that I am exaggerating, or am crazy. Neither one. This was vintage Howard. He must've demonstrated his insulin injection technique at least a dozen times throughout the years that I visited him. Occasionally he would actually do the injection cause it was the proper time.

From a distance I could see the cottage was lit up like a Christmas tree. I could picture Howard passed out on the floor and Dorothy wandering around wringing her hands as I've seen her do before. Up to this point, I have not mentioned that Dorothy was in her dotage. In retrospect, I realize she had Alzheimer's disease. Relieved was I, as I saw Howard wandering through the living room, albeit, in his shorts and T-shirt. I approached the door, found it locked and rattled it loudly. Howard promptly opened the door with a greeting that I thought was perhaps misplaced. "Well, Bill, what are you doing here?"

I invited myself in and noticed that Dorothy was nicely dressed in a nightgown and a bathrobe and was babbling incoherently. Howard had no clue as to what was going on. Based on my own personal experience of suffering hypoglycemia, I recognized the situation. Howard has taken his evening insulin dose, maybe more than once and was in severe hypoglycemia.

I pause at this point to utter a warning to any of my potential readers. Hypoglycemia, which means low blood sugar, is frequently a complication of diabetes mellitus. It can also occur in persons, and in families, as an inherited functional disease. That is to say, people who are so afflicted may find themselves feeling giddy, lightheaded or many other symptom complexes you might want to name, wherein you think you might be going crazy. In cases of functional hypoglycemia, it occurs after ingesting a significant amount of carbohydrate, with no fat and no protein with it. The symptoms will start roughly one hour after ingestion of a large quantity of carbohydrate, and any of the above-mentioned symptoms may occur. Your pancreas has been stimulated to produce insulin, which drives the blood sugar down. With no fat or protein in the ingested food, the impact of the insulin is not moderated and your blood sugar drops like a rock. Symptoms began at a blood sugar level of about sixty mg and may continue to drop. If you reach a level of forty mg percent, you will probably pass out.

Recognizing this as the most likely circumstance surrounding Howard's bizarre behavior, I went to the refrigerator, found some orange juice, poured out a glass and convinced Howard to drink it. He sat down at the kitchen table drinking his juice, blinked his eyes a few times looked around, stared up at me and said, " Well, Bill, what are you doing here?"

I tried to explain the circumstances surrounding my unexpected, early morning visit, but he seemed totally unaffected by my words. Therefore, I got him another glass of orange juice, which he dutifully drank, and after drinking, and blinking and looking around, he again stared at me and said, " Well, Bill, what are you doing here?"

We chatted briefly, and again I tried to explain the circumstances, and then got him another glass of orange juice hoping the supply would not run out before Howard woke up.

After one or two more repetitions, I finally ascertained that his sugar level was decent and that he was coherent, and that both he and Dorothy would be able to resume their sleep. I did remember to call Howard Junior and assure him that all was well. I returned to my cabin, fell asleep quite readily and slept in the next morning. After breakfast, and a couple hours of brushing my stream, I dropped by to see Howard and Dorothy. I was not surprised; they had no recollection of the prior evening's festivities.

Another one of the stories Howard liked to tell was of his daily fishing trip. As I listened to him I thought, " So what's the big deal?"

As I write these notes I realize what a big deal that was for a seventy some year old guy. I now think, "How great that was, that this old guy loved to fish so much he would actually take the risk of fly fishing almost every day." So he would go on to explain his every move. I've already alluded to how he had done this with his insulin injections so I wasn't surprised when he wanted me to walk through his fishing caper.

So we would walk out of his house, through the back door, down the steps to his small basement, which was nice and dry. Here he kept all his fishing equipment. As I perused his little catacomb, it was very easy to see Howard loved to fish, had excellent but very old tackle. He would be one of the guys that would be pictured in an old fishing novel. Howard was a classic trout fly fisherman as was his very old friend and fellow fly fisherman, my wife's great uncle, Lloyd Cook. These guys were cut out of the same cloth; they were fly fishing classicists. I was able to watch Howard fly fish a little bit, but on one of my boat trips with uncle Lloyd, I was able to watch a pro in action. To watch him as he fished a wet fly was a thing of beauty. Such grace and form I have never seen. That skill, combined with patience was worth the price of the trip, that being rowing for uncle Lloyd for six hours.

After Howard showed me his well-worn waders, absolutely gorgeous split bamboo fly rod and a classic landing net, we had to walk the course. We left the basement, walked a well-worn path on the south side of the river downstream probably two hundred yards. Here he paused and showed me a piece of rope that he had tied onto a tree that reached out to the edge of the river. "And I take hold of this rope and use it to get into the river so I don't fall down. Then I carefully wade upstream until I get to the bridge, get out on the left side, cross over the bridge and put my stuff away."

Then he demonstrated the walk back to the basement where he kept his fishing gear. "I usually catch two trout, but I don't always keep them." How many times had I heard that story, and thought, "crazy, old guy." Now as I sit here and review these writings, I wonder, "Why didn't I spend more time talking with him and uncle Lloyd and asking them to tell me stories of their youth?"

Note from Sandy: Bill and I had fun going over these stories and going deeper into his story. We realized today that as do most men, he was longing for a father to approve of him, spend time with him and to bless him. What you read in these stories about Grandpa Doctor and his Dad is about all there was: the fishing bond. He never heard the words he longed to hear or felt the embrace of a warm and loving father. He gave up on his Dad, but his heart was still searching and we were able to remember those who stood in his father's place, and were, I believe, messengers from his heavenly Father: Dr.Stan Toussaint, Uncle Lloyd, Pastor Roy Clark, Dr. Vernon Grounds and maybe even Howard Davidson.

26

Taming the Shrew

When I first heard this term used, my thoughts went to the famous Shakespearean play called, 'The Taming of the Shrew.' When I explained my predicament to Rusty Gates, of Gates Au Sable River Lodge fame, he explained to me that the phenomenon I had experienced on the river must have been a shrew. He said, "No! You're not out of your mind." In my ignorance, I silently claimed intelligence by keeping my mouth shut since I had no idea what he was talking about. The chain of events that led to this amazing discovery is as follows.

When I first started fly fishing for trout, I was very young: probably thirty-five or thirty-six. In those days I still had most of my hair, and most of my five senses, especially my hearing. So as I slipped into the stream very quietly, the second or third time, (you don't want to hear about the first time), all of my senses were on high alert. First of all, when one is trout fishing away from the sounds of the city and highway, one begins to realize how many different and peculiar sounds await such a person.

The emotions and sensations that are encountered by a fly fisherman who is in a stream all by himself are rife especially one who is fishing alone on a very dark night. My first and foremost thoughts were, "What if I get my foot caught under a log or worse yet a man-eating bog sucks me down until I drowned. What about my wife and children? Would they miss me? Would they even know I was gone?" There were other almost as severely morbid thoughts, like, the wind is blowing tonight. Uncle Lloyd told me about how big rotten oak trees dropped limbs or fell over on unsuspecting souls, especially dumb trout fisherman like me, and stunned or even killed them.

And then there are the large wild creatures; squirrels, skunks, coyotes, rabid deer, and even, God forbid, black bear. After all, I had a patient who had a cottage in Baldwin near a swamp. He said he stayed there one winter and experienced multiple visits by black bears. Actually my cabin was on the edge of a swamp. What would I do if I encountered a bear in the middle of the night? He can see better than I, so running was fruitless. Besides with all the bushes and low branches I stood a good chance of putting my eye out so I couldn't run. I would just have to pull out my trusty Swiss Army knife and do battle on the spot.

Another very frequent nocturnal interruption in my otherwise quiet evening might come from a beaver. Now the beaver that live in and around streams, are usually very quiet, unassuming, and certainly not threatening. However as I will relate in another story, their presence and activity can drive shivers up and down the spine of an unsuspecting soul, and cause a near panic state. The normal noise associated with beavers is that of gnawing on a stick or a small log. I could phonetically reproduce the sound, but I can't think of any terminology, which could reasonably replicate that sound.

With all of those thoughts running around in the back of my head it is little wonder that I first missed the very slight noise that I was later able to identify fairly frequently. The normal sounds around the stream at night would be the wind blowing lightly through the bushes, or through very tall pine trees, a soft whistling of the wind through the pine boughs. Not a fearsome noise but as I gained experience in the river, it was very comforting because it frequently told me where I was in the river. Depending upon my location in the river, I could almost always hear a very soft gurgling of water over logs, around branches or down a rapids. These became well-recognized and very comforting and soothing noises at night.

Other nocturnal noises include an occasional snort of a nearby buck, the rustling in the bushes of a bird and the unnerving raucous behavioral noise of a flock of turkeys nesting overhead in a tall pine tree. It is of little wonder that I totally missed the noise of a shrew. The noise of a shrew is not one that would come from his tiny lips, as far as I know, but, a series of very tiny splashes, perhaps I should call them splishes, as though a tiny creature is skipping across the top of the water. My cognitive brain said, "Of course, that is impossible." So I dismissed that thought totally. I then recall my days in physics, although I almost flunked it, I did retain some of the information; such as the concept of surface tension on a body of water.

Would it be possible that a tiny creature could actually run on water if he was so light or so fast that he did not break the surface tension? Preposterous! I returned to my common sense brain which said this is really impossible.

In my early days of fly fishing for trout I was extremely interested in the contents of the trout's stomach. That might give me a clue as to what kind of fly I should use. The olden days of 'flop a slimy worm into a deep hole and wait for the tug at the end of the line,' did not require any modicum of intelligence. The village idiot knew trout eat worms. I knew! But what form of naturally occurring fare tickled the fancy of the feeding trout was a mystery to me. At the end of every successful fishing trip, I would faithfully take out my shiny Swiss Army knife and slit the trout's belly, from the cloacae up to the gills. I would then sever the gills from the base of the mouth and from the vertebral column and strip out all of the guts from the trout beginning at the head end.

Just for the sake of completeness, I must explain that in the trout's circulatory system, the blood flows back to the heart, which incidentally is a two-chambered structure, along what is called the dorsal vein. The accomplished fisherman who is not a biologist, is prone to call it 'the mud vein.' I was taught by my father to take a thumbnail and run it along the vertebral column from the head end down to the cloaca thus expressing clotted blood; this is rumored by some, to enhance the flavor of the cooked trout. I cannot vouch for that, but following tradition, which is somewhat unusual for me, I routinely did it to the slain trout.

As I am re-reading this epistle, I'm wondering if we all know about the cloaca? In case a neophyte should stumble across this writing, I would hasten to explain the evacuatory system of a lower vertebrate. The cloaca is the holding chamber at the end of the digestive system, into which flows fecal material. It also accumulates, from a rather rudimentary renal system, urine. Thirdly it serves as a storage chamber for eggs and semen. All of which leads me to note another sequence of which most non-fisherman are unaware; and frankly don't give a rip. Nonetheless I feel compelled to explain a little bit of the reproductive cycle of most fish, at least many of the fresh water fish that I am familiar with.

Most everyone who I know who has ever been in a boat on a freshwater lake has seen the light colored circles in shallow water in the spring. Freshwater fish do not cohabitate or have intercourse. Their sex life does not involve passion, compassion or any thrills. It is, in fact very mundane. These light-colored or whitish circles which in my earlier days, I thought were white sidewall tires in the water, are not so. They're not tires of any kind, white or black. They are circles made by female fish. As I write this I'm thinking mostly of bluegills but it also pertains to bass. I don't know about perch.

Anyway, these female bluegills (sunfish, crappy, rock bass and black bass) swim in circles, two to three feet across, very close to the bottom so that their fin action sweeps away debris from the bottom. This allows the whitish sand or gravel to show through to the surface and appear as white circles. When, as dutiful females, they are happy with the appearance (it looks clean), they start dropping their eggs, or squirting them out through the cloaca. The eggs are encased in a gelatinous substance so that they tend to stick to the bottom and to one another.

Thence cometh the males. I have to say that I haven't the foggiest idea as to why the males are attracted to a glob of gelatin on the bottom of the lake, but they are! I have imagined all sorts of reasons why the male is attracted. It could be the odor of the egg gelatin. Smells have a definite effect on me. I could imagine it might have an effect on male bluegills. It could be the sight of the white circle. It could be this sensuous appearance of a female bluegill fanning the bed. I really doubt the latter, because, when done dropping eggs the female disappears. The male has two functions.

The first of which is to fertilize the eggs. The second appears to be to protect the eggs from predators. Witness! All fishermen know the aggressive behavior of a male fish on a spawning bed. We have all been the recipients of this aggressive behavior. I hold up the fish frying pan as evidence to this rather predictable fish attitude. They attack anything which appears to be a threat to their future offspring, or tries to somehow impede their sexual activity.

As I have already launched my diatribe on the fish's sexuality, I feel compelled to advance to one further step. On the sexuality of anadromous fish, I have witnessed the following. Upon the occasion of fishing the Pere Marquette, in shallow water in the fall of the year, for spawning salmon, I have witnessed the following. The spawning bed for these very large anadromous fish is always a gravel bar.

The female appears first on the bar and vigorously uses her tail to clean the gravel and scoop out a trough. At a later time she drops her eggs into the hollow or bed that she has created. The appearance of this bed is very similar in function to the white circle of the bluegill, except this is a long trough or hollow into which the female salmon drops her eggs.

We fisherman understand that the gravel is not a solid bottom. In fact, it is a surface with many cracks or holes. We know that the eggs dropped into these cracks or holes are thus protected from predators and current. In the case of the salmon, the males are always nearby. I have personally noted and in fact seen movies of what I am about to describe.

The female opens her jaw or beak and at the same time she vigorously beats the bed and drops eggs. At that very instant the waiting male moves right up against the female and sprays the dropping eggs with sperm. That form of sex will never sell on Video

It is my assumption that trout probably reproduce in a similar method even though they are not usually anadromous. Steelhead, or rainbow trout are anadromous. Not just in the Great Lakes, but very noticeably on the West Coast of the United States. I have also experienced anadromous Brook trout in Newfoundland. That is most unusual. Brook trout in local streams, seldom exceed sixteen inches in length. I have caught anadromous Brook trout in Newfoundland up to twenty inches and that is a hoot!

One would be tempted to think that this whole process is very chancy. It is in fact very chancy. And for that very reason the number of eggs in any fish's skein is unbelievably large. Similarly, if one were able to view the sperm bank of the male, one would be flabbergasted. This of course has been confirmed by scientific investigation. Another amazing fact is that every egg is a life and surrounded by gelatin. Each sperm is incredibly small but also extremely active. Pictures of the sperm would make one think of a small tadpole swimming very rigorously. In so doing, the sperm finds the egg and penetrates the gelatinous shell. The sperm goes on to then penetrate the egg itself. The amazing thing is, that once the shell has been penetrated by a single sperm, that shell becomes impervious to other sperm. Think of the implications; if this were not so, a single egg could theoretically be penetrated by several sperm thus giving rise to a three headed or three tailed salmon. This whole phenomena is evidence of how incredible our God is. Just think what would happen if every egg dropped were penetrated by three sperm. We humans would be up to our eyeballs in three headed salmon.

All this to say, once I had cleaned all of the entrails from the trout I carefully incised the trout's stomach. It was not at all uncommon to find this voraciously feeding fish was empty and was very hungry. Surprise! The fish ate your fly not because you were so clever and skilled, but because he was just plain starving, and that ugly fly looked like his next meal. On the other hand, most fish, that is trout, have some kind of food substance accumulated in their stomachs. It is also interesting to note that ingested food remains in the fish's stomach only a few hours: their digestive process is very rapid in the summer. And I say in the summer because in the winter the digestive process in fish is much slower and a fish may eat only once or twice a week.

I realize that this is a very long run for a very short slide. I had originally planned to list some of the material/substance that I had recovered from the stomach of trout, but I thought that exercise would be too dull. And since some of this material is quasi-scientific, I thought I might avail myself of some of the really scientific material that I might find on the Internet.

Boy was that a shock. So I googled 'content of a trout's stomach.' The first thing that amazed me was there were so many articles available. My joy was short-lived. As I read one article after another, I realized how many idiots have access to Google. Maybe one out of ten articles was written by a fisherman or at least somebody who claimed to be. I realized how many catch and release fanatics think they are real fisherman. There were numerous references to pumping the trout's stomach. Had I not experienced some of these catch and release clowns in my own travels, I would not have believed what I read.

Pumping a fish's stomach is standard fare among the catch and release détente. It's not as though I have never caught and released fish, especially trout, but among other reasons for fishing, one of mine is to catch and eat trout. As I travel around to various fishing sites and sporting-goods stores I see many signs, 'catch and release.' My personal motto is,'filet and release.'

The technique for pumping a trout stomach is quite simple.

1) Catch a trout. You can't believe the number of comments that have been entered in Google about catching a trout.

2) Grasp the trout gently. That in itself is a feat. Trout, unlike other fish, have very fine scales and are covered by a thin coat of very slippery liquid; better known as fish slime. In order to hold the trout one must use a glove which damages the slime, or squeeze the crap out of the trout, which is also probably not good for the trout. Having said that….

3) Thrust the plastic tube into the trout's mouth and down into the stomach.

4) Either squeeze the fish or attach a small suction device and extract some of the stomach contents.

Sounds simple doesn't it. What I'm about to reveal to you will help you to realize how ludicrous the whole process of pumping a trout stomach is.

One must realize that Brown trout are carnivorous; they are not vegans. On a warm summer's day in the state of Michigan one can expect to find a great number and variety of bugs, flies and other critters. I will list a few: June bugs, ladybugs, beatles, tadpoles, fry of other fish, salamanders, freshwater clams, fish eggs, copepods, scuds, nymphs of many kinds of flies including dragonflies and finally all sorts and sizes of actual flying creatures. Can you imagine sucking up a salamander through a five mm plastic tube?

The reason I wrote the above was in the stomach of a large trout I found a pair of very tiny feet. Based on what little I know, I thought they might belong to a baby mouse. Of course there are many wild mice in the northland. Evidence my cabin when left unattended for significant periods of time. The mice have been everywhere, chewed up everything chewable and have left tiny turds everywhere. But, as the internet suggested, I placed the stomach contents into a white pan and teased out the individual pieces. What I discovered was not a pair of tiny feet but rather a pair of tiny legs to which were attached, relatively speaking large feet with soft pads.

Eureka! The mystery was solved. I had found the remains of a shrew. These tiny pads on these relatively large feet enabled that creature to run or skip across the water.

From Miriam Webster: shrew 1: Any of a family Soricida of small chiefly nocturnal insectivores related to the moles and distinguished by a long pointed snout, very small eyes and short velvety fur. 2: an ill- tempered scolding woman. Interesting but not my first choice.

From Wikipedia, some interesting facts. They are indeed very small; they can eat up to ninety percent of their body weight per day. Their brain is about ten percent of their total body weight which is the largest percent of brain to body weight of all mammals. So they are no dumb bunnies. They can reproduce up to 12 times a year. Thank God that brown trout like to eat them or we might be inundated. How shrewd of

God! One additional fact that I feel you ought to know is, that some of them echolocate. I leave you with that teaser. Well, not quite.

I have to leave you with a word, sound picture. I've said it before, but I just cannot emphasize too much, how lovely is an evening on the middle branch Pere Marquette river in the middle of the summer. It has been a hot day on the river. Many flies have hatched from the bottom as nymphs, wiggle up to the surface, burst through the surface tension to the top of the water, split open the shell of their nymphal body and then ride on the floating shell casing as they stretch and dry out their wings above the surface of the water.

On this particular night it is very warm, with no threat of rain. The wings of the insects are dry almost as fast as they unfold from the body. Only a few seconds pass before the fly flops his wings and rises from the surface of the water. The wily trout has sensed the motion in the water and is trying to locate this fly. Perhaps by sight directly or more likely indirectly from the little waves that are reflecting odd beams of light down into the water, those waves having been created by the emerging insect. More likely something similar to echolocation, but in the case of the trout, it's because of the sensitivity of its lateral line. I really do not understand the patho-physiology of the lateral line but I do know that it senses pressure change, from the surrounding water and enables even a blind fish to feed on a moving object.

That hungry trout has sensed the presence of an emerging insect. He didn't get it on the way up from the bottom, but somehow he can see or sense it on the surface of the water, as it sits there drying its wings. So he slashes up to the surface of the water to slurp that fly. But as I said, it's a warm dry night; that fly is already in the air. So all the trout got was a dead casing. That's like eating cellulose. He's not happy. It's a beautiful night and flies are popping everywhere and they are off the water in a split second. That trout is going nuts as he is starving and he needs a good meal.

Enter the shrew. He is hungry too. By echolocation, he senses some large flies on the water and he proceeds to skip his way across to his banquet, Hexagenia Limbata. Dinnertime! Spaloush. That shrew is already in that trout's stomach. Burp! Too much fuzz. End of shrew and shrew story!

27

Lost in the Swamp

Tonight I'm sitting in my easy chair, listening to "my kind of jazz, " and talking to my Dragon. Today I braved the elements with my courageous wife to walk thirty minutes with the other old people, better known as the Senior citizen exercise variant at Hick's Street gym. The snowpack around our driveway is down to three feet and tonight the temperature is up to twenty-two degrees. Summer must be just around the corner, somewhere. It's hard for me to imagine a hot summer night near my cabin in Baldwin.

As best I can recollect, this evening was in June or July of about 1968. I had owned the cabin with Jim Glessner, for a couple of years. I had ample opportunity to wade up and down the stream in the daytime, in order to learn about the stream. I knew a fair amount about the middle branch of the Pere Marquette River, the surrounding swamps and banks. But as the story unwinds, it appears I had a lot more to learn. It was a Tuesday evening, which means I had worked most of the day after rising very early. The reason being, I had long anticipated this fishing trip.

The weather was warm and I anticipated a fun evening of fishing, from somewhere downstream of my cabin, all the way up to my cabin. I somewhat knew the terrain and river, however, I did not have a good idea the amount of water that I could cover in one evening. I donned my waders, which at this point in time, in my fishing career were heavy rubber waders, which I had purchased from Herter's, Inc. Waseca, Minnesota. If, according to their literature, George Leonard Herter, hadn't discovered it or invented it, it wasn't worth owning. It was a mail order catalog, which was the best source for outdoor supplies for a poor boy like me. I had not yet become acquainted with Charles Orvis and his wonderful shop in New Hampshire, or L.L. Bean in Freeport Maine, which at that time was a series of loosely connected buildings. Charlie Orvis was an up and coming quality sporting goods store, but L.L. Bean was just a young upstart company. At this point I must mention that there was a quality sporting goods store called Abercrombie and Fitch. They were located in San Francisco, New York City and Chicago, Illinois. The latter location was reasonably close, as I am about to explain.

'Bunny trail' number seventy-six; at that point in my medical career, I was an employee of John L. Kihm M.D. I was either on salary, or was engaged in a buy-in situation. I barely had two nickels to rub together. But John L, Jack Kihm, had several nickels to shake in a bag. It didn't seriously harm Jack to have a father whose name was Otto Kihm, owner of Otto Kihm Tire Company of Kalamazoo. Historically, Jack and I were in medical school together and were fraternity brothers.

Jack was married to Flo, and had little time for the brothers. We really didn't know one another except as speaking acquaintances. We went our separate ways.

Unbeknownst to me, after his internship, Jack applied for and received a preceptorship with, no one less famous than Homer Stryker, of Stryker Corporation fame. At that time, Homer was the senior partner of Stryker, DeLong and Scholl, of the Scholl foot care company. Jack had finished his residency, passed his boards and was happily engaged in the private practice of orthopedic surgery in Kalamazoo, Michigan. So in practice time, Jack was two ½ years my senior, although younger by a full year.

In 1961, there was not exactly a glut on the market of orthopedic surgeons in Kalamazoo. CH&C, better known as Maynard Conrad, Curtis Hanson and Russell Cashen, had a corner on the orthopedic market at Bronson hospital, were a little older, hated night call and wouldn't travel across town to Borgess hospital.

The Borgess guys, Homer and partners similarly did not like night call or traveling to Bronson hospital. When this young upstart, John L Kihm said to the ER people, "I'll go anywhere, anytime," he was everybody's friend and busier than a one armed paper hanger.

A brief digression in the midst of another digression goes this way. The practice of medicine in Kalamazoo in 1963, the year I arrived on the scene, was relatively archaic; especially the emergency rooms. To enter the Borgess emergency room, was much akin to coming into the back door of the hospital. It was not well marked, nor presentable. To unload an ambulance of its passengers at Borgess ER was to subject them to all of the elements of 'out of doors.' There were no walls, nor roof over the entry way to protect the wounded. I almost felt there should be a sign over the door stating you enter at your own risk.

Once inside that emergency room, the patient encountered a small waiting room, where smoking was permitted. Opposite the waiting room was a small reception area staffed by one clerical person. Across the hall were located two very sparsely furnished examination rooms. There was one very small additional room that could be utilized in an emergency. The daytime staff consisted of one RN, one LPN, and an aide. Orderlies needed to be called from the floor. X-ray services were just down the hall and laboratory services were just around the corner. The evening shift was augmented by an additional RN.

My recollection was Bronson emergency room was a small step up. There was a drive-through approach to this emergency room, so patients were not subjected to rain, snow and strong winds. The inside was quite similar to Borgess in that there was a receptionist, a waiting room that also allowed smoking, one large emergency room that was divided by a curtain and two smaller ones, all of which were sparsely supplied. There was one antique anesthesia machine in each emergency room. This machine frequently was utilized by general practitioners; anesthesiologists were occasionally utilized in those olden days.

There were no emergency room physicians. All of the physicians in town were placed on a roster, and call was assigned alphabetically. When your name came up, you had to supply the care for the patient. Three things became very obvious to me early in my practice:

1. The emergency room nurses held great power. Let's say that Dr. George Hoekstra had a patient show up at Borgess ER with an obvious broken wrist. The clerk would come out and gain information from family; "Your doctor is Dr. Hoekstra?"

"Yes, would you call him?"

"Yes I will." The RN makes the call. Ring, ring.

"This is Dr. Hoekstra."

"Dr. Hoekstra, Charlie Brown is here with a broken arm."

"You know that? "

"Yes sir, it is pretty obvious."

"Who's on call for Kihm?"

"It's that new guy, Burdick."

" Well, let's give him a shot."

So I learned quickly; be very nice to the ER nurses. That paid off in spades.

2. Get to know the local family doctors, especially at Borgess. Local medical doctors ran the medical profession when I came to town in 1963.

3. I don't want to deliver babies therefore when I am on call I need to line up my friends in the various specialties. That is how the ER functioned in 1963.

When I walked into the practice I found Jack to be more than fair. He said to me, " I've been on call alone for two years. Now, you get to be alone on call for the next three weeks."

So, as of September 1, 1963, I experienced immediate success as one of the two orthopedic surgeons in Kalamazoo who would go anywhere, any time. At the end of the three-week period, my exuberance was reduced to a single word, " Help!"

Yes, we were young, foolish but enthusiastic. We realized that we needed further training and from that point on, we sought out special short courses in orthopedic surgery to further our education. One such meeting, was a monthly evening sponsored by the Chicago Orthopedic Society. That's a long way to go for one evening meeting. But Jack, who is multitalented, had learned to fly, and purchased his own Cessna. So once a month we traveled to Chicago, either flying or occasionally driving. This entire bunny trail is simply to explain how I was able to experience that marvelous store in Chicago called Abercrombie and Fitch.

It was a six story building in downtown Chicago, quite near where we attended the Chicago Orthopedic Society dinner. Several times we went early just so we could experience six floors of the most exotic sporting equipment that one could imagine. The displays there would equal the biggest and best of the Cabella's stores today. As I think about the store I cannot imagine how I could relate to my reader the sheer ecstasy I experienced walking through the floor of fishing equipment; four hundred dollar split bamboo fly rods, three hundred fifty dollar fly reels, fishing vests that would hold all of the fly fishing equipment that I processed at that time, seventy dollar fly fishing hats, fifty dollar rain jackets and one hundred dollar light weight waders.

So on that very hot summer evening, as I slogged through swamps, climbed up and down sandy hills, and crashed through thick brush, in those ten pound, heavy rubber waders, I drooled over the thought of a pair of lightweight canvas waders. As it turns out, I would ultimately drool over the thought of some other fishing equipment, which I know now is absolutely essential to a night fisherman.

I stumbled down the last hill, mushed through a small feeder stream and walked the last stretch of tara firma before crossing a large swamp, and then carefully entered the wonderfully cooling water of the middle branch of the Pere Marquette River.

The scene is very difficult to describe, because sound and smell are all an integral part of the trout stream, especially so at this time of the evening, when the sun had just dipped out of sight. A few scud clouds drifted across the sky indicating a moderate breeze. The night air should be a little cooler than the eighty some degrees that I was experiencing at that moment. The water was refreshingly cool but not cold. It would typically run about sixty-three degrees this time of year and this time of day. The air was filled with a myriad of creatures and sounds. The birds made their presence known with a few distant calls, particularly raucous was that of a crow. The rippling water noise was low enough to allow me to hear the birds nestling into the nearby bushes for their evening perch. I could still hear the distant drum of a partridge.

The noise was so low, in fact that I could hear the drone of the hordes of mosquitoes that were lurking in the bushes, ready to attack an unsuspecting wader. To enter this situation at this period of eventide, without "Off," was akin to suicide. I harken back to the pre–Off era, and I recall a number of non-efficacious mosquito treatments, such as oil of citronella. As I recall everything else we tried, attracted, more than repelled, the mosquitoes.

Very few of my readers can realistically contemplate what I am about to disclose. I have fished in various locations where it was not uncommon to have a virtual cloud of bugs around one's head. This was especially true in the woods of Newfoundland. Mosquitoes were bad enough, but much worse were the little black flies and no see-ums. Mosquito bites would raise a small bump and itch, but black flies left a small bloody sore that was beyond irritating. They were particularly bothersome when they flew into one's eyes and even worse into one's ears where they couldn't be touched by human digits.

To counter, or better said prevent, this miserable state, my father employed, rather, tried to employ a head net. As you might imagine this net allowed one to see, but the mesh of which was small enough to keep out even little black flies. Hooray!

But, alas, there was a small shortcoming. We learned that the material was flammable. And my father was an avowed heavy smoker. There was a small split in the front of the net that would allow a cigarette to stick out while the smoker puffed away. I viewed this net as a double edged sword, and sure enough it was. Somehow, my father managed to burn a large enough hole in the front of the net so as to render it useless. Fortunately for him, he carried a spare. However this required a decision; to die of bug bites, or to die from a lack of nicotine fit. Nicotine won.

My father learned that if he lifted the front of the net up and promptly lit a cigarette, the smoke would keep the bugs away until he was done smoking. Then he would quickly drop the net back in place and he could do both, smoke and fish. But consider the cost: he died at age sixty-six of advanced coronary arterial disease. At least dying from a heart attack was faster than dying from bug bites.

The surface of the water, was disturbed not only by the ripple produced by overhanging branches, or stumps in the water, but also by bug activity. I could see many flies hovering just over the water. I could visualize tiny, very tiny dimples on the water. I later learned that these dimples were tiny packets of eggs dropped from the hovering mayflies. Occasionally I could see a mayfly struggling on the surface of the water.

If it were an emerger, an emerging fly, it would flutter a foot or two down the stream and then take off. This fly would then join its fellow mayflies in the air, hover, mate and then drop tiny packets of fertilized eggs. These eggs would drop through the surface of the water to the bottom of the stream and were carried along until they fall into a crevice, either around sand or gravel. Sometimes these eggs would stick to underwater objects such as stones, rocks or branches. They would then spend from one to seven years in the water, as water creatures until maturation and their time of hatching, as airborne, air breathing mayflies.

Every once in a while a fly would flutter and linger too long and be spotted by a hungry trout. Usually, 'the take,' was subtle to the point of not being heard and barely perceived by the eye. It would be a dimple, and nothing more. That was the usual chain of events for most of the mayflies, the one exception being the giant Michigan mayfly called Hexagenia Limbata. By mayfly standards, these guys were huge. The body, complete with three tiny but long tails, were up to an inch and a half long with a wing span about the same. For a trout to take one of these he had to create quite a commotion. This commotion is what we fly fisherman longed to see and hear. But at this time in my life, I had no idea what a mayfly was, and especially a 'Hex.'

The smells present that evening were 'Ode 'D' Off'— musty swamp, and occasionally a very pleasant whiff of Balsam Pine. Occasionally on an evening such as this, I could perceive a distant, and faint odor from a disturbed polecat, better known to the uninitiated, as a skunk. This may sound very crude to most of you readers, however, occasionally, I find a faint, distant odor of the polecat to be quite 'titillating.' If you should happen to share this very weird sensual experience, snap your fingers twice and phone me.

There is one other visual aura that I frequently encounter and that is of a very docile muskrat swimming down stream towards me with a mouth full of fresh, green grass. I tend to think of this as the pizza guy of the stream bringing home supper to share with his wife and brood. I always freeze so I will not disturb this very quiet critter. As he finally perceives my presence, he quietly dives and swims past me until he is safe from the intruder, me.

Permit one more divergence since experiences like this are rare. It was a very similar time of the evening and this time I was wading upstream from Davidson's cottage. I was tired from a fairly long wade, and had a significant backache. I plopped my rear on a very nice grassy bank and was looking straight upstream, into a dark stretch of water. The water was overhung by Tag Alder bushes from each side creating a dark tunnel through which the water was rippling and creating a significant contrast between the dark water and the light ripples which combined to create a rather eerie effect at that time of night.

Again, I spent a long day working, had driven two hours to get to my cabin and had already waded almost an hour, so I was fatigued. I pulled out my trusty corncob pipe, stuffed and lit it. As I was inhaling the pleasant rum flavored tobacco smoke, I must have drifted off a little. I was aroused from my stupor by what I perceived to be a trout noisily slurping up a fly. I opened my eyes to peer into the direction from which I thought the sound had arisen. To my amazement and fear, I thought I saw an alligator swimming down stream towards me with a gigantic head, a huge wake and shiny crocodile eyes. No, I was wrong, I knew there was an alligator coming for me.

You might well say, "you've been in the sauce again," and I wouldn't blame you for saying that. But I've long since learned you stay away from alcoholic beverages in several circumstances; when fly fishing, or wading the stream for any reason, when tying flies and when engaged in card playing for serious money. So I was sober and I knew that this wasn't an alligator in the middle of Michigan in July. But, there was a broad head, bright eyes and a wake that spread from one side of the stream to the other. My sphincters tightened which was a really good thing; otherwise I would have soiled my underwear severely.

As my reason quickly returned, I noted that this creature dove under water and made a huge 'smack,' with his very broad tail. This was none other than a friendly beaver returning home. My problem lay in the fact that, although I knew beavers inhabited streams, I had never encountered one on my stream, so this was a complete surprise, which fortunately, ended well.

Returning to my swamp story of an evening fish somewhere down stream from my cabin, I had entered the stream and was very slowly moving up stream. One always moves slowly in the stream for a variety of reasons. Most importantly, fish can feel vibrations of your boots on the bottom. That is one of the reasons that you always fish up stream. It diminishes their ability to perceive your boot steps in the water.

When wading in gravel, the bottom may be somewhat slippery, so it's much safer to move slowly and plan each step. And lastly and most significantly is the fact that when you're in water that is almost up to the top of your waders, you present a large baffle for the oncoming water, albeit it's only traveling at five or six mph. It takes some strength to wade upstream in a river of that depth. One side effect is the faster you try to wade, the more forward you have to bend, and if you have a tendency toward back pain, you're going to aggravate it more by wading rapidly than if you move very slowly and cautiously. Not to mention the fact that if you stumbled and lunged forward, you would fill your waders very rapidly. Cold water inside your waiters is always discomforting.

In those early days of my fly-fishing, especially night fly-fishing, I was singularly unaccomplished; translation, I was pretty much a klutz. I was fishing with a nine foot, eight weight fly rod, with a Pflueger medalist reel, and a crappy fly line. However the stream was so small that I could not stretch out a cast beyond about fifteen feet so the line, or should I say, the sinking tip of the dry fly line was not a big factor. I customarily fish with seven ½ foot tapered leader at this time of day, and use a relatively large dry fly, a size twelve Adams or a Boerchers Special. These both were general imitators and very effective in the evening when the fish were not too discerning. I had not yet discovered the effectiveness of a large white Wulff, and therefore didn't own or carry any.

I had caught a few trout and generally had a wonderful evening of fishing. I trudged along slowly, and I would like to say cautiously, but that would be a lie. I was tired, my back ached, and my hips were bothering me. Unfortunately, at that time in my life I didn't realize that I had rotten hips. Only later was I to discover that severe malady. All I knew was that I wanted to get out of the water, stumble back to my cabin and slip into happy land. As I had mentioned earlier, I was not yet familiar with my stretch of the river but I did realize I was surrounded by swamp. I thought that if I got out on the right side of the river I could easily walk to my cottage.

At this point in time it was quite dark and even though I have good night vision I could hardly see my hand in front of my face. Unbeknownst to me a cloud cover had settled in. There was no ambient light tonight. So I reached for my handy dandy clip-on flex light and turned it on. "Oh no! I didn't turn it off the last time I used it. No light!"

Lucky for me I always carry a spare. But what I also don't always do is check the spare. It is deader than a doornail. "Well, I'll just pull out my regular flashlight." It was very dim but at least I could see the bank and the bushes on the bank. I found a spot between bushes and crawled up on the soggy bank. I quickly realized that I was walking into a swamp.

A swamp with heavy bushy overgrowth is no place to carry a nine foot fly rod. It didn't take me too long to realize that I had to break my fly rod down before I broke it up. I took the rod apart and laid it side-by-side, cranked up the reel until the fly was caught in the end guide at the tip. I realized that if by any chance, I dropped the tip and it was not locked into the rod, I would lose it, or break it. I started walking very carefully, as near as I could tell, away from the river. I twisted and turned to go around bushes, dead falls, and swampy holes. I soon realized I had no light at all. The last semblance of a battery in my little flashlight had just died. I could see absolutely nothing. As I continued to twist and turn as I walked through the bushes, the branches grabbing at my creel, my landing net and my folded up rod, I came to a stark realization; I was lost! Not just disoriented and wandering. I was totally lost, and in my own back yard, so to speak.

What does one do when lost in a swamp with no idea of what is where? As I sit here tonight and dictate this I have no better idea of what to do tonight than I did that night in the swamp. I figured I probably would not die from exposure to the cold, but perhaps my body could be consumed by mosquitoes, raccoons, or more likely crows. I did remember one of my patients who had a cabin about ten miles from mine, tell about the winter he spent in that cottage. He saw several bears; that thought lurked at the back of my mind. "Would a bear eat a dead body, or worse chase a live body?" (We just saw the movie Revenant and the answer is yes.)

A myriad of bizarre thoughts raced through my mind. I'm getting tired, where can I sit down or lie down? Nowhere in this swamp. I need to get out, keep moving. So I kept moving even though I became more and more tired, and had more and more pain from my back and my hips. What were my options? Keep moving. I stumbled, ran into sticks and stepped into suck holes. Thank God for the rotten heavy rubber waiters, they did not tear. On the other hand, I needed to get out of those waders long enough to take a whiz. "Is my urinary stream still strong enough to clear the waders or will I end up peeing in my own waders?"

I am sweating profusely, which means, I'm sweating away all of my Off. The bug bites are getting worse, but given the hopelessness of my situation, I could care less. I kept on moving but I'm not getting anywhere going to the right, so I turned to the left. After repeating this inane exercise innumerable times, I figured I was probably going in circles. Logic was starting to return. If I just walk a straight line, I'll either fall into the river, in which case I can swim downstream to the bridge, or I'll hit a high bank and get out of this miserable, rotten swamp.

So I began my trek on what I thought might reasonably be a straight line. Only God knows where I went that night. After an hour or two, since I couldn't look at my watch, it felt like half the night, I stepped on solid ground. I walked up a bank until I reached level ground. Another huge decision, turn left or right or go straight ahead. My choice was left, and I have no idea why I chose left.

All of a sudden I was in the woods with big trees, there were very few low bushes. But of course since I could not see, I had to feel my way along the course. Actually, I had spent the whole evening with one arm or the other out in front of me, so that I would not be impaled by a stick, or worse yet, have my eye impaled by a stick. Thank God I did not drop my glasses, or I would not be writing this tonight. I hope my readers will understand my circumstances, because I had long since become irrational. Be warned, it could happen to you, and it is a horrible feeling; to be lost, and worse yet, possibly on your own property. I could never tell a single soul about this humiliating experience.

As I cautiously made my way through the forest, constantly looking left, right, behind and straight ahead, I spotted what could be a light! Civilization. I was filled with hope that I might live to fish another night. But it was simply a light and I knew not from whence it came. My thoughts went to my own response to a weird fisherman knocking at my door at 2 o'clock in the morning. What would I do with such a threat on my doorstep? I would get a gun or a knife before I opened the door, because there's probably a lunatic out there waiting to jump all over me.

Now I was really filled with fear, how would this kind, gentle unsuspecting cottage owner greet me? My mind went everywhere. I conceived so many stories to tell this person that I could not begin to relate them to you. My last and probably my best response was to be honest. "Help! I'm a poor stupid fly fisherman who got lost tonight." Yes, that had to work, I had no other defense.

What do you expect to read next? That I found myself 17 miles downstream at the Pere Marquette Lodge, or that somehow I walked around to Davies' cottage? As I approached that 'light in the night,' I could see very little until I got very close to the back door----of my own cabin. I chuckled at the irony of it all, took a placidyl and hit the bag.

28

Midnight in Idlewild

Just east of the town of Baldwin, Michigan, there is a settlement named Idlewild surrounding the lake of the same name.

Wikipedia: *Idlewilde is a vacation and retirement community in Yates Township, located just east of Baldwin, in South East Lake County, a rural part of North Western lower Michigan. During the first half of the twenty-first century, it was one of the few resorts in the country where African – Americans were allowed to vacation and purchase property, before such discrimination became illegal in 1964. It surrounds Idlewilde Lake and the headwaters of the Pere Marquette River run through the area. Much of the surrounding area is within Manistee National Forest*

Called the "black Eden," from 1912 through the mid-1960s, Idlewilde was an active year-round community and was visited by well known entertainers and professionals from throughout the country. At its peak, it was the most popular resort in the Midwest and as many as twenty-five thousand visitors would come to Idlewilde in the height of the summer season to enjoy camping, swimming, boating, fishing, hunting, horseback riding, roller-skating, and night time entertainment. When the 1964 civil rights act opened up other resorts to African Americans, Idlewilde's boomtown subsided, but the community continues to serve as a vacation destination, retirement community and as a landmark of African American heritage. The Idlewilde African American Chamber of Commerce was founded in the summer of 2000 for the purpose of promoting existing local businesses and for attracting newer ones to the Lake County area.

This place, as described by Wikipedia, was just east of my property by a few miles. I had no idea that a place like Idlewilde actually existed. I recalled a few stories that I heard from uncle Lloyd, Howard Davidson and quite a few of the Baldwin natives; everything has been nicely summarized in the Wikipedia story.

In the early days of my fishing, the middle branch of the Pere Marquette River was relatively shallow and easy to wade. Since I had just invested ten thousand dollars in this little cabin in the words, I thought I would like to learn as much as I could about 'my river.' My river began downstream at the Forks Bridge which was over the middle branch of the Pere Marquette River about one hundred feet upstream from the entrance of the Little South Branch of the Pere Marquette River- From that Forks down, it was known as the Pere Marquette River. It remained a moderate sized river for about fifteen miles until receiving the Big South Branch. For me, my river began some where east of the Good Shepherd Camp above which it was too small to support any fly fishing for trout.

I had obtained a number of maps of Lake County in which most of my river was located. I scouted various parts of this river on foot and by car in the fall and spring before and after the trout season. I had a very good idea of every access point for entering and leaving the stream. It only remained for me to actually don waders, arm myself with the appropriate dry fly fishing equipment and enter the stream. For the most part I had divided the stream into two or three hour sections. That was important because, when I fished with another person, we had to plan and coordinate our getting in and getting out.

The section of river through Idlewilde, was very pretty indeed. I entered the river from the north side at the end of a peninsula, which extended south into a bend of the river. Thereafter the river meandered a little and made a sharp left bend at one point leaving a deliciously deep hole, which I was convinced held many large trout, even though I never saw one in the middle of the day. But again, I never saw much in the way of any trout in the middle of the day, ever. And I hearken back to prior words, brown trout are very suspicious, and are spooked easily. The one exception being Davies signal trout.

I had learned from Uncle Lloyd and others that this was owned and inhabited by a very nice African American widow lady whose name was Alma Hall. I was particularly interested that my presence might not be intrusive in the middle of the night. I heard many rumors about how some of the natives are particularly restless and are known to carry knives and guns. Not wishing to encounter that type of behavior, in that neighborhood, I got out of my car, knocked on the door and introduced myself. Alma Hall was an extremely gracious lady, and so kind that I asked her if she would be willing to accept my gift of trout, should I be so fortunate so as to catch a few. In return, could I have the privilege of walking across her property? You would've thought that I had offered her a gold coin. "Yes, I would be more than happy for a gift like that." And, "Certainly, feel free to get in and out of the stream on my yard," Thank you, kind Alma Hall.

I then proceeded to park my car, walked down to the end of the peninsula, entered the river and experienced an outstanding day on the river. The sun was up, a breeze was blowing and made a very pleasant rustling sound as it whistled through the pine trees and Tag Alder's. There were a few black flies, but no mosquitoes. It was truly a gorgeous day. During much of this trip, the sun was slightly to my back, so that I had almost perfect vision of this stretch of water, which was shallow enough for me to see the bottom most of the time. Even with such great visibility I was absolutely amazed at the fact I could not see most of these trout in the water, until they had hit my Borchers fly.

At that time in my life, I was fascinated by primarily two flies; the Adams and the Borchers. The wing pattern was that of tiny feathers placed upright on the front of the fly, at a forty-five degree angle from one another. When looking at the front of this fly, these two feathers would almost look like horns sticking up from the top of the fly, in the midst of the head hackles. The pattern for the two flies was very similar, differing only in body material; the Adams was medium gray, and the

Borchers was a tan body with peacock ribbing. Although I was a fairly good fly tier, it took me a long time to tie one of these, eight to ten minutes each.

I had learned about these flies from one of my meetings of Trout Unlimited, which was held on a monthly basis. At that time this meeting was the highlight of my month, at least as a fisherman. These meetings were especially interesting in the middle of the winter, when spring trout fishing seemed to be three years away. Every meeting reminded me of Art Neuman's fly shop, Wanigas Rod Company.

From these meetings I learned about the Boercher's fly. Art would mail out flyers highlighting his specials. That is how I came to purchase a lovely, seven and a half foot split bamboo rod. I also learned about the special on, 'the Boercher's fly.' Twenty-five cents a piece! I couldn't buy the material let alone tie one for that price. So, guess what? I bought one thousand of them.

On that particularly gorgeous day, I managed to pick up many small rainbow trout and browns. I actually caught a number of medium sized brown trout on my trip up stream, to the high bank at Alma Hall's cottage. As I passed one deep, dark hole, in a long bend in the river, I experienced not one whit of trout feeding activity. This cemented in my mind the fact that it was occupied by very large trout, who were not so foolish as to come out and grace the presence of a neophyte fly fishermen such as myself, with a slurp of a fly.

As I left the river and walked up the bank, toward Alma's house, she spotted me and greeted me at the door. "How y'all do?"

"I did fairly well, thank you," and presented her the four specimens that I had caught. I asked if I could clean them for her and she acknowledged that she was very capable of cleaning her own fish. It was a wonderful exchange and a marvelous experience of fishing on this beautiful stretch of river and meeting such a truly gracious woman.

As I headed back towards my cabin, I recalled a very interesting tale told me by Uncle Lloyd Cook. I have been racking my brain to try and remember how I first became aware of Uncle Lloyd. Although his last name was Cook, he was not a relative of my wife, Sandy Cook, or her grandfather, Harry Cook. Rather, he married Grandpa Harry Cook's sister, whose name was Catherine. So a Cook married a Cook, and I became a distant relative of Uncle Lloyd.

I'm going to give a brief history of what I know about uncle Lloyd and his upbringing, because it's a fascinating story I wish to convey to my grandchildren the importance of respecting and listening to your elders' stories. They can be very interesting, and informative; there are many lessons to be learned, if you will avail yourself of family mysteries.

Uncle Lloyd was born into a very poor family that was involved in agriculture in or around Bailey, Michigan. That is a very small town, through which I passed many times on my way to Baldwin. There was some good agricultural land in that area but from what I gathered, Uncle Lloyd's family occupied some pretty poor land and eked out a living raising potatoes. I do not recall much about his family i.e. whether there had been mother, father, brothers or sisters. Upon graduation from high school he moved to Grand Rapids, Michigan where he took a very menial job as a laborer, working for the Grand Rapids Press ✗

I remember him telling me that he had to bind up packages of newspapers to be delivered to the outlying districts around Grand Rapids. My impression was that he started at the bottom rung on the ladder of success. I don't recall a lot of the history in between, except for the fact that he was a hard worker, obviously very bright, but he made some wrong choices along the way. The major one was that he married early, had two children and divorced early in life. Much later, he found and married Aunt Catherine Cook.

As he worked his way up the ladder of success, the major factor was that he did what was necessary in whatever job he found himself until he was employed by the Grand Rapids Showcase Equipment Company. If you go to Wikipedia you might get some background on this company, but when I was but a wee lad, I was aware of some of their display cases. They were the very most common type of display cases in the United States. The mainstay of this production was a show case with an oak base and top frame into which, was fitted a fairly large piece of plate glass as the display area. There was a top of oak from 6 inches to a foot wide and the length of the case. The back consisted of a pair of sliding glass doors set in wooden frames. Had you gone to a bakery anywhere in the Midwest you would have seen one of these showcase displays manufactured by Grand Rapids Showcase Equipment Company.

This company, as were probably thirty-five other furniture companies, was centered in and around Grand Rapids. At that time in this era, Grand Rapids was known as the furniture capital of the United States. In the forties and fifties that all changed and much furniture manufacturing moved to the Carolinas, which, as far as I know, is still the center of current day furniture manufacturing.

All of this was happening in and around the 1920s', before the great depression. Uncle Lloyd was sent to Dallas Texas where he was in charge of the sales of this equipment to the Southwest, and later moved to New York City, which you can well imagine was one of the larger users of this type of showcase. Shortly before the big depression, he was moved back to Grand Rapids where he assumed the role of Director of Sales of all of the Grand Rapids Showcase Equipment Company for the United States. He worked hard for and invested in this company, and according to his own words was a self made millionaire; all with only a high school education. He was extremely bright, and an avid reader of important books and magazines. He read himself into becoming an extremely well-informed man.

Enter the great depression. The Grand Rapids Showcase Equipment Company went belly up; uncle Lloyd lost his job, his fortune, and suffered, in a three-year period, three coronary artery occlusions. The only treatment for the problem, at that time was rest and aspirin. He survived along with his wife,

Catherine, son Lloyd Junior, and daughter, Marilyn, who went on to marry a cardiologist Ed Harris.

For several years uncle Lloyd worked where he could, doing what he could, but apparently just making a living until, he got a job with Rose-Patch & Label Company. So what the heck is that company all about? Again this company was located in Grand Rapids and I had no idea that such a company ever existed.

It manufactured cloth labels. "So what?" you might say, big deal. In those days, every piece of clothing manufactured in the United States had a cloth label sewn in it someplace. Today we look at a piece of clothing and we see a stamp somewhere on the fabric to identify the manufacturer, the name and the size. How they stamp that on to the fabric, without run-through, I have no idea, but in the olden days they manufactured a cloth label with all that information on it, which was then sewn into the inside of the edge of the piece of clothing. Somebody within the organization of Rose-Patch & Label Company had invented the machine that manufactured those labels. So not only did they own their own machines to manufacture these labels, but they had a copyright on that machine. And so every such machine owner, as far as I know, in the whole world, had to pay for the copyright in order to use the label making machine, again, which was invented, by somebody, at Rose Patch & Label Company. What a sweet deal.

Uncle Lloyd never told me the details of his employment but when I first knew him, he was chairman of the board. He readily acknowledged he had made his second million. I could see how this had happened. This guy was as tightfisted as anybody I had ever known, to the point of being ridiculous. But he could also be quite generous. Case in point. When we fished together, he made a point of having Aunt Catherine, cook a beef pot roast the night before we fished. He would then pride himself in bringing the left-over beef up north with us, so he could make us beef sandwiches, on my wife's homemade Swedish rye bread; wonderful sandwiches.

Uncle Lloyd owned and loved to drive his Cadillac. In those days, the Coup DeVille, was more a boat then a car. It was gorgeous and occasionally I got to ride in his around town, I don't think he ever trusted me to drive it. When we went north, to Baldwin to fish, it was always in my car. He was perfectly happy to let me do all the driving. As I am dictating, I have a sudden memory that makes me shudder. He was driving us up north in his car, when he went to pass a car on a very straight stretch of road between Bailey and Grant. As we cleared the back end of the vehicle in front of us, all three of my head hairs stood on end as I viewed a large truck bearing down on us from the opposite direction. I gasped, and then screamed. I think he got the message, because that was the very last time, we drove anywhere in his car.

On the other side of his tightfistedness, was his foolishness. He really loved his Cadillac which was really one of the most plush vehicles I have ever ridden in. Even in those days we had some problems with gasoline prices rocketing up without apparent reason. Today's market is no different from the sixties. Let's say that the price of gasoline went up a nickel a gallon, something as ridiculous as that. As I drove to his apartment off of E. Paris Ave. in Grand Rapids, to pick him up for our fishing trip, he bounded out of his apartment and said to me, " Would you like to see my new Buick? I just bought it because it's more gasoline efficient." He had just turned in his three year old Cadillac, which had about fifteen thousand miles on it, for a brand new, more economical Buick.

" The dealer was very happy to get that Cadillac."

At this point I'm thinking a number of thoughts about what I had just heard. A couple of them are as follows, " I'll bet that dealer was happy, you just gave him a gift of about $3000." And "I would have died to have paid that small amount for your old boat." And so the stories go on and on, but uncle Lloyd was truly a gem, who I did not fully appreciate at the time.

This is really a sweet time for me. I'm sitting at my computer, weeping and talking into my Dragon. I am so happy that I can still recall so many details of my life experiences. And as I picture them, I'm thinking of my children and grandchildren, as they read these words. I have to give you a word of advice, as it were, almost from the grave. "Look around you at the people that God has put in your life. Appreciate them and thank them for their life experiences, which they have shared with you. You cannot speak into the grave, or hear from the grave except through stories."

The reason I am bringing up my recollections of Uncle Lloyd, was a story he told me. Many years ago, he used to rent a cottage on a little lake, south of Baldwin, where he would bring his wife and two kids. He would, according to his own words, "abandoned them" and sneak over to the Pere Marquette River. One evening, as he was returning from the Idlewild stretch of the middle branch, late in the evening, he encountered a large, luxurious sedan, pulled off to the side of the road. Since it was late, he assumed that the driver may well be in distress, and, being the gentleman that he always was, he stopped and inquired as to the circumstances of the occupants of the car. He perceived they had a flat tire, and the occupants were two well-dressed African American women.

They quickly confirmed that his observation was correct, indeed they had a flat tire and didn't know what to do. Mind you now, this was in the 50s. There were no cell phones, it was nighttime, and for these ladies, walking down a dirt road in Idlewild at night was highly risky. Uncle Lloyd, very gallantly offered to help and his offer was received graciously and with great appreciation. Upon the completion of the change of tire, the driver of the car requested Uncle Lloyd's name and address to wit, he wrote out the information, having no idea that anybody would ever acknowledge his gift of kindness to these African American ladies. You can imagine his surprise and appreciation when he received the delivery of a large TV set, to his home, with a note of thanks, signed Mrs. Nat King Cole.

Nor was that the only story, of note, related to me by Uncle Lloyd, but another, I considered quite humorous. He apparently was well known around the Grand Rapids area, but also, and especially through his associations with the Peninsular Club of Grand Rapids, or Pen Club for short. That was the good old boys club of Grand Rapids, and to be invited to be a member of the club, was a singularly impressive achievement. There he established his lifelong friendship with Howard Davidson. Another noteworthy member of that club was Gerald R. Ford, who would later become, president of the United States. Lloyd invited Jerry to be a member of the board of directors of Rose Patch & Label Company, even though uncle Lloyd acknowledged that, "Jerry wasn't the sharpest knife in the drawer." Uncle Lloyd was probably the kindest, most humble, and yet the shrewdest man that I ever knew. I only wish that I could have known him and fished with him over a longer period of time. Some of his genius may have rubbed off on me.

Back to fishing at night, near Alma Hall's cottage. It was only midday, and I had not yet visited Ed's tackle shop, which I just had to do every time I went to Baldwin, in addition to sampling the wares at the Jones's Ice Cream Shop. So I drove to Baldwin, tried the chocolate ice cream and visited Josephine Sedlecky, who was the owner of Ed's tackle shop. Ed was Jo's former husband. Jo was one of the best known inhabitants of Baldwin, and the very best fly tier I have known. Jo was always cheerful and full of the latest fishing information. To go to Baldwin and not visit Ed's tackle shop was, to the fisherman, akin to a tourist not visiting Jones's ice cream shop; it was unconscionable.

But the real interest in my visit to Ed's was Ains Borsum. Ains really ran the fly shop, and knew everything about fishing that was to be known. He not only tied flies but he built rods and knew who was catching what, where and how. I mentioned to Ains that I had planned to fish around Alma Hall's cottage that night and ask if he had any advice. " Just hide your car well, and don't let anybody know you're there."

" Sure," I said knowing that I had already tipped my hand to Alma Hall. It seemed to me that Ains had a twinkle in his eye as he gave me his friendly warning, but later I wonder if that was a twinkle of humor, or a twinkle such as, "Watch out! You're going to get yours." He also mentioned that there were some fairly large brown trout in that area since it was so uncommonly fished. African Americans didn't go for trout fishing as Ains and I did and few whites cared to venture into Idlewild, especially after dark.

I returned to my cabin, brushed a short stretch of stream, took a nap and ate my sandwich. There was no such thing as TV at the cabin and radio reception was poor, so I read for a short period of time until dusk had descended. When I deemed the time to be appropriate, I loaded up my car and traveled over to the Idlewilde area. My car was not hidden but it was alongside the dirt road in a very isolated part of Lake County. In spite of some of the tales, probably very tall tales, how could being associated with Alma Hall do me any harm?

As I stepped into my waders, I remembered to check both clip-on lights and my backup flashlight. See, you can teach an old dog new tricks. Never again would I be caught without a serviceable flashlight. I checked my canvas Creel to make sure the repair job I carried out was still intact. The reason I repaired it in the first place was I had lost a very nice brown trout, because the seam in the canvas Creel had ripped out. The mesh bag of my landing net was in good shape, and the elastic cord that went over my shoulder was still very springy. It was a hot night so, I freshened up my body odor of sweat with a thick layer of Off.

I slid down the sandy, grassy bank to the water and carefully stepped into the river. The river was cool, and I immediately sensed a problem. Cool anything has an exhilarating effect on me, and in addition to exhilaration, I frequently feel a sudden urge to micturate. And that is what happened to me, immediately upon entering the cool water. To the un-initiated, that means, I had to take a leak real bad and real fast. So I had to climb out of the water, took off my net, my creel, and lowered my waders and tried to pee over the edge of the waders. I usually try to lean forward on a tree trunk, which will allow me to clear the waders. If that doesn't work, then I figure, "What the heck, I'm going to get back in the water and that will wash my waders clean." That whole process is a minor irritation, the cost of which is insignificant in light of the potential joy that I will experience in embellishing this tale to people such as you, the readers of this epistle.

As I finally faced upstream, I stripped out my line and flipped my fly. The sun had set and dusk was upon me. I saw a few minor rises, cast to them, and was rewarded with several small rainbow trout. Time passed and I moved slowly up stream, casting to rises, some real and some imagined. But that's the way evening fishing is. You see some strange and unreal things, some rising trout, that don't exist. However I was not disgruntled because this was fun fishing, even though I had not yet encountered a significant fish.

As a matter of fact, I was quite enthusiastic. The lack of decent fish hitting my fly might indicate that there are some real hoopers in the area, just waiting for me. So I carefully picked my way through the Tag Alder's, finding fishing quite difficult at this point, because the stream had narrowed, and the Tag Alder bushes formed an arch all away across the river. I had to employ my slingshot method in this particular area. If the slingshot technique is a mystery to you, and wish to learn more about it, especially budding dry fly fisherman, on small streams, call me and I can give you an hour or two lecture on the subject.

I just cleared the cathedral of Tag Alders and was looking right directly at my super deep hole, drooling, with the hairs on the back of my neck rising. To say that I was anticipatory or excited is an understatement. I was hyped up beyond reality, ready to catch a trophy Brown. As I inched forward, just a little more so I could clear my back cast and drop a fly on the lower half of the hole, I heard, just around the bend ahead of me, an explosion. This was not a muskrat seeing me and splashing into the water, or a large fish spaloushing a big fly, nor was it any critter that I could remember or ever imagine.

Realize my state of mind, if you can, given your lack of enthusiasm toward fly fishing, wading a stream on a hot summer night amid flies, mosquitoes, sweat and Off. I was running on a full tank of high-octane gas. I was hyped out of my mind. I was already seeing a twenty-six inch long Brown trout engulfing my beautiful, number 12 Boercher's, setting the hook and feeling the solid pull of that huge Brown. My epinephrine level was immeasurable.

What happened next was reflex; I had no control of my mind. I visualized the scenes that I had heard about, that ostensibly occurred in Idlewild, during the deer hunting season. The deer hunting season, around Idlewild I heard, was simply an excuse for people to go wild. And when I say people, I don't mean African Americans. I mean all red-blooded American males. I had heard, on very good authority, and you know exactly what I mean, as you have used that same term, you rascal you, that Idlewild rocked. The bordellos were packed, since many ladies of shady character were imported to Idlewild for that fifteen day stretch of raucous behavior. I knew that some of this activity was real, because a man, who at the age of fifteen was dragged into the middle of all of this by his 'reprobate' of a father, had reported it to me personally.

I had been taught by hearsay evidence, that all of this stuff has happened and could happen again. Added to this I had heard many stories, and rumors, that some people in northern Michigan participated in such activities as dynamiting rivers, so as to stun and kill fish. They then netted them, downstream from the blast for purposes of eating or selling such stunned and killed fish. I'm sure all of you have heard rumors such as this, so I quickly dispelled them as just " rumors."

What went through my mind at this instant was, " My goodness, it's true, somebody is dynamiting this river just upstream from me."

Rationality was a word I couldn't comprehend at this point in time. All I could think was, "I've got to get out of here as fast as I can. If these guys find me, they'll kill me, to keep me from reporting them."

Even in my stupor, I realized that I was in the middle of a river surrounded on all sides, by swamp. I had fairly recently gone through an episode of trying to walk away from the river through a swamp, and that was nearly a disaster. If I just followed the river downstream, I'll find the high bank on the right where I can crawl out and get to my car. So I put my Boercher's fly into the keep of the fly rod, turned around and started downstream, with some haste. With what happened next I thought surely I was going to die.

There was another explosion downstream before my take out point. It was a darn good thing that I had taken time to empty my bladder before I got into the stream. For if I had not done so, I would certainly have wet my pants at that point. Swamp be damned, I had to get out of here. So I crawled up on the right bank, headed straight for where I figured the car was, and found it. I unlocked the door, stuck the rod in the best I could, climbed in with my waders on and ripped out of Idlewilde, back to my "little cabin in the woods."

As I realized that I was at last safe, I started to reason out what had just happened. I had lost all objectivity. I had allowed stories, rumors, thoughts and suggestions to feed into my overly active mind. That probably wasn't a stick of dynamite, or even a hand grenade. That stretch of water was so small, nobody would ever try to stun those few small trout that live there. This was the middle of summer in Idlewilde. There were no evil characters inhabiting Idlewild in July. In fact, I don't think there were ever any evil characters inhabiting Idlewild at any time. Idlewild was simply full of kind, generous and friendly people. It didn't make any difference whether they were Afro-Americans, Spanish Americans or just dumb white guys. They were just nice people, and I suddenly see how rumors, a state of mind and other factors could severely influence the behavior, of otherwise sane, rational people.

So what was this all about? As I drove, initially quite rapidly, my brain returned to reasonable function, I slowed down. I had heard that noise before! Where was it? Oh, yes! It was in the North Woods, in the Border Lakes Wilderness Area. In the late spring of 1963, Jack Crawford, Marshall Patullo and I drove up to Ely, Minnesota and packed into this area in an eighteen foot canoe. It was an uneventful trip of paddling, hiking over five portages, and then more paddling. When we hit our first campsite, about fourteen hours later, Jack and Marsh crapped out; that's an old way of saying, they were whipped, and hit the bag.

I was exhilarated by the whole trip in, although tired. I was too excited to sleep. So I took our eighteen foot canoe out onto the lake, alone, and was casting for the Great Northern Pike. After all of the unkind things I've said about pike this may seem quite strange to my reader. This, however, was very early in my semi-professional fishing career, and I was very eager to catch a pike, especially after a long hard day of paddling and hiking.

It was an overcast evening without a hint of breeze. The lake was flat as a pancake and covered with a gray sheen that was almost eerie. As I fruitlessly cast my red and white dare-devil, again and again, I found that the pike were singularly unimpressed. As I write these lines, I realize that I was fishing in the wrong way, in the wrong part of the lake. There weren't any pike in the middle of the lake. They make their living cruising the edges looking for minnows, small perch, small pike and any other small fish that inhabited that lake.

Back in Baldwin, Michigan, I remembered that night in Canada and that event. As I was about to again cast that dare-devil into the depths of an empty lake, I heard what sounded like a rifle shot. Realize, it was dusk, there was no wind and the water was flat. I turned to look in the direction of the shot and saw a large disturbance behind me with the waves spreading out from a single point, confirming what I had thought, some-one was shooting a rifle at me, and missed by a mile. Never mind, I screamed at the top of my lungs, " Don't shoot!" And I repeated that phrase several times until my reason started to return to me.

Here I am in the middle of nowhere, with my two buddies sound asleep, and we are miles from any other human. And somebody was shooting a rifle at me? As I carefully watched the center of the receding ripples, I saw a strange thing. A very broad head with beady eyes was moving directly toward me; he was curious. So was I, but more afraid than curious at this point. I realized I didn't need to tell people, "Don't shoot," anymore. But I do need to scare this thing away, whatever it is.

So I waved my arms back and forth. The critter saw me, dove into the water and as his rear end was about to go totally underwater, his huge broad tail smacked the water so loudly, that it startled me. However, the mystery of a lifetime was solved.

In that moment of enlightenment, as I recalled my Canadian fishing trip, I had a tremendous sense of relief overcome me, and quite frankly, humiliate me. I had allowed my imagination, fed by rumors, and probably many lies, to overcome my rational mind, and had in reality, panicked, beyond belief. The noise in the river that caused this panic was none other than a friendly beaver, or two, or perhaps a whole family.

As I better visualized and thought out the entire scenario, I realized that the far wall of that deep hole that I had savored, as a large trout hole, was made up of a beaver lodge. When I visualized that lodge earlier in the day, I had not registered in my mind it was an integral part of the middle branch of the Pere Marquette River, in an area known as Idlewilde.

29

A Soggy Day at Warner Lake
or Rub-a-dub-dub

It was a beautiful day early in the spring of 2012. I had planned to go fishing with Jim Visser in my little aluminum boat on Warner Lake. I had mentioned to my buddy Bill Stoub that I had been catching some very nice sunfish. He indicated that he thought it might be time for him to try Warner Lake again. I insisted that I was not going to use my big boat but rather fish in the small aluminum boat. I had noted that there was a larger flat bottom aluminum boat right next to mine. I had never seen anybody use it and I thought it might be a whole lot more stable than my little V-bottom boat. So I checked with Jim and it was okay with him that the three of us go fishing together.

We arrived at the lakeside in my trustee Rave-4 Toyota. The flat bottom boat, also called a pram, that I had noted, was about fourteen feet long and had four seats in it. My grandsons had used this earlier in the year, and even having no oars they paddled it around the lake very easily. So I knew it wouldn't sink although it did leak, somewhat. They both viewed the two boats and decided that the pram would be a whole lot more stable for the three of us. So we turned the boat over and dragged it into the water. The bottom of the lake at this particular location, was mostly gravel for about five feet and then tapered into mucky or muddy bottom. I fitted the oars, which I always carry with me to Warner Lake, into the oarlocks and was assured that they would work.

We proceeded to load all of the paraphernalia into the boat, and then donned our life preservers. It was agreed that since I knew the lake fairly well that I would sit in the middle and row the boat. Jim Visser being the lighter of the other two was relegated to the bow of the boat. It was his job to shove us off once we were all in the boat. I weighed approximately one hundred sixty pounds and Jim probably tipped the scales at two hundred, which was considered quite svelte, considering all the circumstances that we encountered that day. Bill Stoub has been a very good friend of mine for twenty years. I have, on many occasions, been very concerned about his weight. The problem of his weight has seldom been a topic for discussion. He does readily admit that he loves to raid the refrigerator before bedtime. Although he has probably committed this sin in seclusion, the results of his nightly escapades are readily apparent. On this particular day they were even more apparent. I would hazard a guess that he would readily acknowledge that his weight may exceed 250 pounds. The sequence that follows would evidence that statement.

As I took my seat in the middle of the boat, I looked ahead, which was toward the rear of the boat, and noted that Bill was standing and facing me. When he is fishing, and I am rowing, he needs to be facing the rear of the boat so that his line will be in the water trailing the boat where it should be. One cannot fish upstream when you're sitting in a boat on a lake. Basically you are fishing downstream so that all lines will be aimed toward the back of the boat. I didn't need to explain the circumstances beyond the statement of "Bill, you dummy. You're fishing backwards." He immediately grasped the significance of my kindly suggestion.

Here I must digress to confess my naïveté. A very light weight square ended pram, albeit fourteen feet long, is not very stable when loaded with upwards of six hundred pounds of beef, not to mention six fishing rods three tackle boxes, lunch, coffee, water, etc. What I'm about to relate to you is not so much from memory, because everything happened so fast, I virtually have no memory of what happened, but rather by reconstruction of what must have happened given the outcome.

I was seated in the middle of the boat; Jim was standing in the bow of the boat getting ready to push us off. Bill was standing in the rear of the boat facing me when he realized that he needed to heed my admonition; turn around and face the rear of the boat. Oh my! I saw him start to turn, (I needed to stop dictating because this dragon does not record laughter), I saw rods fly, arms flailing, some muted noise from the rear of the boat, followed by a very large spaloosh. I next found myself standing in the water up to my belly button, and assumed that the boat had tipped over.

With age, one's senses are somewhat dulled. It took me a few seconds to figure out where I was and what had happened.

I looked up and saw Jim standing alongside the bow of the boat with wet legs. The boat was upright and had a very large amount of water sloshing around on the bottom. Most of the stuff in the boat was floating, on water in the boat, including my tackle box. I heard a cry for help behind me, and saw Bill floundering in the water. He couldn't stand up and he couldn't reach the boat. I grasped the boat, which was considerably heavier than the eighty pound empty boat, and shoved it out to sea towards Bill. He gratefully grasped the edge of the boat and was able to drag himself up. I never did figure why he could not stand up in the water because the depth where he had fallen in was only five feet and he is five feet, ten inches.

It took all three of us several minutes to figure out where we were, what we were doing and what had just happened. Bill had in his hands, both of his fishing rods when he fell. He fell to my left landing on the left side of the boat before he flopped into the water. As he hit the side of the boat, the boat violently tipped and catapulted me into the water. Jim had witnessed the whole thing and simply jumped out of the boat into the water. He was only wet only up to his knees, I was wet up to my waist and Bill was soaked up to his Adam's apple.

Bill was missing both of his fishing rods and had a soaking wet tackle box. I found that indeed everything that I was wearing below my belly button was soaking wet. That included my billfold and my cell phone which was in my right pants pocket. Unfortunately, I did not realize that my cell phone had taken a bath; otherwise I might've saved one hundred dollars. As it turns out, I didn't realize that, so I didn't open and shake out the water. I didn't put it in the sun to dry. I simply left it in my wet pants pocket. Very costly error!

My tackle box unfortunately was not waterproof, so everything inside my tackle box was soaking wet. The rest of my material, fishing rods, bucket for miscellaneous fishing junk, the marker buoys and my worms were unscathed. Jim's stuff was unscathed. Bills tackle box had no lead in it so it floated. Later we looked around into the gin clear water, found and retrieved both of his fishing rods.

At this point I expected both of them to say, "We've had it, let's get out of here." But instead I was flabbergasted by their attitude. They both agreed that the fourteen foot pram was too unsteady to fish the rest of the day. Instead they looked at my little tin boat and said, "How about that boat?" That was the very boat that I deemed to be too tippy to be safe to fish in, or rather out of.

So we totally unloaded the pram, loaded all of the junk into my twelve foot, V- bottom, tippy boat and launched out into a gin clear lake on a beautiful sunny day. This time Bill was facing me because there was not room enough for him to sit backwards. As per usual I sat in the middle of the boat so that I could row the boat. It's not that I love to row; rather I just want to be in charge.

Today, especially, I did not enjoy rowing the boat because it was like rowing the Queen Mary, or a garbage scow. However, there was a modicum of saving grace. Neither one of them gave me orders; I was free to row where I wished. They were especially attentive and kindly when I announced we were in

26 feet of water. That's quite sobering even in the face of life preservers. Bill would fish off of one side or the other and would very carefully announce that he wanted to turn in his seat. He asked if it was okay for him to turn; I needed to give him permission to turn in his seat. Was I ever in control! His turning was extremely careful, with his hands he lifted his butt and turned about seventeen degree either to the left or to the right. At no time did he or any of us ever tried to stand up. That would have been another disaster.

So I very carefully rowed around Warner Lake, announcing my every move and every intent to move; we could not risk another capsizing We very slowly and intentionally circled the areas where I had anticipated an abundance of bluegills, and some sunfish. Our patience and persistence were duly rewarded. We kept the fish in a floating bag at the side of the boat. But even placing the fish in the bag required one of us to lean toward the other side of the boat, so we had to coordinate our efforts. When one of us would throw a fish in the bag to the left, the others had to lean to the right. As I look back on that day, I still shudder. Would I do it all again? The most disturbing part of the whole day is my answer. Yes, I probably would.

The day ended very well. Because we were wet, Bill and I both suffered a near, severe case of crotch rot, but we managed to boat forty-four large sunfish and bluegills. We were actually quite dry by the time we quit fishing, and we had no more untoward incidents. We are still friends and we all lived to fish another day. Unfortunately it will not be another day on Warner

Lake for Bill Stoub. He has sworn off Warner Lake unless he is in my big unsinkable boat.

> Rub a dub dub,
> Three fools in a tub,
> And who do you think they be?
> The butcher, the baker,
> The candlestick maker.
> Turn them out, knaves all three.
> (1842 James Orchard Halliwell)

30

Dan and the Steelhead

I have mentioned in an earlier story Sandy and I had gone to Dr. Dan Allender for counseling for a period of approximately nine months; once every week. That afforded us ample time for discussion before and after our counseling sessions because we had a two-hour drive each way. In the middle of these counseling sessions, our associate pastor had arranged for Dan Allender and Larry Crabb to present their seminar in our church, Westwood Baptist Church, broken into two weekend portions, two weeks apart. By the time the seminar was supposed to take place, our associate pastor had quit. The senior pastor knew that Sandy and I were acquainted with Dan Allender and so he invited us to facilitate the seminar in our church. That afforded us the opportunity to become better acquainted with both Dan and Larry. During this period of time, on one occasion our conversation had drifted towards fishing.

Dan's opinion of fishing was not withheld from me as I invited him to go fishing with me. He related a story of his only prior fishing episode. His oldest daughter prevailed upon him to take her fishing in Winona Lake. I hadn't thought to ask him about where he got the boat, the fishing rod, or the bait. Only later, did I realize what a problem that must have presented to him at that time. As I listened to the story told in his own inimitable way, I realized the significance of ir. Apparently he was slowly rowing the boat when the unthinkable happened.

"Daddy, I have a bite!" And worse yet, she had hooked a fish and then proceeded to reel it in.

I don't remember Dan's exact words but they amounted to this, "I saw this wiggly, slimy creature on the end of her line and she wanted me to grab it and take it off the hook." I don't remember if he said he grabbed the hook and flipped the fish off or if he'd simply cut the line. It really didn't matter to me because I got the point. He had no interest at all in fishing.

In approximately December, 1986, after he and Larry had presented their seminar in our church, Dan announced to us that he had just written a book, The Wounded Heart, and had prepared a seminar to present the contents of the book, sexual abuse. Sandy had been very active in Bible studies for women for many years. Many women came to her with problems of all sorts. And being the kind soul that she is, she endeavored to walk alongside the women. She sensed there was a whole lot more in their stories than she could identify. So when Dan asked if we could hold his seminar in our church to allow him to introduce his book to our area, we quickly accepted the invitation. That was an event that has had a huge impact on our lives, and on the lives of many of our family and friends. It also began a long, albeit long distance, relationship with Dan and his wife, Becky.

With that background you can imagine my surprise when, on one of his visits to our home on West Bridge he announced, or rather asked, "I want you to take me fishing."

It was the fall of the year, late October or early November and the only fishing available at that time was for steelhead. I briefly explained to him what fishing for steelhead was all about and then took him down to our basement where I had a large freezer chest. I opened the lid to the chest and took out a whole steelhead, one about 6 pounds, that had a lovely pink stripe down the side and showed it to him. He was impressed and said, "That would be fine."

You can imagine what kind of fishing equipment he had available to him; nada, zilch. So I rummaged around in my basement and came up with enough equipment to keep him from freezing to death. He had my bright orange ski pants, a surplus Air Force parka that cost me a loaf of bread in New-foundland, huge mittens, ice fishing gloves, a large fur cap and huge pair of old Air Force 'Mickey Mouse' boots We started from our home in Plainwell very early in the morning, stopped at my cabin to pick up my 14-foot aluminum pram and pro-ceeded to Irene MacDougal's home on the mainstream of the Pere Marquette River. Irene had not moved down to her daugh-ter's home in Grand Rapids for the winter yet, so she was able to spot us, and was very happy to meet any friend of mine.

The drive between Plainwell and Baldwin was just under two hours and I was thrilled to have the opportunity to speak with Dan all the way up and all the way back. I'd rather hoped that I could teach him some of the basics of fishing for steelhead both with plugs and with Spawn bags but I was soon to realize that he had been deprived as a young lad. No one had ever taken the time to explain to him the concept of fishing, what it was all about and how to do it. I accepted the fact that my chore for the day would be 'on the job training.' Fishing with a plug is relatively simple and I hoped that would be successful. Fishing for steelhead with a delicate nine foot spinning rod, eight pound leader and a spawn bag, is a whole different matter and as I reflected on the length of time it took me to perfect that technique I realized how difficult it would be for him to comprehend that concept and technique.

The day was very pleasant for a fall day. There was a light overcast and a very mild breeze with no apparent threat of either rain or snow. The few maples along the river had long since shed their colorful leaves, but the oaks still maintained many of their leaves although they had turned from a pleasant maroon to a dull brown. Contrasted with the bright green pine trees, it was still an impressive and pleasant sight. We had not had a lot of rain, so the river was still running medium height and almost gin clear. We jumped a few ducks from the river, and saw an occasional goose headed south. There was sometimes a crow both to be seen and heard with his raucous cry and in the distance we could barely hear the drumming of a partridge. It was a pleasant day to not catch fish.

I used the oars to carefully manipulate the boat side to side, through rapids and around windfalls and brush along the bank. I would carefully position the boat alongside a deep run so that we could both run a plug through the run and then roll a spawn bag down the run. As I am thinking and writing, I recall a similar trip down the Pere Marquette when I first introduced Bill Stoub to steelhead fishing with a plug. We were fishing the same way, and I had provided Bill with a spin casting rod with a flat fish on the end. He had a number of good hits from steelhead, but did not hook a single one. I had been making all sorts of accusatory comments, and he was feeling increasingly forlorn having hooked no steelhead after what appeared to be vicious hits. At the end of the trip he finally inspected the lure and found that the bottom hooks were missing. He then accused me of sabotaging his fishing trip by removing the hooks so he couldn't catch fish. We were both wrong, I shouldn't have ridiculed him, and he should have checked his own plug to make sure it did have hooks. Having previously experienced that unfortunate day, I checked the hooks on Dan's plug several times.

At lunchtime we pulled up on a sandy bank, got out and each had one of my world-famous sandwiches along with lukewarm coffee and a couple of chocolate chip cookies. I must digress to explain my recipe for sandwiches, which I heretofore have not described. I cook a chuck roast for two hours, remove it from the pot and allow it to drain and cool. I cut it into strips, put it in a blender to grind it up. I then place one measuring cup of this meat into a sandwich bag, express the air and seal the bag. One good-sized chuck roast will make about ten bags of sandwich meat. These are double bagged and put in the freezer until needed. At that time the bag is removed, the meat is thawed, placed in a bowl and mixed with mayonnaise and sweet pickle relish to the desired consistency. This mixture is then spread on a well-buttered sandwich made of Sandy's delicious homemade Swedish rye bread. After lunch we both puffed on our corncob pipes, boarded our vessel and proceeded downstream.

After we carefully fished run after run with no hint of steelhead in the river, let alone hitting on our plugs, I began to get quite discouraged since Dan was counting on me to show him the joy of fishing. I was a failure as a faithful fishing guide; the weight was heavy on my shoulders. Our minds and conversation drifted from fishing to many other aspects of life, none of which could be as satisfying as a firm tug on the end of your line.

But in the back of my mind I still had an ace in the hole. The big horseshoe-shaped bend just above Peg's cottage almost always held a steelhead or two. Even though I had never taken a trout out of that hole I knew there were big fish there most of the time. I pulled the boat to the right side of the top of the hole and dropped the anchor for our first set. We diligently fished the upper hole with no hint of anything. I carefully raised anchor and moved the boat around the short pier to the lower part of the hole again, pulling off to the right and dropping the anchor.

I checked the glob of spawn on my nine foot spinning rod, and carefully swung it to the middle of the hole. I was very carefully walking it down through the hole when I felt it. Almost as sure as I could see into the bottom of the hole, I knew what was happening. A large fish had picked up my spawn bag making the rod tip wiggle, but didn't take it and I didn't set the hook. I knew he was there and I knew he would hit again. I told Dan to bring in his rod and set it down out of the way. I told him what had just happened to me and said, "When I set the hook, I'm going to hand you the rod. Keep it pointed straight up in the air and when he stops running, lift the rod tip higher and then crank down as you lower the rod tip toward the fish. Keep doing that until he tires and we can bring him up to the boat."

It was a great plan for a three or four pound steelhead. We had a broad area of relatively calm, deep water below the boat which would allow for ample space to play a small to medium size steelhead. It was a combination of events and actions that was doomed to failure. I had underestimated the size of the steelhead and this freshness. Fresh run steelhead from Lake Michigan that are still very silver, are also very strong and prone to take long, hard, fast runs when hooked. Here we were on the Pere Marquette River some thirty miles upstream from Lake Michigan. I would never have expected a fresh run steelhead to be this far up the river at this late date. My other mistake was expecting that Dan would understand what I had just told him to do, never ever having had in his hand a rod like I had just given him, with instructions that he had never heard before. Without knowing, I just set him up for failure.

After Dan was vaguely aware of my plan, I asked him to sit patiently and quietly. I checked the Spawn bag to make sure there was an ample amount of spawn and then I deftly flipped the bag of spawn and sinker across the hole near the far bank.

I could readily feel the sinker dragging along the bottom of the hole. What I had not anticipated, was the hard hit that followed. That steelhead hit the Spawn bag so hard that even though I was prepared, I was still shocked. No sooner had he hit the bag and hooked himself, he was off down stream like a rocket. Dan sensed the excitement that I had exuded and leapt to his feet. I practically threw the rod to him and shouted, "Keep the rod high and don't let him run into the rapids!"

By now Dan was standing in the boat holding on to that rod for dear life while the steelhead took off downriver. He first ran to the other side then ran back to our side and headed for the rapids at the bottom of the slow steady water. Once he got into the rapids he was not coming back, he was a goner. I realized that this was probably the biggest steelhead I had ever hooked in that little river, at least ten pounds. And I had placed on Dan's shoulder the awesome responsibility of pulling that big steelhead in. He was doomed to fail. In the meantime, I had not realized all the circumstances that I'm now relaying to you and so I too was standing up the boat and practically screaming at Dan, "Don't let him get into the rapids, you'll lose him."

He did and he did; the fish got into the rapids downstream and pulled the hook out of his mouth. No comment, no con-demnation, just dead silence.

We were practically at the end of the line. There were a few more holes to fish but they were as unproductive as the whole upper river was to us. A few more hundred yards and we pulled up to the landing, unloaded the gear from the boat to the car, loaded the boat onto the trailer and headed home. I have no idea what we talked about, but I suspect that Dan took a nap for part of the trip. Once we got home we related our journey and our big disappointment to my wife and the girls. They were duly impressed or at least said so.

As we were sharing a glass of wine while waiting our supper, Dan turned to me and said, "Show me that steelhead that you have in your freezer again."

I thought that was a very strange request, but nevertheless I acquiesced to his suggestion. I went to the basement, lifted the lid of the freezer and took out my six-pound steelhead and brought up to the kitchen. Dan said, "Throw it to me."

I thought he was too heavy into the wine already, so I said, "What did you say?" He repeated himself, whereupon I threw him the dead, frozen steelhead.

He deftly caught it in his arms and said to me, "The day is not lost, I just caught a steelhead."

And I quietly thought to myself, "He just made a silk purse out of a sow's ear."

31

Fishing with the Grandchildren

I have always enjoyed fishing. As I am starting to write of my fishing adventures with my grandchildren, I'm trying to put into words the things that motivated me to do so. In order to understand, I had to reflect on my own childhood experiences of fishing. I'm going to try and summarize them here to give the reader some consistency in my thought process. I have related my first recollections of fishing in Lemon Creek. I had several occasions at which time I accompanied my father to fish along the south pier in St. Joe, Michigan. We had to park our vehicle in the Silver Beach amusement park lot. We would then carry our equipment through the boardwalk of Silver Beach. It was always daytime so there was no activity at the amusement park. I did note and later remembered the many times that my family, friends and I went there. There was a roller coaster, booths where you could throw baseballs at milk bottles, toss rings over figurines and receive cheap prizes. There were many other booths but most importantly of all was the fun house.

The fun house had a whole bunch of crazy mirrors which made one look tall, fat, big headed, and many other distortions always worth a couple of chuckles. There were two features about the fun house that still stand out in my memory. One was a very long wooden slide with a hump in the middle. It was constructed of highly polished hard wood. We sat on a burlap bag and scooted down the slide at what I considered breakneck speed. We would run around, climb up the stairs and slide again and again.

The other feature was a very large wooden bowl. We would all climb in and sit in the middle. The operator would start the bowl turning. As the speed increased, we found our bodies slipping from the bottom of the bowl, up along the sides until we were firmly plastered against the side of the bowl and could not move. We could not even lift our head from the side of the bowl; was that great or what!

At the north end of the runway was a large wooden frame building called 'Shadow Land.' I was told it was a dance hall where big people would gather on Friday, Saturday and Sunday nights while swing bands would come in and play music for the dancers. It was a little beyond my comprehension, but it sounded like it could be fun. In my teen years I did indeed dance in Shadowland with my girlfriend even though it cost fifty cents to get in.

Just past Shadowland, was the pier itself, which ran way out to the lighthouse. The channel for the St. Joe River was on the north side of the pier, and we would fish on the south side in fresh lake water where we would catch perch. This would always be on a Wednesday; because that was the day we closed the store at noon. My father, and sometimes his friends, would go with us to the pier where we would always catch some perch. I have many fond memories of days like that, because time spent with my father having fun was not common for me. Most of our relationship involved work, not just at the store, but also around the house when my father would undertake a project. He was always the boss, and I was always the gump. Gump work became more strenuous as I grew stronger.

I will list some of the chores since most of you have had very similar experiences with your fathers, and I say that, not in a derogatory fashion, but with a comment that it was probably good for you and your development. Most of these projects occurred long before I was old enough to drive, because getting behind the wheel of the red panel truck was the most liberating thing I had experienced until the day of my high school graduation.

The first chore with my father was building a split rail fence on the backside of our spare lot. That was the time I mastered the post hole digger. Following that maneuver, we put shrubs all along the fence. By this time I was a professional post hole digger. Upon finishing that chore my father decided he was going to build an outdoor grill. When he told me about the project I had no idea what this was all about, and I'm sure you don't either. It was going to be made out of small field-stone, roundish type rocks from the size of your fist to the size of your head.

"Wherever could we find rocks to do this?", I queried my father. At this point in time, I was driving and my father had the use of a flatbed trailer. Al Brett, who I've mentioned in other writings, had an abundance of this size rock on his property on Lemon Creek. I was instructed as to how to hook the trailer onto the truck and how to back it up. I proceeded to Al Brett's house and loaded the trailer with rocks. In my mad youth, I did not visualize this as a chore, but rather an opportunity to have extra fun.

So at age fourteen I wheeled that trailer right out to Al's house, backed it up with no instruction from anyone, loaded it with rocks and left for home. Upon leaving the country road upon which he lived, I had to make a right turn onto US 31. I had learned to look both ways, but I hadn't quite commanded the resolve to come to a complete stop at every stop sign. As I viewed the highway as clear of traffic on my left, I came to a 'rolling stop' and whipped onto the highway not noticing the state police officer coming from the other direction. The red gum ball came on before he reached me, and I pulled off the road before moving fifty feet from the intersection. I learned humility very quickly. As a result I received only a severe warning and no summons.

Back to the field rock grill that I had difficulty in visualizing. Apparently my father had the same problem, but I thought he had talked to some very intelligent people and so we started. I first dug out the grass and made a flat base about three feet wide, and five feet deep. It was my 'privilege' to mix the concrete and fill the forms with cement for the base. After I had unloaded the trailer and carried the rocks across the yard to where we were building the grill, I was then instructed as to how to mix 'mud' mortar. Since we had to allow the mortar to dry, we put the fireplace together in layers.

We had two parallel rows of rocks about one foot apart and about two feet long. At about one foot high we put on a metal grill and mortared that in place. At the back end of this grill we built a stone chimney about three feet high. The idea for this whole grill was to fire up some chunks of wood under the grill, and when the flames were out and we had only coals left, we would grill our steaks. "So what's the big deal?"—you're asking.

This was about 1945. Charcoal briquettes as we know them today, had not yet been invented. It was still the war years and my father ran a meat market. There was food rationing in those days and steak took a lot of red points. Most people were unwilling to waste their red points on steak. When we slaughtered beef, we always had more steaks left over than any other part of the cow. It would be a shame to throw away T-bone steaks, so we suffered; the Burdick family had to eat a lot of steak. In those days one could cook steak two ways; either fry it in a pan or put it in the broiler oven, which we did most of the time. My father, at a very early time in history, had visualized the concept of charcoaling steaks.

His idea to build the grill in the form that we did, was the smoke from the fire would go up the chimney, and only the heat from the charcoal would cook the steak, no smoke. As it turns out, my father was half right. The heat cooks a steak, but the smoke gives it flavor. I started out writing this story, to give my grandchildren an idea of why I enjoyed fishing, and therefore tried to involve them in my lifelong pastime, and I've just come to realize that my father had some original ideas in his lifetime, for which I have been unable or unwilling to give him credit. So as I reflect, and write my fishy tales, I find the whole process to be redemptive.

I had several insignificant fishing episodes with my father on local lakes, but since we could only fish together on Wednesday afternoon and occasionally Sunday afternoon, our experiences together were limited. I intended to use the title, 'Tales of Round Lake,' as separate chapter to allow you some insights as to what really stimulated my interest in fishing.

Round Lake was the first place where I was able to fish and was really on my own for all of my fishing and other adventures, away from home, mom and sister. It was a real guy thing. So, as I visualized all of my grandsons at home and under the tutelage of their mothers, I began to empathize with them, and thought back to my youth. I could not wait to get away from my mother and do things that I wanted to do rather than things she thought I ought to do. If this rings a bell in any of your heads put the reading down and send me a text. If I'm dead, send it to grandma, because she is my editor and is sharing this whole process with me, with a few chuckles.

Although I realized that all of you had your own stories with your fathers, none had fishing stories, so I wondered if I might enter your lives as a fishing mentor and a releaser from familial obligations; a chance to be real, wild boys. My cabin in Baldwin, Michigan was perfectly suited for boys and exploration. Having been part of a family of four women and me, I was well aware of the need for 'guy time,' but had zero experience in dealing with young men. I had watched all of you play, 'jam pile,' in our yard at Thanksgiving time and wasn't sure I knew how to handle rough and tumble boys. But I had a friend who was a Phys. Ed. teacher and coach who dealt with boys all the time; John Hamilton.

So I enlisted him as I contemplated a trip up to Baldwin with eight-year-olds to 12 year old boys. I chose eight years of age upon consultation with John and decided that any boy younger had to be accompanied by his own father. I think that worked out very well.

The first guys were Jeremy, Andrew, Austen, Parker, Erik, and Joel. We traveled in my suburban, because I had to pull the boat. When we arrived at the cabin, all was chaos as the boys ran around picking out their bunks or sleeping area. We had one bedroom, which belonged to old Gpa. John took a lower bunk in the bunk room. I don't remember any fighting and everybody seemed to find a great place to sleep. The loft was a favorite because the guys liked to lean over the edge and watch me cook and try to drop things in the fry pans and pots.

I was grateful that John had a lot of experience with young men. It seems like he was always organizing some activity, which was a little beyond my capacity to enjoy. I think I did go for a few walks in the woods where the boys were looking for anything out of the ordinary. I remember each kid had a stick and would beat on something: a tree, a bush, a weed, and occasionally on one another.

The swamp right next door was always a point of interest. There were always frogs to chase, catch or shoot with their BB guns, and if I'm not mistaken there was an occasional snake to be tortured. Of course everybody got dirty several times a day and some even fell into the swamp; that's big-time dirty. But the solution was always the same, go jump in the river. I did have a hot water heater, but it was only about ten gallons so we saved that for washing dishes and Gpas' shower in the morning.

Either John or I or both fixed bacon and eggs or sausage and toast every morning. Lunch was sandwiches and I cannot imagine what we had to eat for dinner because we never had enough fish to eat. We did try fishing one day in a nearby lake into which I dumped my huge boat. We rowed around and tried to fish and I don't think anybody got a thing. I never even considered fishing for trout on that trip.

The highlight of first trip was when Erik broke the middle finger of his left hand. I knew immediately what it was, a Salter -II of the distal phalanx. Although I knew what it was and what had to be done, I panicked considering my alternatives. The closest medical area was Big Rapids, Michigan. That was a long drive, for a 'short putt,' as it were. I called my buddy, who practiced orthopedics in big Rapids and said, "Jerry, what do I do with my grandson?"

"Hell, Bill, you taught me how to do it. Just crank it back."

"Without anesthesia?"

"You want to drive all the way to Big Rapids just so I can freeze it a little?"

I was afraid of hurting my grandson and having him hate me for the rest of his life. Although he had some degree of pain, he was the center of attention of all his cousins, and he was eating it up. So I explained to him what I would like to do. Or rather what I felt I ought to do. Pull on his finger, crank it back and then tape it to the next finger. "Will it hurt, grandpa?"

I couldn't lie to the kid so I said, " It'll hurt like hell for a couple of minutes, and then it will be all over."

I looked around the room and I have never seen so many wide eyes. Everybody there was terrified, except Erik. So he said, "Do it, grandpa!" So I shooed everybody out of the room, washed my hand and Eric's finger to get all the grease off the fingers so I could get a good grip.

As I reached out to grab his finger he said, "Can I watch?"

I said, "Sure." I knew that when I grasped his finger he would not be able to see a thing so I grabbed it and said. "Now!" However, I had actually reduced it before I said now because I didn't want him to jerk when he heard me say, "Now."

There was an ear piercing scream, and then, "Is that all?"

"Yep, it's fixed!"

"That wasn't bad."

"Thanks, Jerry," I murmured, and then "Thank you, Jesus!"

The boys all came back into the room, still wide-eyed with a million questions, "Did it hurt? Does it hurt now? Is it straight?"

There was an obvious air of respect for Erik for having submitted to this barbaric treatment. John looked at me and asked, " And how are you, feeling?"

"I think I need a beer."

"Me, too." That obviously, was the highlight of that trip. It was a good start and the kids responded very well. John and I were grateful to have survived with no more trauma then one broken finger, but realized we could do better on a fishing trip for the grandkids. "Jay's Resort, here we come ."

32

Cousins Camp at Jay's Resort

Following our fun trip with the grandkids up at my cabin, I realized this was something I really wanted to do; I wanted those boys to learn how to fish. As I reflected on the several times I had gone fishing with my father and the weird ideas he had about fish, fishing and how to catch fish, it made me realize, that I had better study fish and the art of catching fish. I had spent a large part of my adult life fishing for game fish. I started with the Atlantic salmon during my two and a half years in the military in Newfoundland. I learned a lot about Atlantic Salmon fishing by reading several books, and talking to a lot of Newfies, particularly fish wardens. There is a lot of information that can be gained before you ever wet a line.

Upon returning to Grand Rapids to finish my residency, Dr. Jim Glessner invited me to join a group of attending physicians from Grand Rapids, for the opening of trout season on the Au Sable River. I had the equipment that I used in Newfoundland, and it was reasonably suited to trout fishing in Michigan. So I went with Jim to Grayling, Michigan, for the opening of the trout season on two successive years.

I knew all of the doctors who would be attending, and they all knew about my fly-fishing experiences in Newfoundland, so they did not consider me to be a novice. Since I did not have, so to speak, 'two nickels to rub together,' I felt very fortunate to be included in their company. It turned out that they were using this occasion to party rather than really fish. John and Wilma Ludeman, owned a beautiful log cabin lodge, where we were housed and a delightful log cabin dining room where we dined royally with genuine German home cooking. It was truly a weekend to remember and to avoid as a way of life.

Promptly at 12:01 AM, Saturday morning, the opening day of the trout season, I donned my waders and made my way down to the river with the aid of a flashlight. After whipping the rapids to a froth for more than an hour, I decided I didn't like this kind of stream fishing. I returned to the Lodge almost frozen, had a whiskey sour and called it a night. The next morning I waited until the sun was shining before I went into the river. In the course of the day I managed four keeper trout. I was top rod, and every time I went fishing with those guys I was top rod; it wasn't that I was that good, it was that they were that bad.

It turns out Jim Glessner didn't have the slightest idea about fly-fishing. I had brought enough equipment to supply him, and gave him lessons during the daylight hours. He was hooked on trout fishing and that led to our eventual partnership in the little log cabin on the middle branch of the Pere Marquette River. We bought that twenty-seven acre lot with the cabin in 1964 for ten thousand dollars. Later, I bought his half so that he could upgrade to a much finer cabin, more to the liking of his wife.

All of this to say that I found I could teach other people how to fish. In keeping with that concept, I took Jeremy, my oldest grandson, fishing on the main stream of the Pere Marquette, and started him out fly-fishing for trout. So I realized I had developed a certain expertise in Atlantic Salmon fishing which was transferable to stream fishing for trout.

Sandy just reminded me that four of our grandsons have taken up fly fishing. As their interest and expertise in fish grows I find the increasing loss of rods, reels, boots, flies and vests to be redemptive. My old stuff is going into the hands of those I love.

But what did I know about fishing for bluegill? Only what I had learned from my father, and that probably wouldn't grease the skillet. That thought propelled me into reading about the various kinds of fish common to our Michigan waters, methods used to catch them, information about lakes where we could actually expect to catch large numbers of fish.

So, back to the books. I had another big advantage over most people who wished to learn something about fishing. This source of information came in the form of live people, called, 'my patients.' I knew a lot of them fished, so I simply asked many questions. I received a plethora of information and had only to figure out how to put it all together.

Enter Larry Moon—voila! Larry was 'the head he-weasel' of Friendship Village Retirement Home. I knew he had taken many fishing trips with our fellow parishioners from Westwood

Baptist Church, so I figured he would be a great source of information. He was!

One of my sixteen year-old female patients, spoke very highly of wonderful fishing adventures in the Thousand Lakes resort area. Larry and I investigated and decided to take a trip as a potential fishing site for us and our friends. We investigated, made phone calls, and then drove the 10-hour trip through the Upper Michigan to Jay's resort, where we rented a very small one room cabin. It was September, warm and beautiful, but it seemed that all the fish had gone on vacation, away from One Thousand Islands Lakes. We explored most of the lakes on the Michigan side of the border and learned a lot about the area and the lakes themselves. During the time we spent fishing, we had sufficient fish to eat and more.

What impressed me more than the quantity and size of fish that we caught, was the layout of Jay's resort. It was a very short boat ride from the public launch to Jay's dock, with ample room for boats. There was a very small but nice sand beach, and a raft, which would become a great platform for King of the Mountain, and the King would be my oldest grandson, Jeremy Kuiper, hands down. The other selling point I was particularly enthused about was a large pontoon boat, which I could rent. It would hold all the kids that I could possibly bring. Done deal! I just had to figure out the fine details.

When I first proposed my daring mission, to extricate my eager young grandsons from their doting mothers, I was met with a variety of responses. These responses ran all away from, "Oh, my precious boys on a fishing trip with you?" To, "How many do you want and for how long?" A number of grave matters, gradually begin to seep into my, not yet, senile mind such as what will they want to eat? That meant a food checklist. What kind of fishing gear must I have for each boy? Tackle list. What will they wear? That was a stupid question. Their mothers will fill in those blanks. A travel check list was also needed that would cover the vehicles, boats, motors, trailers and miscellaneous.

The day finally arrived when we assembled and packed the vehicles and boat with enough stuff to last a month. The mothers, my daughters, stood around wiping tears from their eyes and wringing their hands. I thought, "How sweet and loving and tender is this scene." Only later was I told that the whole scene was an act. They used their handkerchiefs to cover their mouths so that they would not laugh out loud. They were already planning their freedom and their first of many, shopping trips with our one granddaughter, Maddie. They were more excited about this trip, and getting away themselves, than were the kids and me about going fishing.

I well remember the many road trips that Sandy and I had taken with our three daughters to Colorado, Florida and to college, and elsewhere that I may have forgotten. There was one common denominator in every trip that we took. Would anyone like to hazard a guess before reading the next line? The formal terminology is, "An eructation involving the anal sphincter. In the vernacular it is known as the common fart!" Being a relatively healthy male, I have spent my share of time with fellow males in locker rooms for six years of athletics in junior and senior high, fraternities, laboratories, medical school, all pretty much segregated from the fairer sex. So you can imagine my surprise when our family set out for our first long road trip with our daughters. I was shocked! Aghast! Flabbergasted! All this noise and odor could not be coming from those sweet young things in the backseat, could it?

As I reminisce, I would like to interject that we have always driven a station wagon or a suburban for our long trips. My first station wagon was a brand-new 1968 Chevrolet with this newfangled device called posi-traction. This resulted in constant turning of both rear wheels all the time which was a new concept for vehicles and excellent for those of us who drove in snow. I did not realize the benefit of this invention until the big snow of '68. Betty Schafsma, our young neighbor from Grand Rapids was spending some time with us and was working part-time in my office. We started out early in the morning and headed for Borgess hospital. Betty waited in the car while I ran in to see a couple of patients very quickly. In less than half-an-hour I returned to Betty in the station wagon to find a fresh fall of 1 inch of snow. Weather forecasting in those days had a long way to go, so this was a little unexpected. We drove to my office and we both went to work. Throughout the morning I heard ghastly tales as my patients slid in to the office, complaining about the horrid road conditions.

The girls in the front office started listening to radio reports and by noon, the handwriting was on the wall; terrible blizzard. We, the other doctors and I, decided to close the office and send everyone home. I promptly jumped into my 1968 Chevrolet wagon, with posi- traction, and started up the hill from my office toward home. The state of Michigan had just completed the section of the brand-new divided 131 Highway, between Kalamazoo and Plainwell and so we struggled to get on that road. As we wended our way around slide offs, and stalled vehicles, I counted the number of cars that were stranded at forty-three. We made it home without incident, and as I pulled into the entrance of our driveway and stopped there, I said an audible, "Thank you, Jesus."

The next morning, I shoveled out behind my station wagon and started out of town on the completely plowed streets of Plainwell only to find every road out of town was unplowed and stayed that way for three days.

Our new Norwegian Elkhound puppy, Tryna, was being toilet trained but we couldn't open our door to let her out. We simply opened a window and dropped her, onto a snowdrift and hoped that she could find her way home. It worked, we didn't lose Tryna, but we didn't get out either until the third day. We didn't suffer too badly during that snowstorm, because I had stocked our wood chute with an abundance of firewood.

That winter was remarkable also for the introduction of the snowmobile into our community. Several of the Lake Doster boys had them, and they were more than happy to be of service to pretty young ladies in our community; Beth, Sue and Amy. We wanted for nothing if the grocery store had it. It was a real fun time.

That incident proved to me the value of large and heavy station wagons. That Chevy wagon was replaced in time with two Olds 88 station wagons, and finally with a series of suburban's. All of which have served to transport a great number of people, boats and different kinds of trailers.

Alas, I have again strayed, but I return to the last theme from which I departed, noxious vapors. Standard fare for our long road trips for each person included the following items; books, a reading light and extra batteries, a pillow and a blanket. We carried several spray cans of pleasant smelling vapors. I became accustomed to hearing from the rear of the vehicle, "Aarugh! Who did that? P U!" And on and on. On one occasion Grandma Cook was traveling with us, when an offense occurred, Sandy rolled the window down to air the car out, then Grandma complained about being cold. She was old and could hardly smell anything, so she was totally clueless as to what was going on behind her. Well, enough of the dirty, family laundry, back to the boys fishing trip.

All of the above was reported with the intent of informing you as to my background traveling with young people. Nothing that I have ever experienced, could have prepared me for the first "guy trip" up north. Passing gas was not incidental, or accidental for these boys, it was intentional. It was a way of life. It became a contest. I was astounded when I learned that Erik Anderson could pass gas on command. That appeared to be the highest calling that any of these boys could seek. And try as they may, no one could match Erik. I do believe there were a few cases of messy underwear during the attempt to match him, but no one would ever confess to such an atrocity. That trip up to Jay's resort, was my initiation into the brotherhood of grandsons and cousins.

The trip always originated at our house because that was the location of the boat which was a necessary and critical part of our fishing trip. We prayed for a sunny day because packing the boat and car in rain would have been very messy. To the best of my recollection, we always started out with non-rainy weather. On several occasions we encountered rain on the trip but our trusty boat with it's covering tarp always seemed to suffice in keeping our stuff dry.

Early on the morning of departure, John and Jeremy and I would load the boat. As the years went by, I was happy to be relegated to the role of supervisor. When you have all the food and drink for about eight of us for a whole week, all the clothing and sleeping bags to get into the trailer and car, in an orderly fashion, I am very much reminded of the phrase, 'Trying to herd cats!' My grandchildren are either brothers or cousins. With cousins, they frequently have not seen each other for a while and so the anticipation of an all boy trip, without mothers, and virtually without control, was more than they could hope for in their wildest dreams. John Hamilton, being a coach of young boys was much more prepared for this whole trip than I ever could be.

"Thanks again, John, for saving my butt."

Once the gear was in the boat, we carefully placed, on top of everything, the rod carrying case that I had made just for this trip. It held twelve rods and transported them safely up and back for at least ten trips. I don't think we ever suffered a broken rod. A couple 'fell overboard.' I anticipated that and had a large collection of bargain, kid proof, spinning rods. They were different lengths and thicknesses with different types of reels, but they all worked. Before we left home, I set the rods out and let each kid pick his own. Once that was done, we taped his initials on that rod, and that became his rod for all the years we fished. I still have a number of them with the boys initials taped on.

Once the trailer was covered, we did a final check of air pressure in the tires, the running lights on the trailer, the hitch and safety chains. We would then start the engine and pull out of the driveway. I would turn to get one last look at the ladies standing around, ostensibly crying and waving. I'm pretty sure I caught a glimpse of them running into the house, smiling or laughing, to do whatever they had waited so long to do.

Once we were on the road, I dialed the excitement down in order to pay attention to driving. And then the barrage began.

"I'm thirsty."

Followed by, "I gotta pee."

Or, "I'm hungry."

If I heard it once, I heard it 100 times every trip, "Who farted?" followed by, "You did."

"No, you did"

Then, "Grandpa, (or John, or Curt, father of four of the boys) he hit me," then sounds of a scuffle in the back, moaning, groaning, hollering and screaming. How would you like that for ten hours straight? I have to confess it wasn't that way for ten hours straight. We usually had several breaks along the way: rest stops, lunch stops and a few miscellaneous stops.

I was always glad to get to Jay's resort. On our first trip, we were situated upstairs in a building away from the shore. We could see the lake and the beach but had to walk about a hundred feet to get there. "No swimming until the work is done." I'm sure you can imagine how fast the stuff got upstairs. Then the boys headed for the beach. John and I launched the boat about a half a mile away, and I drove it to our assigned boat dock. I joined John on our deck for a well-deserved bottle of beer, as we reviewed the unbelievable amount of activity that had gone on with our charges. As the wind died and the sun slowly set in the west, we were serenaded by loons from across the lake. It was warm there in 'loon land,' and for a moment, I wondered if I had gotten to heaven a little early.

33

Cleaning the Catch

It seems I have spent a proportionally large amount of my lifetime cleaning fish. As a little kid, my father taught me how to clean fish according to his method. Like so many other things that my father taught me, it was simply the technique that had been passed down to him, from his father, old Bill Burdick, or by some other miscreant. It is because of this process, that I learned to hate the phrase, "We've always done it this way." It took me a long time to break out of that mold, and, "He's such a nice little boy."

As I look back on my life, I realize my father actually taught me a few things that were good; work hard, pay your bills and obey the law. However, he could hardly drive a nail straight, or cut a board with a sharp saw. I have already alluded to his difficult time of trying to build a fieldstone outdoor fireplace or fire pit. I had forgotten to mention that he wanted to extend our driveway, when we finally got a second car. It was simply widening the drive just before it went into the garage. He borrowed a trough, a hoe, and a shovel. We mixed the cement in the trough, three to one gravel to cement. We dug out some of the dirt and tried to level the ground with a flat edge shovel. Next, we tried to level the poured concrete with a board. When finished, it looked fairly nice. But after one winter of driving on the concrete, we ended up with a flat gravel pit. The concrete completely crumbled, and it was still that way when I left home in1948. I think the concrete should have been thicker than one inch!

As I mentioned elsewhere, my father insisted I learn to drive so I could run the delivery route for the grocery store. Up to that point in my life, he had never even let me steer the car while he drove. Upon hearing of my desire, and need to drive, Uncle Ray offered to teach me while visiting us from Grand Rapids. I was thrilled, because uncle Ray was my favorite, and I knew he was an excellent driver. He put me at the wheel of his own car as we left my house and headed south. The lesson was abruptly ended at the end of the block when I barely missed a telephone pole while making a left turn. Uncle Ray promptly resigned, my father never offered, and it was my mother who taught me how to drive.

My father's method of cleaning a bluegill in those days was fairly simple. Using a special tool; hang on to the tail of the fish, scrape the scales off from the tail toward the head. A reasonable alternative was couple of bottle caps nailed to a stick Next cut off the head, cut the belly down to the cloaca, and reach in with your finger to scrape the guts out of the fish. Make sure you scrape all the blood from the dorsal cavity with your thumbnail. Fry the fish by whatever is your favorite method and eat. Note: the fish my father cleaned, and you ate, had it's tail, all of it's fins, all of it's skin and all of it's bones.

The meat had to had to be very carefully teased off the bones. Failure to do so produced a very sore mouth. When I was a kid, eating a fish was a lot of work, for something that didn't taste all that good. This skin did not have a good flavor. My father would always make sure the fish was fried crisply because he claimed that the tail was especially fine eating when very crisp.

I thought that was a bunch of crap, but I was smart enough not to say so. I grew up not particularly caring to eat fish. I loved to catch them, I hated to clean them and I disliked eating them. So what changed me? A guy by the name of Don Mason.

He had driven his wife Mary Jane, into my office for me to fix her foot, and we got to 'talking,' as was frequently the case before Obama care. The old name for the practice of medicine was, 'patient care.' It worked well for me for 49 years. Obama care and resulting cumbersome governmental paperwork, robbed us all of the golden era of medical care for patients.

Don lived on this relatively newly created, man-made lake called Lake Doster. I readily accepted his invitation, to join him to ice fish for blue gills, following which he took me into his garage and showed me how he cleaned fish. It revolutionized my whole concept of catching, cleaning and eating fish. Without having to deal with all those tiny fish bones, the rotten taste of the skin and no tails or fins to work around, I found eating fish was second only to eating steak.

Although I considered myself to be a skilled surgeon it took me quite a while to master the Don Mason technique of fish cleaning, which I'm about to describe. It is suitable for all pan fish, bass and Walleyed Pike. Cleaning Northern Pike is something totally different because of a funny thing called the Y bone. Figure out your own way to clean that sucker. The best way I have ever seen a walleye or a pike cleaned is the method that Denny uses. I mention it but I cannot describe it. Dr. Timothy Reineck is truly 'the master' of salmon cleaning.

The technique for cleaning pan fish for a right-handed person, is as follows:

Step one. Cut the throat. Make a cut just behind the operculum, that begins from the dorsal side of the fish, alongside the operculum and exiting the body just behind the pectoral fin. Cut through all of the flesh but not the spinal cord. Flip the fish and do the same on the opposite side. This is about a thirty degree cut from cephalade to caudad (head to tail).

Step two. Turn the fish right side down, and with a very sharp knife, cut on the left-hand side of the dorsal fin as close to the fin as possible, so that the blade goes as deep as the rib cage. As the knife blade slips past the last of the rib cage, aim the point of the blade directly at the cloacae. Push the blade out the cloacae. Turn the knife blade about fifteen degrees down and complete the cut along the vertebra to the tail. Return to the head of the fish and turn down the flap that you have cut away from the dorsal spine. With short strokes cut the meat away from the rib cage being careful to bevel the knife blade down, again, at about fifteen degrees. When you reach the belly, cut the flap loose. You should have one solid piece of meat. Flip the fish and repeat the action on the other side, however best suits your technique.

My technique is as follows; with a sharp, pointed knife, I enter the fish at almost the end of the dorsal fin, aim toward the cloacae and cut toward the head keeping the knife blade as close to the dorsal fin as I can. Once I reach the rib cage, I complete the cut up to the head end of the fish, turn down a slab of meat and again cut it loose from the rib cage. At the tail end of the rib cage, there is a small area where the meat is very thick. If you do not follow the rib cage carefully, you will tend to slide over this area and lose a nice little piece of meat. Once the second side is released, cut into the cloacae and sweep the meat off the vertebral body to the tail. Always try to bevel the knife blade nicely into fifteen degrees into the area you're cutting and hopefully that will enable you to avoid loss of meat especially around the rib cage.

Step three. You should have two pieces of fish with the skin on. I place the fish on a flat surface and grasp the tail portion of the fish with my thumbnail or a salad fork. Holding the skinning knife at, again, a fifteen degree angle, I cut the meat away from the skin with short, slicing movements.

Step four. Wash the filets to remove loose scales and place them in containers for safekeeping. Unless I am going to eat them within four days, I place them in a container, cover it with water, place on a lid and label either with the number of fish or the number of filets and the approximate size; small, medium large, very large.

I use a couple of gauges to see how I am doing in my fish cleaning effort. When the fish has been removed from the skeleton you should be able to hold up the skeleton and almost read a newspaper through it. When you have skinned the fish well, there should be no white fish flesh left on the skin. For fish seven inches or more, if you have filleted and skinned well there should be a very thin piece of flesh over the rib cage, or where the rib cage was. I note all too often in cleaned fish, this thin piece of meat has been lost. It either was not filleted properly or was not skinned properly. If you think this critique is a little critical, you're right. I aim for perfection but sometimes have to settle for mediocrity.

Trout are handled a little differently. They do have scales but they are so fine that they are never a problem. They all need to be gutted but the head can be left on for cooking purposes. If you choose to leave the head on, the operculum and the gills' need to be removed. Then the fish is prepared and cooked. When eating trout, you can carefully tease the flesh away from the bones and end up with a complete skeleton of the fish, none of which is in your gut.

I taught as many of the grandsons as wished, how to clean fish by this method. I have personally witnessed the skill that they have acquired. I occasionally hear a comment like, "Thanks, Dad" from daughter Sue, and "Grandpa, I'm the only one here who knows how to clean fish." And that has been the stimulus for this portion of the treatise.

As I have racked my brain to try and remember certain incidents and observations from these fishing trips, I am hoping that these words will be an encouragement to "Fish On."

One other technique I use, is called the Swedish Method of

removing a fish hook from a human body. Consider that the hook is firmly embedded in the flesh past the barb. Place a loop of very sturdy fishing line under the shank of the hook and draw it toward the curve of the hook. Firmly depress the eye of the hook into the flesh of the victim, and with the sturdy fishing line, jerk the hook out. Be violent! You can't pussyfoot around with this one.

Evening time was my favorite of all, because the boys would give up their running around, and would be happy to gather around and share the stories of the day, play games or play cards. John would usually have some games that we would play but we often settled for one of two card games, Up-and-Down or Scum.

Day in, day out the favorite game was Up-and-Down. As the younger boys would join in our card playing, there would always be a hiatus between beginning to play the game and mastery of the game. Bidding was usually the worst problem that any boy faced. Austen seemed to struggle more with bidding, than any of the other boys. In fact, the title ascribed to him. 'Austen's style of bidding,'was a form of slander that occasionally was applied to anyone who appeared to be having trouble with the game. He now deals with high finance, so I think he figured it all out. He actually won a game at Christmas time this year.

Some other comments about card playing have been suggested to me, once the boys learned that I was trying to write about our fishing trip. Some of the guys had certain reputations that were usually well-earned.

No one wanted to sit next to Ryan because 1) he was wearing the same bathing suit all week 2) his farts were worse than most and 3) he cheated by looking into other people's hands. As you all read this, I want you to understand these are not my words, I'm simply repeating rumors that have filtered in to my computer, from unnamed sources.

Many had recollections of how seriously I took the game and that I was 1) A poor loser, 2) a worse winner. I guess I'll have to own that one. But maybe that was because I was being constantly heckled.

Certain grandkids like Seth, would sneak over and punch the light switch on my watch. I didn't want to wear the battery out on my watch light so I reacted accordingly. Another trick that I do recall, I think was invented by Joel, and that was catching me with my arm flexed, and vigorously rubbing the hair on my arm so it would become knotted and pain me when I straightened out my arm

I was reminded by several of the grandkids that our fishing trip was the first occasion for sipping beer, always from John's bottle, never mine. They wanted to refer to that as Panther Piss. I can't imagine where that gross terminology came from. They also took great delight in having a puff from a cigar that was being enjoyed after dinner.

There were a number of singular instances that bear mentioning, if for no other reason, but to tickle the memories of the participants, so that each may consider some of the stories, and write to me about additional stories or memories that occurred. Very early in our fishing adventures we were subjected to a heavy lightning storm, during which time Joel was severely traumatized. He was seriously afraid of lightning, to the point where several of his brothers/cousins told him to be careful where he sat because the lightning could strike the chair and run right up his butt. Kindly John, remembered that incident and said he felt moved to hold Joel on his lap until the lightning storm was over. And I don't remember the lightening going up his butt.

On one of our trips back from Jay's resort, we stopped in the middle of the night near Lake City, for all the boys to get out and take a whiz. Son-in-law, Curt, as per usual, checked all of the tires of the vehicle and the boat and incidentally noticed that the tongue of the trailer was cracked and sagging. I thank God for Curt's habit of checking vehicles, which I assume he learned after working for years with Wandering Wheels. It was difficult to explain to the boys that we needed to wait until daybreak and then get the trailer tongue fixed. What was worse than trying to get them to understand, was trying to get them to stop burping, farting, arguing, and fighting. We had to spend the rest of that night locked up together in that vehicle. It clearly was one of the worst nights of my life.

Through all of that, we were quite fortunate. We had stopped on the south end of Lake City and very near that spot was a store that had all the parts that we needed. So we unhitched the boat and trailer, drove to town, picked up all the parts and returned. John took the boys to a MacDonald's, while Curt and I changed the trailer tongue. We lost a few hours of travel time, and of sleep, but that fortuitous stop, probably averted a tragedy. Thank you, Lord.

We took a number of road trips from our base camp at Jays and on at least two occasions we visited a water fall in the Upper Peninsula. As per usual, we would load up one or two cars, travel up North through Watersmeet and on a devious route until we arrived at the parking area for the falls. We would then disembark and walk a trail through the woods mostly downhill on the east bank of the river. I remember walking under a railway bridge that towered above us. As I looked at the bridge, I couldn't help but wonder, "How in the world did they ever span that gorge to build that bridge, probably in the 1800s?" We finally reached the lower end of the falls and scrambled down the bank to the river's edge. That was just the beginning of the adventure.

The boys had to jump back and forth across the stream, walk through the water as it splayed over the rocks and finally walk up to the column of rock over which the falls dropped. They were surprised to find that they could walk behind the falls and get to the other side of the river on dry land. Of course everybody had to swim, and I know that there were many pictures taken of that event. I struggled to get back up the bank, and then back up the trail to the car. As I think about the trip now, I'm grateful that I was only in my 70s then. I couldn't even think about that trip now.

On our circuitous route home, through the Northern Woodland, it was all very pretty, but after a half hour of driving through those woods, it all looked the same. We found another tourist spot where there was another river and several very small falls that were also very scenic. Hopping over and around all those rivers and falls occupied quite a bit more of the boy's time. At the last falls, we had ice cream and headed to the cottage with only John and me awake—and that, barely.

I asked the boys to read this over and respond. I think you might enjoy what they said.

This is a copy of Austen Comfort's email response. He is now thirty years old and is a bond trader for Fifth Third Bank.

The first year's trip to the cabin (before Jay's resort)—the morning I remember to this day, waking up in the loft above the kitchen and looking down to see you standing in your holey underwear cooking bacon. I remember thinking, "Isn't my grandpa a doctor and doesn't he have lots of money...why does he not buy himself some new underwear?"

I don't remember catching many fish that year, but I do remember you setting Erik's broken finger while we waited outside, terrified. And that was also the year we convinced Joel, as he was crying, that lightning was going to come up from the ground and through the chair and zap him in the butt.

As far as Jay's resort, there are too many fond memories to recount, but here are a few:

You always did an amazing job shopping for your grandsons. Yes, you've always loved shopping, but you always showed your thoughtful side in the vast amount of junk food and drinks you bought for us. The terrible part we dreaded was being bossed around by you and my dad as we tried to load and unload it all. But we were lazy boys, we didn't know how good we had it.

Leaving the mom's in the driveway crying as we drove away, happy to be free and dirty boys for a week.

The traditional stop for McDonald's breakfast on the trip up. Relentless farting and shooting of spit balls at fellow cars on the highway. Also, Erik filling up numerous Gatorade bottles with urine.

Our first taste of Corona beer. To this day I vividly remember you referring to it as "panther piss." We laughed, but mostly because you had said "piss."

Big chief skinny wahpoo, eat a birch log, shit a bark canoe. I still don't know what that means.

The prep and cleanup schedules. God bless the meal where you weren't on either.

We always ate loaves and loaves of bread. And the others always tried to hide the Oreos from me because they knew I would eat them all myself.

The card games, one of our fondest memories. Dirty jokes and lots of laughing. You're a sore loser and an even worse winner. Not much changes I guess.

Cleaning lots of fish. You were so good at it, but very patient in teaching us. To this day I can still clean a fish thanks to you.

Sunsets on the pontoon while listening to loons.

Watching bald eagles grab the fish we'd stabbed in the head.

Someone always getting snagged by a hook.

You cooking amazing fish. Amazing.

Now that it's all said and done, I will always remember just how much you actually did for us. I can't even name it all. Time, money, literally blood, sweat and tears. You taught us many things on those trips, but in hindsight, it's easy to see your true intentions: you wanted to teach us, show us, how to be men. Godly men. Your tough exterior built character in us, and played a significant role in molding us into the strong husbands and dads we are today. In those days you weren't always the best with words when it came to telling us you loved us, but we knew. As the saying goes "actions speak louder than words"...and I will never forget those actions grandpa. You're a Godly, selfless man, and I will always love you.

An email from Jeremy Kuiper now an MD and a general surgeon.

1) I hope you talk about Irene McDougall and her car ferrying service.

2) I remember the first time you took me fly-fishing when I was eleven or twelve. We were wading in the Baldwin river, we came to a deep hole and you had to carry me on your back so that I didn't get water over the top of my waders.

3) I remember eating the same thing for breakfast – English muffins, fried eggs and sausage while listening to Blue Lake NPR.

4) Fishing in the Sanborne Creek with crawlers after it rained.

5) The first kid fishing trip we took to your Cabin. Joel was afraid of thunderstorms, Erik broke a finger, we hardly caught any fish but had a blast. We shot frogs with BB guns, played stupid games in the cabin and lots of card games.

6) Jay's resort and feeding the loons one evening while fishing. We would take the small fish and you would pith them and throw them in. A loon probably ate four or five fish that we gave him. We didn't catch many fish that year either but it was a blast being so far away from home. We swam a lot, went on hikes to waterfalls. Fried onions and potatoes.

7) I remember fishing with Tom Bennick and Big Wayne Schense on Lake Doster and all the times on Big Lake and Warner Lake.

8) Cleaning fish was the first opportunity I had to wield a knife and dissect things out.

9) On our trips to Baldwin we talked about life, money, God, being a man and even being a respectable man and at the time those talks were pivotal in my life and definitely shaped who I am and who I have become.

10) Regardless of how many times we went fishing and did catch something or didn't catch something your overall excitement and love of fishing and spending time with us and passing along your hobby always seemed to be on the forefront of the experience.

11) I love telling people that I fish and fly-fish. So many of my friends and colleagues don't have hobbies. It makes me/us a rare breed to have a hobby and that hobby.

From Preston Comfort....

As the youngest on both sides of my family, I have come to realize how much I love fishing. This is all thanks to my grandfather. Most or some of you may know I work at a place called Viking Village. This is a huge fishing export and import industry on Long Beach Island. Basically my job is offloading huge boats that come in after long trips at sea. If it wasn't for my love of fishing I wouldn't have taken this job, considering I'm always covered in fish blood and guts.

The story that I have involves Seth, Grandpa, Bill Stoub, and me. Several years ago when I was thirteen or fourteen, I had taken a trip out to Michigan for a few weeks to go fishing and hang out with the cousins. We had planned to go fishing early that following morning, six am or so. We planned to meet Bill Stoub out at Gun Lake where his house is, and go out on his boat. Bill had told us about this hot spot he had for perch. So we got onto the boat and headed to the fishing hole, we all know grandpa's famous phrase as we are about to cast out our lines. FISH ON!! Well yup, he said it. The fishing began, at first we were pretty unsuccessful, not hitting much, its all about drifting with current. So we brought up anchor and proceeded to fish. That's when we really started to hit. It had been a solid hour by this time and he had caught a few keepers, but grandpa for whatever reason was catching a lot of small fish. Seth and I thought it was hilarious, of course, because he was getting mad. If I can remember there were only about three seats on the boat and Seth and I decided to share one up in the front. Below it was Bill and Grandpa sitting next to each other. After a while of non-stop fishing, Seth and I, not really paying attention to the other two, wanted to take a break. To this day I still think this is funny. Seth and I proceeded to turn around and found out that grandpa, not knowing this was happening had thrown half the fish he meant to throw back into the water, into the boat. He would catch it, throw it over his shoulder and miss. We counted about 10 or so fish in the boat that didn't make it into the water. This is one of the many good memories that I have fishing with GPA.

Fishing Tales from Seth Anderson (graduate in zoology, and a spear fisherman).

1. Oftentimes when someone got snagged, one of the kids would use that as an opportunity to jump in and unhook it. If I remember correctly, Joel was usually the first one for this.

2. Once while reeling in a tiny bluegill, Joel had a huge pike come and bite half of his fish off.

3. The older boys would always volunteer the smaller ones (usually myself and Preston) to be launched off the blob. After a hefty Joel and Parker combo would jump on the other end of the blob, we would be launched a pretty good distance in the air, and it seemed even further when I was so young.

4. Grandpa mentioned heading to a waterfall nearby every trip and playing around in the falls. I have a distinct and vivid memory of John Hamilton walking under the powerful falls and disappearing behind them. Upon reappearing, he was hunched over and walking like an old man using a stick as a cane. We joked he bore resemblance to Yoda. I recall as he walked through the falls with water pouring down on him hunched over, he then turned around and we discovered that the power of the water had pulled his pants down just far enough for us to see a good amount of crack-age! Of course to us kids this was the funniest thing that could ever happen.

5. One day we decided to go to the "rock pile" in the middle of the lake and catch some smallmouth bass. After an hour or so, Erik had dropped his pole in and somehow someone else managed to snag it and bring it back up. Erik also caught a 2-inch fish that was about the same size as the lure he was using. I (Seth) managed to catch an 18-inch smallmouth, which back then was just the biggest thing ever. Grandpa subsequently caught a 17-inch smallmouth and he named the two Walter and Esmeralda after some movie or show that nobody had ever seen.

6. Often when fishing got slow, we would entertain ourselves by lobbing small fish from one boat to the other or from one end of a boat to the other in an attempt to bean someone in the head. It often worked. I remember Parker being able to chuck a tiny bluegill a seemingly impossible distance at the other boat and would always yell some sort of battle cry while doing so.

7. I remember hearing the story from a previous trip where they had a lot of trouble pulling up the anchor. After a lot of heaving and ho-ing, they pulled up an entire tree with the anchor.

8. I recall upon getting to Jay's, the unloading process was always long and strenuous. Grandpa would like to pull up a chair in front of the fridge and prop the refrigerator open and sit and organize the whole thing. It was quite a sight to see. I also recall grandpa mak-

ing coffee in his holey underwear, which was also quite the sight to see. I also have good memories of fishing with Grandpa and Bill Stoub (also known as "sweetness"). Grandpa and Sweetness would bicker and argue just about the whole time about the most trivial of subjects. I often wondered how those two were friends. We rarely caught many fish, but it was a good time none theless. I recall one day (Preston loves this story), we were fishing with Sweetness and Grandpa and Sweet ness had decided to take a lunch break while fishing. He sat in his chair eating an apple and would watch his rod. He would see his rod tip move and then quickly lean forward and try to set the hook. It was quite the spectacle and I don't recall how often it really worked. Grandpa would sit with a rod in each hand and would often catch two fish at a time.

34

Cousins Camp Relocated

Shortly after we started our annual trek to the resort, Jay built a beautiful log cabin and offered it to us. Most of the logs were eight inches thick or greater, peeled and finished. It was two stories with large rooms, two large bathrooms, and a loft to sleep a bunch. The second story porch afforded us a beautiful view of the lake and occasionally, of the loons swimming by our dock.

We had earlier agreed on a basic plan for the daily activities of the trip. Realizing we didn't know all of the things that were available to us in this beautiful northern country, we allowed for additions and changes, subject to the vote of the majority; John and me. Breakfast was obviously the first order of the day and that always consisted of eggs plus. The boys have rightly reminded me, of John's time at breakfast, where he would faithfully scramble two dozen eggs.

I would think, "This guy is crazy. We will never eat all those eggs." We always ate all of the eggs and we never ran out of eggs. Other choices were toast, bacon, sausage patties, sausage links, juice, milk and coffee. Erik took great delight in making toast every day. I did not count, but one of the cousins reported that he ate four or five pieces of toast every day. I didn't remember that, but I surely could believe it.

The first year John and I made up the duty roster. Of necessity we had boys setting the table, clearing the table, doing the dishes and putting them away. Sweeping the floor was a many times a day chore since our feet were covered with sand and we wore no shoes. After the first year, the boys did their own duty roster. That eliminated a lot of bickering; "That's not fair, I did that this morning."

The next order of the day was the devotions brought faithfully by Pastor John; occasionally by me, Curt or Greg (Sue's husband). That was basically the only quiet I experienced all day long. They were even noisy in their sleep. It is to be noted at this point at no time during any trip did we ever tell a kid what he could or could not wear. We occasionally had a suggestion, but that was it. Case in point, Ryan wore one bathing suit all day, every day the whole week we were there. He went home with a bag of clean clothes. We never asked anyone if he had done his duty yet today. The favorite urinal was off the back porch. There was no such thing as showering required of the boys, since they spent several hours every day in the lake; if that didn't clean them off, no shower would.

On non-rainy days, we would load up the pontoon boat and head out. Although our lake was at the head of a chain of lakes, we would concentrate our fishing efforts on our own lake.

Though we would occasionally cruise around to see various sites, fishing eventually boiled down to one of a few places. We frequently had a late evening trip on the pontoon boat down to the ice cream shop. We never had to ask a kid twice to get ready for that trip.

When we initially started fishing, we called our lake, Jay's Lake. I know it had another name and if I find it in my records I will insert it, otherwise our lake is Jay's Lake. We would simply pick a spot, try it and if not successful move on to another. We probably had six or seven spots where we could realistically expect to catch fish. When I say fish, I'm referring to bluegills, sunfish and perch. That's pretty dull fishing for young active boys. They would rather catch pike or bass. Later in the trip, the boys could go out by themselves and try for that type of fish. Northern pike, although large and fun to catch, are slimy, smelly, have very sharp teeth and taste awful. Only on our Canadian fishing trip when we had nothing else to eat, would we eat pike.

Largemouth black bass are also fun to catch and are somewhat edible. Small mouth bass are fun to catch and are good eating but hard to find. For our fish eating purposes these smaller pan fish were more readily available and tasted so good, that our mealtime was limited to bluegill, sunfish, perch and the occasional small mouth bass. They were still relatively small and we had to have at least fifty of them for each meal.

Not every boy really liked to fish, but every kid did fish just so he could be part of the group. Because interest in fishing varied among the boys, John took it upon himself to make it interesting. Every fishing trip would be a contest. John would set the rules for the day or for part of the trip. The rules would vary and might go as follows, "For the next 30 minutes we're going to see who catches the most keeper fish, or the most fish or the most sunfish."

He would set the rules and keep tabs, or make sure each kid kept his own tally. The rules varied, so the boys never really knew what to expect, trip to trip, day-to-day. He kept the boys focused, as much as was possible. I was always the judge of whether or not a fish was a keeper. Although I did have a ruler, I mostly eyeballed each fish. A fish was judged to be a keeper or not, based largely on how many fish we needed for the evening meal. A seven inch bluegill, and an eight inch perch were the minimal sizes. Sunfish, because they were thicker, could be smaller and still be a keeper. On a very lean day, we might stoop to six and ½ inch long fish being a keeper. That would be a hard day because cleaning those little suckers was a real chore.

The boys would be verbally keeping score, on themselves and one another, so there was constant banter. John would keep score, or at least pretend he was keeping score and I was never really sure if any of us had any idea who was ahead at any time. John would always make up prizes for the most, the biggest and on and on. At the end of the day, nobody really cared because we all had fun.

On a slow, hot day, if I made them stay out too long, they would start swimming around the boat. They were usually wearing their swimming suits so changing was not a problem.

I remember a time or two when some of the boys went skinny-dipping. On especially slow days when the sun was not out, and the water was deemed too cold, we would occasionally revert to a contest in which the boys would see how far out they could extend their micturition attempts; better known as a pissing contest. Yes, such things really exist.

On a separate occasion, another such contest ended in a somewhat unpleasant circumstance. It was a typical warm evening on the beach at Jay's resort. We had a small fire pit and the boys loved to build and feed the fire in the evening. As the flames died and the embers remaining glowed sufficiently, the boys would bring out their ingredients and make s'mores. If there were other kids in the camp, they would be drawn to the celebration, and there would be one big party. The whole event was boisterous and sometimes obnoxious to the other adults in the camp. Or they simply preferred to drink their martinis in silence at their own party.

On this particular night, it was very late in the evening and the boys circled the campfire alone. This is all hearsay, because I was not present. One of the boys came up with an unusual suggestion, let's pee on the fire and put it out to which all responded in the affirmative and proceeded with the action. At this point I must ask you adult male readers, "When was the last time you had the strength of stream to be able to do that?" The answer certainly escapes me. Nonetheless, they proceeded and came up with an unusual response. That many boys peeing on an open fire, did little to quench the flames, but did a lot to raise a most unpleasant odor. At that point, they agreed to never try it again, the stink was terrible, so I hear.

After the morning fishing contest we returned to the cabin,

ate lunch and then it was free time. For me, if I had a beer before lunch, I was assured of a nap. I simply could not stay awake after a beer and lunch. Most often, John and I would simply try to stay out of the way until dinnertime.

One of the favorite beach time activities was, " King of the mountain." The functional beach at Jay's resort was very narrow because of two factors. The sand had to be trucked in for the beach and the drop off was very fast, so the beach was very short. It was a very short swim out to the floating raft, which became the center of most of the activity for the rest of the day. The boys made up all sorts of games to be played off the raft, but the favorite of all was 'King of the Raft.' Jeremy being the oldest and by far the strongest, was always the King to dethrone. As I think back on all of the time spent in trying to dethrone King Jeremy, I am amazed at how strong he was, and yet how kind and gentle he was. He could have seriously maimed any of those boys, but to the best of my recollection, no one ever received a serious injury. After Jeremy out grew the fishing trip, Andrew, and then Parker replaced him. It remained the favorite game for all of grandkids, forever.

The dock at the north end of the beach was only about twelve feet long, but at the end of the dock, the water was already over eight feet deep. It was off this dock that the smaller kids would spend hours catching the littlest bluegills that I could ever imagine. They were present in such great perfusion that Erik found he could catch them on a shiny hook with no bait. They took great delight in catching them and then torturing them in all sorts of ways, including blowing them up with firecrackers. Firecrackers, which we usually had in abundance, were utilized to blow up everything imaginable. There were many small crayfish that inhabited the lake. There were good ones and bad ones. The good ones would be sought out by bass and other critters for food. The bad ones had an orange spot on their back and would not be eaten by any type of animal life or fish. So when the kids took to blowing them up by the hundreds, I felt they were doing the lake a big service.

As the boys grew larger, stronger and more adventurous, they would cruise the shallower water off the boat docks with nets and spears looking for large bass and pike. I don't remember if they ever actually speared any of the fish but I know they caught quite a few of these larger fish with the landing nets. It's strange how these fish would view the boys in the water with nets. They were not particularly alarmed until the boys got very close or actually touched them. I don't think they actually caught one large enough to eat, but the pursuit of these larger fish occupied them for hours on end.

On one of our very first trips where we were using only my boat, we had traveled around a couple of islands and were in a very secluded backwater area. I had four fairly young boys with me who were doing the usual amount of squabbling, bragging, raising heck and not particularly paying any attention to the fishing; it was lousy anyway. We were catching a bunch of very small bluegills. I looked up from my intense fishing and saw a loon swimming about thirty feet from the boat. This gave me an idea which I had to explain to the boys; it is called 'pithing.' You grab a fish so that the dorsal side is up. Take a knife with a very sharp short blade and stick it in the fish's skull just behind the eyes, and twist it around several times. The fish will twitch several times and then die. Dead fish don't swim, they float.

So I said to the boys, "Throw this dead fish as close as you can to the loon and let's see what happens." I purposely gave it to the oldest boy thinking he probably had the strongest arm, and he threw it toward the loon. After several tries he finally got a fish close enough to the loon to interest him. He swam over to the dead fish and gulped it down. The boys were so excited, that they forgot all about catching keeper bluegills, fighting and bickering with one another. They had a whole new game called 'feed the loon.' They all got real busy trying to catch fish, taking turns pithing the fish and throwing it toward the loon. I cannot believe how many fish the loon ate that evening. The loon slowly moved our way and before he got filled, he was about fifteen feet away from the boat. The boys talked about that incident for days and couldn't wait to tell their mothers all about that trick.

The pursuit of loons provided an almost unlimited source of activity for all of us. Since we were located on the east shore of the lake with the prevailing west wind and slept with our doors and windows open every night, we could hear the loons calling from all over the lake. The first time I heard a loon crying at night, I was reminded of the saying, 'crazy as a loon.' The sound is a little eerie, but after a while it becomes very comforting or soothing. It reminds me of the beauty and complexity of our northern, wooded state. We have encountered a few loons in our Canadian fishing waters, but with a strong wind and our cabin position mostly north of the lake, we were not privileged to hear the loon crying at night very often.

On one of our pontoon boat trips, John was at the wheel and we were moving right along. I was almost asleep in the back of the boat, when someone in the bow hollered out, "Hey! Look at the loons right ahead of the boat. I think we're going to run over them."

Immediately, everyone was alerted and ran to the front of the pontoon boat. "So what?" you say. "What's the big deal?" Two or three years before, it would not have been a big deal. But now that we have sizable young chaps aboard the speeding pontoon boat, and they all rush to the very front railing to be sure and see the loon, guess what? Something that I had never conceived as possible happened.

The front end of the pontoon boat was thrust under the surface of the water by the weight of the grandkids, and we started shipping water over the entire front end of the pontoon boat. I thought we were going to sink. John calmly pulled back on the throttle, the boat leveled out and the water ran off the deck. But not before it had washed a few ice chests out into the water, as well as a few pair of flip-flops and a bunch of water bottles. We had to scurry around for a while to retrieve our ice chests, which contained our bait, our lunch and our drinks. There were several startled, if not scared young men on board. One of my faithful reporters, Austen, noted I was sitting in the back of the boat, laughing as everybody scurried around to pick up their stuff. As far as I know we did not lose any fishing rods or kids.

At another time, and at a different location we were having similarly poor results with trying to catch keeper bluegills. They were far and few between, but we possessed a never ending supply of undersized fish. After an hour or so of catching fish that were not keepers, the mind games began. Taunting, teasing, name-calling, and lighthearted fistie cuffs; I feared the worst. I was cheered when one of the young lads screeched at us, "Look at the top of that dead tree! Is that an Eagle?" We all looked and agreed; it was indeed an American Bald Eagle.

"Can we feed him?"

Several of them remembered what we had done with the loon a few years before. So they skillfully pithed a couple of bluegill and threw them out, off the back of the boat. It was not toward the Eagle, since we knew he would not swoop down to pick up the fish if our boat was in his flight path. So we threw the dead fish far as we could at approximately a right angle to where he was sitting.

The dead tree, on which the Eagle was perched, was close enough so that the good eyes of the boys could see him turn his head to look towards us and toward the fish.

"He sees the fish!"

But no action. Not until we had thrown several fish out behind the boat did we see the action. As all eyes were focused on that beautiful bird, we saw him gracefully lift off the tree, glide down toward the water, reach out with his talons and pick up one of the fish. He proceeded to fly back to his perch on the top of the dead tree and pick the fish apart. We were all thrilled. I'm sure some of the boys have pictures of that unique incident.

The process continued for some period of time. And of course, the boys wanted to get prizes for the fish that they threw that was eaten by the Eagle; another contest for the boys.

To the delight of all concerned this process continued on through the retrieval of several dead fish. All of a sudden we spotted a second Eagle who wanted to join the feeding frenzy. We were all excited beyond belief at our good fortune. The party abruptly ended when we saw each eagle diving from a different direction for the same fish. They appeared to collide in midair. The dead fish remained on the surface of the water. The Eagles retreated to their own secluded safe place, and that was the end of our fun for that fishing day.

35

Wintering Lake Discovered

Larry Moon and I had been acquainted for at least twenty-five years. It began when we both found ourselves attending Westwood Baptist church. Sandy and I were looking for a new church after having a difficult time at our first and briefly second church. The fact we were still looking at Baptist Churches at all is a monumental tribute to my stupidity. Nonetheless, we found ourselves happily engaged in the late seventies at Westwood Baptist church, which in retrospect was probably the greatest church I ever attended. Had I only recognized that fact, I would have fought harder to save the church and the fellowship we enjoyed there. Larry was the director of a retirement home, Friendship Village, and I was just starting out with some new partners in orthopedics.

We became friends and shared many social events in and outside the church. We knew of each other's affinity for the spiny denison of the freshwater deeps; we both liked to fish.

We discovered and scouted Jay's resort which resulted in the cousins' camp. This adventure led to not only a series of trips that provided immeasurable fun and fellowship with my

grandsons but also provided a fellowship that I had not anticipated. It started off with John Hamilton as my buddy and
crowd controller but through the years we added other adults
who offered another level of fellowship. Joining us in the ensuing years were my sons in law, Curt Anderson and Greg Comfort and John's son, Jeff, and son-in-law, Tom Senna.

The good times that all of us enjoyed through the years at
Jay's resort, was a confirmation to me, that all of us guys long
for fellowship with other men. I saw this desire for relationship
as a driving force I encountered in many men through Open
Hearts Ministry. The stories I heard in group were in many
ways like my own; a deep longing for a relationship with their
father. As I have related earlier, my desire for such as I was
growing up, was found in school with guys my own age. Perhaps having buddies later in life might help each of us compen-
sate for the father relationship that was not there.

With that in the back of my mind, I started talking with
Larry about some of his fishing trips with guys in Canada.
Could we take men who knew nothing about fishing up to
Canada, teach them about fishing and have some good Christian fellowship? Yes, we could, but since they didn't have
bluegills where we wanted to go, I'd have to learn about fishing for walleye. Is that reasonable, Larry? Yes, it is but it will
involve a lot of planning. Planning and lists are my middle
name; let's do it.

As I continued with my practice of orthopedic surgery and
continued inquiry into my patients' fishing experiences, I was
pleasantly surprised when I heard a happy story about fishing
for walleye in Canada. I launched an investigation into a fish-

ing camp located on Wintering Lake, Ontario, Canada. After I had gleaned sufficient information, I again approached Larry and asked if he might be interested in another wild goose chase. Absolutely! So we started planning for another trip into the unknown.

In my mind, I made up basically four check lists. One for the vehicle and boat, the second one was for food, my choices of course. Next category, the fishing gear, followed by clothing. The first two were pretty well-defined because they fit any location, travel needs and food needs. The latter two were much more of a guess because we were going to be in Canada somewhere around September 15, therefore, weather was an unknown. The last was fishing equipment, and since I have never seriously fished for walleye, fishing equipment decisions were a crapshoot. As a result I had much stuff that I didn't and couldn't use, and was very short on the stuff I really needed. Just remember, necessity is the mother of invention. The whole trip was pretty much trial and error but it provided me with a basis from which I would operate for the next fifteen years

We had to leave late in the day on a Friday. I assumed that we would easily find a place to spend the night. By saying that, I inferred a motel, hotel or room to let. Even though I had traveled through this country several years previously, I had forgotten how isolated it is. The motels and gas stations are hundreds of miles apart. If you don't understand that, you will have real trouble while traveling in Canada.

Somewhere in the middle of the night, as I was getting increasingly sleepy, I realized that we were a long way from civilization. When we finally encountered a rest stop somewhere on the east end of Lake Superior, we pulled in and parked. We were to learn the view to the West was extraordinary, but at midnight it was just plain black. What we did not realize as we pulled in, this was a local hotspot for lovers. There were cars, trucks and all sorts of vehicles in and out of that rest stop all night long. I was more than a little concerned for our safety. So we rolled up the windows, locked the doors and pretended to be asleep, resisting all temptations to respond to knocks on the window. I have never been so grateful to awaken and find that we, our car and boat were still intact. The view west was indeed spectacular; a beautiful, shiny lake with islands and wooded shores all around us. Nonetheless, we did not dillydally. Wintering, here we come.

My first impression of the camp at Wintering was the first owner had built one or two cabins on the lowest budget possible. There were a number of very small cabins, each one in poorer repair than it's neighbor. The cabins had been constructed as the need arose and as the building material became available at wholesale prices, plus leftovers. The roofs of the buildings all appeared to be at high risk, the leaky roofs may have been the only source of fresh water for that Cabin.

A few cabins had running water whereas some only had access to running water through an outside tap. Hot water was available only after you heated it on a butane stove. Buckets and pans were provided. There was an inside drain to help with washing dishes, and washing hands. Each cottage was equipped with a path to the local outhouse. Several cabins were assigned to each outhouse, but gratefully, each outhouse was a one holer. There was one community shower; one room, one shower head and a drain on the floor. My feeling was that if you could get out of there cleaner then when you went in, you would be very fortunate.

It was almost like being back in high school athletics. We had a common shower room, several shower heads, with no dividers. Every shower allowed each person to be humiliated and shamed. As I'm sitting here writing this, I realize that was the norm for every young boy and perhaps every young girl who participated in athletics; taunting, ridicule and shame.

Wintering Lake Resort had just been purchased by new owners, Dennis and Deb Cowan, who were quick to note that there would be big changes in the camp over the winter. At the point I entered the camp, I wasn't at all sure if I was interested in any change they might make to this camp. Let's see how the fishing is.

We received a crash course in the navigation of Wintering Lake, along with a map which marked many dangerous rocks. Since my boat would travel thirty-five miles an hour in open water, I was terrified to travel more than ten or fifteen miles an hour. The thought of running up on a sharp rock and ripping out the bottom of my boat was ever on my mind, in addition to worrying about a broken prop, because I did not have a spare. We tried to fish very close to the camp but sat in wonder at the several boats ripping by us, full speed ahead. They had to be insane, drunk or both. At the end of the week, we managed to travel about only one half the distance to the far end of the lake.

We made three trips away from the camp in order to find large numbers of edible fish. The first trip was made by dragging my boat by trailer all the way to the south end of the of the main lake. With fear and trepidation we navigated a tiny channel to a larger lake and drifted around with no success. We were told that the walleye would be lying no deeper than twenty feet and up to five feet depending on the sunlight or lack thereof. Walleye are basically nocturnal feeders but they may be caught in deeper water in the middle of the day. If the day were overcast or rainy, the walleye may move into very shallow water, that is five feet or so.

The usual method used to catch walleye is back trolling. I learned that back trolling was limited to smaller boats and smaller motors. You simply started the motor and ran backwards. The back of the boat would slow down the speed so it was reasonable. Forward trolling usually results in too rapid a speed. Well, my seventy horse motor would not allow for either forward or backward trolling at a satisfactory speed. So we had to drift.

Drifting, of necessity, surrenders accuracy. One picks out a spot where he wishes the boat to travel. Then you drive your boat into the wind to a point where you feel that the wind will carry the boat over your selected spot. It is reasonably accurate however you never get a straight drift. Because of the shape of the boat, a narrow bow and a broad stern, there is always a forward thrust to any drift. The force of the wind determines the speed of the drift. The speed of the drift is not usually very important because fish are carnivorous. For most game fish, a moving bait is a great target. The fish are aggressive and accept motion as a challenge. Some days, the faster the motion, the better the action.

After an hour of drifting over what appeared to be sterile water, we carefully picked our way up a winding channel to the main part of Wintering Lake. The lake itself was so large, we felt we had no chance to catch fish unless we picked out a bay or somewhere with a well circumscribed portion of water. That we did and drifted along large reed beds, in shallow water to deep and then from deep water back to shallow. We tried all sizes and colors of jigs; I used crawlers and Larry used minnows all to no avail. At one point I know the depth finder was showing us fish at seventy feet. I thought that was a mistake but later Denny told us those were White fish. You don't catch White fish at seventy feet, but when they come up to shallow water to spawn, you may catch them with a jig. Well that I did and in the end I was not happy about it.

On that particular occasion, we were returning home from Wintering Lake with a boat load of fish. We had a wonderful time at Wintering Lake and on that occasion we had about eight guys, two boats, two vehicles, packed with gear and food going up and gear and fish coming home; perfect! It was a wonderful trip. We had fish up the old waazoo. What I'm about to say now is old hat for all the old wizened and seasoned Wintering fisherman. Canada is a wonderful place unless you are a hungry fisherman and tend to be a little greedy. The goal of every fisherman in our camp is:

1. Catch as many walleye pike as you can.
2. Eat as many walleye pike as you can.
3. Bring home as many walleyed pike as you can.

When we first started fishing at Wintering, there was no limit to the number of perch we could catch, eat or bring home. There was a limit to both Northern and walleyed pike; four per man in possession at any time.

We had all been warned from day one that the game wardens or fish wardens in Canada, just sit around and wait for dumb fishermen like us, to make a mistake on the rules and regulations.

Whereupon they swoop in to take all of your fish, some of your fishing tackle, occasionally boats and motors and I've even heard a rumor that one or two guys lost a car. It is imperative to count the fish caught, and frozen with the intent to take home. The limit per man of walleye in possession at any one moment of your visit to their fair country is, four walleye and only one over eighteen inches. This is so important, that every trip we assigned one person who's only responsibility for the whole week, was to keep track of the number of fish in our freezer. Failure to keep close tabs could be a disaster.

As we loaded our vehicles for the trip home we again counted fish. We had our limit of walleye per man, a few perch and one nice white fish. We were all surprised when we caught a white fish because they're not common. We have eaten a few and they're very good perchance not quite as good as walleye, but nonetheless highly desirable. One of us decided he wanted to take a white fish home for his family to try. I don't remember who he was, but we all paid the price.

Returning from Canada we have to cross the Canadian and then the American border. We have had several different experiences. The most pleasant of which is nobody at the gate on the Canadian side; we are home free.

One other time the Canadians set up camp on the American side. I'm sure they got a few cheaters on that trick. Being stopped at the border is the usual routine and none of us were surprised by that.

The Canadian DNR must supplement their income by catching poachers because they try many ways to do so. Most of the time they set up camp on the Canadian side of the Saute and inspect your vehicle and boat and everything for suspected contraband walleyed pike. They don't care about northern pike and until recently even perch since the limit on perch was fifty. The one time they set up camp on the American side of the Saute was the time that they found a white fish in with our walleye and called it a walleye. We had our limit of walleye +1 white fish and that is the only time we've ever brought a white fish back. Well, it was declared a walleye and I think we owed corporately about three hundred seventy bucks for that one dead fish. We learned our lesson and that is why we had one man only in charge of fish counting for the entire week.

On another occasion, Frank and Bill and I were coming back and we were still quite a ways up north in Canada when we encountered a roadblock on the main highway just north of the Canadian Saute. We were routed around and because we were dragging a boat there was a secondary roadblock where the policeman said that he was looking for open liquor bottles in the car. At that time I had one of my gallon jugs of wine with about a quarter of the wine left and I was basically sitting on it in the back seat of Bill's car. I'm thinking, "I'm dead. How much is a gonna cost me this time?" Then the cop looks back at our boat and said surprised like, " Oh! You guys been fishing?"

Of course we had to confess to that sin and his next question was, "Did you do pretty well?"

The whole roadblock was nothing but a ruse; they were looking to supplement their income. So we hauled out our ice chest and they counted eleven walleye and then they started looking at our huge pile of perch. Right near the top of the perch pile was another walleye, we had miscounted, but we were still within the limit. Never mind, they went through that entire ice chest and counted all eighty or ninety perch looking for one more walleye so they could nail us. We were legal so we escaped with no fine.

The time of acute loss occurred at the Canadian border, where we had been stopped and our fish totally exposed and counted. When the white fish was brought out, the question was duly asked, "What is this?" We all stood around, swearing before all the officers, that this was a white fish, although we could not remember who caught it, and who was bringing it home. Never mind! As I recall, the fine was $370. That's $370 for one stinking white fish.

The incident that was most severe occurred right at camp. Those of us who were early participants in the Wintering retreat experience, found Denny to be most hospitable and help-ful. It seems as time went by, Denny became a little more ob-streperous and his relationships with the local Canadians, in particular the fish wardens, became quite testy. As a result, the wardens took to a policy of in-camp inspections. That means, without notice, the warden would appear in camp to inspect the large freezer in the fish cleaning house and question as to who owned what fish in the freezer. In addition they would walk into any of the cabins to check the refrigerator for a walleye count.

Recall; the legal limit for walleye in possession per person at any time was four. Toward the end of the fishing trip when we are storing up walleye to take home, we might have as many as three walleye per man in the big freezer and two or three more in the refrigerator waiting for the evening meal. This evening, we were clearly over the limit.

It was about four o'clock in the afternoon on a beautiful sunny day in Wintering Lake Resort Camp when John Hamil-ton came running into our cabin, pale as a ghost. "They're here! The wardens are they are checking every cabin!"

I'm guessing that everyone who was on that fishing trip knew exactly where he was and what he was doing when John burst into the cabin. I felt paralyzed as I looked over to the sink and the colander full of walleye ready to be fried. Every last little filet was over the limit. I was about to lose every piece of my fishing tackle, and perhaps my boat, motor and trailer, but I hoped I could keep the suburban to drive home. All of this went through my mind like a flash.

Thank goodness for Mick's quick thinking. Mick grabbed the colander full of our walleye fillets, sneaked out the back door, across to the only empty cabin on site that day and stuffed the fish in the freezer of the empty cabin. The warden beat him back to our cottage and opened both refrigerators and freezer compartments to find no walleyed pike. "What are you guys having for dinner?"

"Larry is cleaning a northern for us right now, and as soon as he comes in we're going to cook it and eat it."

The guy knew we were lying through our teeth but he couldn't find any walleye. Fortunately he didn't think to look in the empty cottage. We survived, kept all our gear, and later had a very well appreciated walleye dinner and a couple of beers.

36

A Perch Day to Remember

Back to our first day of fishing away from the camp. Larry and I were motoring and drifting around the lower end of Wintering Lake to no avail. I don't think we had one hit however we had a lot of action. That is because we were in south Wintering Lake with a series of storm fronts coming through.

As we looked off to the West we spied a big, ugly cloud drifting our way. We had ample rain gear including wonderful rain hats Larry had procured for such an occasion. They were Boston Whaler hats that more than covered our head and shoulders so we suited up. This brief rainstorm was followed by no less than four more. By the end of the last rainstorm, we were starting to get wet all over and cold. Call it a day.

Back to the trailer and car, back to the camp fishless, cold, tired and hungry. Denny was more than kind and provided us with some smoked northern pike. I don't believe I ever tasted anything as good as those smoked northern pike. Thereafter, every trip, I asked Denny when he was going to smoke pike so I can get some more. As far as I remember he never smoked any more pike for us.

The second episode that I remembered from that first trip was a day on Robinsons Lake. Denny took pity on us since we were catching very few walleye, didn't want to eat Northern Pike and hadn't figured out how to fish for perch. This being around September 15, it was the ideal time to catch perch but we didn't know it at the time. We drove to Robinson's Lake with Denny, where he keeps a boat. We just had to provide the motor and the gas.

Denny is a horse,and he simply boosted the ten horse motor on his shoulder and walked back to the lake. It sounds like that could be just a nonchalant stroll. Let me tell you that walking anywhere around the lake is high risk activity: slippery mossy rocks and mud bogs. And that is the easy way into the lake. Larry carried the gas container and I was lucky just to carry me down to the lake and thence into the boat.

The boat was a beater; maybe fourteen feet long, V bottom, no oars, no anchor, just three guys, three rods and a minnow bucket. Dennis is not one for long conversations, so it went something like this, "Get in, sit down, and hold on." Frankly, I was nervous about the size of the boat and what we were about to do. Fortunately, the leakage was minimal, so we didn't have to bail. We just soaked up the excess water with a sponge and kept on with our business.

We motored across the main body of the lake, between two weed beds that I could see, turned the motor around, and started back trolling. Dennis told us which side to fish on and we proceeded to catch walleyed pike. We caught quite a few, and I found that catching walleye pike was a lot of fun. Up to that point I had no idea, because I hadn't caught any. End of a fantastic day!

The third episode is one of the most outstanding days of fishing I have ever experienced in my life, and that includes catching 14 Atlantic salmon in one day on the River of Ponds. For the uninitiated, fourteen Atlantic salmon in an entire year, is something to brag about. But fourteen in one day was beyond remarkable. There are very few salmon fishermen who would believe that could happen. That probably was my most outstanding day and two of us catching 150 keeper perch was a close second.

This was a separate day on our initial trip to Wintering Lake. We had not done well on Wintering Lake itself, or better known as Gamsby Lake. There was a third named lake that we fished frequently and that was called Fectau Lake. There were a number of smaller lakes around Wintering, where Dennis had established a presence. He would use a four wheeler and drag a boat into the lake while the ground was still covered with snow and the lake with ice. He would chain it to a rock and leave it for people like Larry and me.

When we would push to fish another lake, we would take in a motor, gasoline and use the boat that was already there. Sometime during that first week when we got sick and tired of not catching fish on Gamsby Lake, we asked about the possibility of another. Dennis directed us to Wig Lake and assured us we could get in quite easily. I hearken back to what I had mentioned earlier, basically one man's caviar may be another man's poison. That is exactly what I thought about the approach to Wig Lake. We started walking on firm soil, dropped down onto huge rocks and then a bog area. Finally back to small rocks and to the lake with pretty good-sized rocks. We each had to make at least two trips across this terrain, and by the time I had gotten back to the lake the second time I wasn't sure I had enough strength to fish.

'Good, old Larry,' better said, 'good, young Larry.' He's about 10 years younger than I am, about 40 pounds heavier and about three times as strong. I was thinking that he carried the motor in but I was mistaken. Somewhere I had picked up a wheeled motor mount for 'peanuts.' That motor mount turned out to be just the 'cats meow' to haul that motor into the fishing site. Were it not for Larry and the motor mount, I would never have fished Wig Lake and you would have been deprived of a fantastic story.

We loaded the boat, cast off and motored here and there looking for, God only knows what, because I had no idea what I should be looking for. Whatever it was we found a lot of it. The sky was overcast early in the day but the water was so clear we could see the bottom, at what I'm guessing to be twenty feet deep. We motored and drifted and drifted and motored for most of the morning and finally decided to drag the boat up onto some big rocks so we could sit and eat our lunch overlooking this beautiful scene. As I recall we were able to drink the water because it was spring like water.

The sun had come out and it was a beautiful warm day in the middle of September. Larry thought it would be awfully nice to go for a swim. So he skinned off his clothing and dove in rather chilly water, but had a very nice swim. After he dried out on the rocks with the bright sunshine, we entered back into the boat and headed for the other end of the lake.

We had no map of the Lake so any part was as good as the next, as far as we knew. We just wandered around. We were drifting along at a very slow pace when, much to my amazement, I had a tic-tic-tic. "Could that be a perch? Let's swing around and try it again."

We did and on the next try, we both felt the light tapping at the end of the line, jerked the line up and each of us had an empty hook. This would never happen back home because given this scenario, we would be using two hooks each. With two hooks we rarely lost both baits at the same time. But here in Canadian land, it's a different game. It's called 'nail the tourist.' Using more than one hook on a rod is illegal except for fishing for northern pike. And we want to have nothing to do with those ugly, smelly, slimy great northern pike.

We turned around and repeated the float and as soon as we had a bite, I threw out the anchor. Up to that point I had not paid much attention to what was in the front of the boat, but I knew that we would need an anchor if we had indeed found 'nirvana.' What I found in the front of the boat looked like refuse from a landfill. I suspect it had one time been part of an automobile engine; probably a transmission. It was tied on to a fairly flimsy rope, but I knew the anchor was heavy enough to hold us in the strongest gale we would ever experience on that lake. And surely the cry arose from the rear of the boat, "Throw out the anchor." I responded immediately and was surprised to find that we were in about 3 ½ feet of water. It ultimately turned out that we were surrounded by a huge school of absolutely ravenous perch.

We had for bait a few minnows, and maybe two dozen crawlers. We were using fairly small jigs with either a minnow or a piece of crawler that we would drop straight down. We quickly learned that we needed to pick it up as fast as it hit the bottom because there would be a perch attached. We laughed and giggled like a couple of schoolgirls as we proceeded to haul in perch as fast as we could; we had indeed found Perch Nirvana. If we did not pick up rapidly we would have an empty hook and a lost opportunity. After about twenty minutes of hauling in perch as fast as we could, we realized we had to set up some sort of a system or we would; 1.Catch all the perch in the lake or 2. Sink the boat with all the perch in the lake.

We had to make decisions. "How many perch would we take home?" There appeared to be absolutely no limit to the number of perch we could catch. Next question, "How small a perch do you want to clean," or "Should there be a minimum size for keeping?" Third question, "What are we going to do with these perch as we haul them into the boat?" The fourth question, "Can we stay here and fish all night?"

The questions all had logical answers so we just had to consider the circumstances. There's no limit to the number of perch we can take back to the United States but there is a limit to how many perch I want to clean tonight. If we limit the size of the perch we keep, we will eliminate a lot of the problem by throwing back perch under nine inches. A nine inch perch in the state of Michigan is a reasonable size perch. After cleaning there still is a significant amount of the filet left. These Canadian perch appeared to be about fifty percent heavier than our Michigan perch, so a nine inch perch is at least four bites of fish, plenty for my liking. Being an eternally optimistic fisherman, I had brought along a very large white bucket. One that had been filled with plaster of Paris. It was much larger than a standard water bucket. The fish were coming in so fast that we had no chance to use a fish bag or a stringer. We just threw the keeper perch into the big white bucket. All my fishing buddies and grandsons are acquainted with this bucket, and they know it holds a lot of fish.

So here we were laughing, giggling, jerking perch out and throwing them into the bucket just as fast as we could rebait our hooks and drop them into the water. I totally lost track of time, but I guess we had to be at it for at least one hour, but it could have been as long as two. I don't know. Moreover I don't really care. I didn't want that day to ever end.

The next challenge arose when the bucket was so full that every time we threw in a new perch, one would jump out and land on the floor of the boat. It didn't bother me because I had on a pair of boat boots. Larry, on the other hand, became a little concerned, because he had a pair of deck shoes on his feet, and they were starting to get wet. So Larry stood with each foot on a different seat straddling the bucket, so he could keep his feet dry.

Next crisis arose when we realized that our bait had run out. Long before that problem reared it's ugly head, we had cut back on the size of the crawler that we'd use for bait; we were down to a quarter inch of crawler per hook. Even then we ran out. I've heard tales from 'the old guys' and what they would do in such a circumstance. So at this point I ask all you old guys, "What would you do to save the day so that you didn't have to quit fishing and go home with only 100 perch are so?"

You take a very sharp knife or a pair of scissors and cut some perch belly into thin strips about three quarters of an inch long and put them on the hook. Guess what? These perch are cannibals, they ate one another's belly and so our fish catching continued unabated.

I finally got so tired that I wanted to quit. Larry agreed that he had straddled those two seats long enough and he was ready to go home. He took his shoes off to keep his shoes dry and drove the boat back to shore where we reversed that laborious process and hauled back to the suburban; the motor, gas can, fishing gear and now a huge bucket of perch. We had another container of sorts in the suburban so we didn't have to throw fish on the floor of the car. As we drove back very cautiously, because I didn't want to spill a bucket of fish on the floor of my suburban, we carefully planned our reentry into the camp.

We stopped by the office to show Denny our successful day, knowing that he would put the call out to everybody in camp. This news could only boost the popularity of Wintering Lake Resort. We drove back to the cottage, picked up a bunch of knives and returned to the fish cleaning shack. No, I didn't make a mistake when I said we picked up a bunch of knives, because I rather figured what was going to happen. And it did!

Sooner or later every person in camp came over to the fish cleaning table to see our mess of perch. As I remember, we counted one hundred and fifty perch, all of which were over nine inches long.

We dumped a bunch of perch out on the fish cleaning counter and started our work. Person after person came into the shack, looked at the mess of perch, 'Ooood' and 'Aaahd' and said without fail, "I've never seen that many perch before!" Larry and I agreed, we never had either. And then again, without fail each would pick up one of our spare knives and say, "Let me help you."

I'm quite certain that every person in the camp did come by the cleaning shack that evening and each cleaned a few perch. Yes, we had a lot of help, but it still took us three hours to clean those 150 large perch. And we had to put each fish in a separate plastic bag with a piece of skin still on for the fish police. That was clearly the highlight of all of my Wintering Lake fishing trips.

We continued to wander up and down Gamsby Lake, catching a few perch, a few walleye and a lot of little, throw-back pike. We left Wintering Lake early on Saturday morning with our freezer packed, swearing that we would be back. In fact a plan was already hatching under my calvarium.

37

Robinson's Lake

One of my all time favorite memories was a day on Robinson's Lake. I have mentioned that Denny kept boats on several lakes in the proximity of Wintering Lake, so when the opportunity presented itself, when the fishing was rotten on Wintering, we had other places to go. This particular day, Jim Keller, Dan Colley and I drove down to Robinson's Lake. Jim and Dan are both big guys and so they could easily handle the gas and the motor to put it on our aluminum boat.

The method of fishing on Robinson's Lake is back trolling. I was never enamored with that type of fishing, but I'll do what I have to in order to catch fish legally. However, I was not looking forward to running the boat. I was hoping that either Jim or Dan would step up and volunteer. I always knew that Jim was well acquainted with boats and motors and he would be more than happy to do that and rather expected him to volunteer. Much to my surprise, Dan Colley stepped up and said, "I'd like to run the boat." After we had assured him as to how to handle this fourteen foot boat with a ten horse motor and especially back trolling, we cast off and headed for the trolling area. Although we started off on a cloudy day, we had not anticipated rain, but that was always a possibility up at Wintering. We had no reliable weather forecast available to us. Every day was a crap shoot. "What do you think it's going to be like today?" Then we get 3 different answers, and go out and fish anyway.

Today was one of those days. We had started out in about fifty-five degree weather, with a little wind, heavy overcast and generally a pleasant day to fish. We back-trolled up and down the lake and managed to catch six or eight nice walleyes. We were enjoying the day and the fishing and Dan was doing an excellent job of running the boat. Suddenly the weather turned nasty.

A wind came up and slowly grew worse. The rain came as a light mist, then a light rain and then the roof fell in. Heavy rain and strong wind, and even though our boat was fourteen feet long, it was a small boat on the lake at that time of day. We called it quits. Dan swung the motor around and headed back toward shore, right into a wild wind and driving rain. I was so happy that I was not running the boat. I simply pulled my raincoat up high, pulled my rain hat over my eyes and looked down at the bottom of the boat, and of course prayed.

As I did so, I recalled Dan's story from our group. As had so many of my fishing buddies, Dan grew up without a significant father figure. As I recall, he grew up feeling he was not enough as a man. Dan was a tall, strong, good-looking and intelligent guy; a really good guy. He carried this burden his whole life. I never used to understand people like him, until I became a group leader at Open Hearts Ministry, and heard story after story just like Dan's; never quite good enough in his own eyes. I lifted up my head in spite of the rain and looked back at Dan and was amazed. He had a strong hand on the throttle, a determined look in his eyes as he searched for our landing spot, and just, ever so slight a smile on his face. He was winning, he had just cleared a big hurdle. He was a man among men, his peers.

Jerry Kasper was a very pleasant addition to our fishing group. He took a risk, traveled up from Texas, and joined a bunch of crazies like the Wintering guys. I don't recall if he brought a tackle box and a fishing rod with him or we supplied him with such. It made no difference; he was happy just to be up there with a bunch of guys. He volunteered to help out wherever he could and it was just a pleasure to have him around. Being from Texas he fit right in with Richard Lee and Bill Stoub. We offered him the opportunity to fish with others but he declined. He was quite a talker and seemed to have to find something to keep him busy at all times. No surprise that he found himself with Bill and Richard on a dull fishing day. He grew tired of throwing his lure out and catching nothing. After he had consumed his beverage, eaten his lunch and had nothing more to occupy him, he offered to clean out Bill Stoub's tackle box.

Since I have never looked into Bill Stoub's tackle box I have no idea what Jerry found. But I know he fussed and fiddled and offered to throw this out and to rearrange that. When he had completed his chore, and the fishing had not improved, he offered to do likewise to Richard Lee's tackle box. Since Richard had accumulated much less merchandise than Bill, it was a disappointingly short task for Jerry. The fish were still not biting, the day was dull for everybody, and if I'm not mistaken Jerry offered to re-do Bill's tackle box. That became the joke of the trip, if you needed your tackle box cleaned out, take Jerry fishing with you. I didn't want him to get his hands on mine, so I never volunteered to take Jerry out. I often wondered what might have happened had he been released on Mick Kiss's boat.

One of the days, early in our fishing ventures, when Bill and I fished alone, he left the cabin early to get the boat ready. I was still finishing up the breakfast dishes. When I finally managed to make it down to the dock, I went through my checklist. I have previously alluded to the fact that I use checklists to run my life; so this should be no surprise to you. And, it was not totally unexpected to Bill when I arrived and began my questioning. "Did you get the bait? Do you have the minnows? Did you put the net in the boat? Is my rod still in the boat?." And on and on.

"Hey! Does this look like your OR, and am I your circulating nurse? Just shut up and get in the boat." This was obviously after that unfortunate day on the St. Joe River, where we both forgot a landing net. So I got in the boat quietly and that probably was the worst argument we ever had. This fact has to be very surprising to most of our friends who, when we first went off on a day of fishing together, wondered which one would come back alive.

As Dennis continued to improve conditions around the camp, he built a whole new dock system which allowed ample room for all the boats that were in the basin. The main platform was firmly attached to pipes driven into the ground. From that main dock, the individual smaller docks were placed on floating barrels which allowed that portion of the dock to rise and fall as the water did. But they were carefully balanced side to side and no one ever came close to tipping the dock and falling in. Prior to this new dock we had several docks that were strictly on floats with minimal stabilization. Consequently, they were a little tippy.

On one of the very early spring trips, we were coming in off the lake after a miserable day in which we had wind, rain and eventually snow. We were very happy to see the cabins appear in the distance. We carefully matriculated the narrows without incident and pulled up to the east side of a short dock on the west side of the camp. We were all stiff and sore and achy. We've been in the boat a long time and our sea legs were shaky. I was in the bow of the boat, so I got out early and fairly easily and started to walk up the dock toward shore. Just as I stepped off the dock onto the solid ramp, I heard a loud "Whoa," a loud thump followed by a generous splash. I quickly turned and saw flailing arms attached to a snowsuit that was in the lake. "Help, help me." As I steeled myself in preparation to jump into that icy water to help my unfortunate buddy, Bill Stoub, Craig from the next dock hollered out, "Put your feet down and walk out, you dumb bunny," or something like that. It was only three feet deep!

John Hamilton had started his fishing adventures with me as he accompanied me and my grandchildren to northern Michigan. There we spent a lot of time catching bluegills and an incidental bass, but basically no fish of any size. So when I told him of my desire to go up to Canada to catch big walleye, he was really excited. As we talked and he helped me plan our first old guy trip to Wintering Lake, he got really excited about the possibility of catching walleyed pike. Our first trip out into the lake was in my boat with John, Bill Stoub, and Frank Amtower.

Fishing had been slow but Bill, Frank and I each caught at least one nice walleye. John had been blanked all day. He finally got a hit, jerked the rod so hard I thought he was going to break it, and reeled in a 12 inch walleye all the way up to the end of his rod. He was so excited he didn't know what to do with it. Frank volunteered, "Give it to me." John was ecstatic, this was his first really "big fish."

"Let out some line and swing it in," were Frank's instructions to John. As he swung the walleye in, Frank reached out with his left hand, grabbed the fish, deftly unhooked the jig and nonchalantly flipped the walleye back into the lake. John was crushed! That was his first 'big fish' that he had waited a year to catch. He was as proud as a peacock with that first walleye. Frank had punched his balloon with a walleye jig. "It was too small, and besides, you talk too much." John recovered, but I'm not sure he ever fished with Frank again.

Our cabin had a very large garbage can which we managed to fill almost every day with eight guys living there. We asked

Dennis what he did with the garbage as we just set the bags out on the porch. He told us he came around every day, collected all the garbage bags and drove them out to his dumpsite.

"Where is the dumpsite?"

About a half a mile off the drive way. Some of the guys were quite curious about that dumpsite since we heard rumors of bears prowling around dumpsites. A couple of the guys decided they wanted to go out and see if they could find bears at our dumpsite at sundown. After dinner and before the card game, Mick and Dave, Bill Stoub's son-in-law, headed out in Dave's pick up to find the dumpsite and hopefully some bears. When they didn't come back at sundown we began to worry. But not enough to quit the card game, just to talk about it a little. After another hour went by, we really started to get worried and were thinking about getting in one of our vehicles and looking for them, or possibly their remains. I say that because some of us had seen a bear up real close, when one of the DNR guys hauled one into camp on a caged trailer. That bear was big and ugly and stunk. Most of us knew enough to not fuss with bears.

Nonetheless, these two idiots had decided they wanted to see some real bears, alive, and up close. As we considered what to do, we had actually gotten up from the table and were starting to leave the cabin when we heard the screen door slam, and two very pooped troops stumbled into the cabin. "Where you guys been? Weren't you worried about us? Why didn't you come after us? We could have died out there."

Then the story came out. These two guys drove their pickup out to the driveway and found the lane back to the garbage dumpsite. When they got back there, they found no bears and no place to turn their pickup around. So as they tried to maneuver the truck while turning around, they got stuck. Dark was approaching and they were afraid that bears might be approaching also. So one guy held the light looking for bears and the other one shoveled. They alternated until they finally got the truck out and drove back to the cabin, much wiser than when they left.

When Russ Engelhart agreed to join us on one of our trips, he was the youngest guy in our group at about forty-five years of age. I'm sure he felt somewhat intimidated by a lot of gray hairs and bald heads. But he put up a good front and talked a good game. He actually was a good fisherman but walleyed pike offered a different challenge then did big mouth bass in Texas. It took him a good while to figure that one out. But figure it out he did and eventually caught his share of walleye. His enthusiasm was never dimmed no matter how bad the fishing was in general. We all enjoyed his enthusiasm.

His enthusiasm for winning in our card game, up and down, was equally great. He had played cards with the guys at our cottage in Muskegon and figured he could hold his own in any crowd. What he never understood was that our group of hard-core fisherman, were also the best of the hard-core card players. The card table in Muskegon was also frequented by some of the ladies, and some of the neophyte card players. So up-and-down in Muskegon at our cottage was a piece of cake for a semiskilled player. The players at Wintering Lake were all seasoned and hard core, he never had a chance. He played hard, faithfully, enthusiastically but near the end of every game, no matter how good was his lead, he managed to shoot himself in the foot.

We were all beginning to feel sorry for Russell, for he is such a great guy but pity got you nothing at Wintering Lake. Seeing him lose in the clutch, time after time, began to bother some of the faint hearts, and wusses. Most of us simply felt that, "He got his come-up-ins again." But by the last night, we were all pulling for Russell. So when he ended the last game with one third of a win we all cheered and patted him on the back. You wouldn't think that would mean much to most of us, but for Russell in his week with the "old guys," that was a big win.

38

The Big Cabin

When we first arrived at Wintering Lake and were so greatly disappointed in the appearance of all the buildings, we were greatly encouraged when Dennis told us that he was going to build a new office, a whole new enclosed bathroom, and a large new cabin. By the time of our first large group, we had reserved this brand-new large cabin. It was almost forty feet long about twenty-six feet wide and it was two stories with a screened in porch that was eight feet deep and full width. The main floor consisted of two bedrooms in the back, or west end of the building. The stairway was just in front of these two back bedrooms and was steep. The steps were so short that you had to walk up and down with your feet angled so you would not fall off the edge of a step. The upstairs also had two bedrooms situated directly over the main floor bedrooms. In front of the steps upstairs was a large dorm room with a number of single beds or cots.

Downstairs, in front of the stairway, was located a single large room which was our living area. On the south side was a wood burning stove. On the east side was a thirteen foot long counter with a sink and drain. The north side contained a four burner stove and a refrigerator. The dining table was on the west side.

There was a spare refrigerator on the porch where we kept all our bait and cold drinks. Denny had also provided a smaller table to fit in the middle of this area and that became our kitchen work area.

There were cabinets underneath and on either side the sink. There was a set of wall cabinets about three feet long on the left end of the sink. This set of cabinets held our dishes, glasses and cups. By the second trip to Wintering we were happy to supplement this cabinet with our own items that we had all salvaged from garage sales. That was a step up for the cabin. We were always looking for a place to store or set our pots and pans, since by this time, I had purchased all the stuff I deemed we needed because it seemed, at the time, to be a good investment. And it was. So I made a lightweight set of shelves for holding these pots and pans. Basically, we customized this cabin to fit our needs. After several trips, everybody knew where to sleep, to store his fishing stuff, to sit at the table for eating or card playing. For most of us, this was a home away from home for at least a week every year for about twelve years.

Sleeping arrangements were somewhat dictated by who snored and who didn't, who used C-PAP machines and who didn't, and who was too old to climb stairs and who wasn't. The bedroom at the bottom of the stairs was granted to the two Bills. I would be getting up from two to six times a night so I was closest to the side door where I claimed my own pee tree.

The guys upstairs either had huge bladders or they found themselves each a pee jar.

We soon learned that each jar needed its own lid—"nuff said!" Early on in our trips, I thrilled to step outside on a cold, windy, rainy night to take a leak. That soon became 'old hat.' I discovered that when I got up in the middle of the night, I was alone. So I simply shuffled over to the sink, urinated into one of the plastic glasses, dumped it down the drain, turned on the water and washed the sink clean. To some of you this may be news, even very repulsive news. Don't be too quick to criticize, your time may be coming. For those of you who already knew, thank you for not ratting me out.

Nighttime produced a few more predicaments. When Bill and I first started sleeping together, that is in our separate beds in the same bedroom, I was occasionally awakened by his snoring. I simply emulated his wife and hollered at him, "Turnover!" That worked and fortunately it didn't happen very often. Because he had sleep apnea, I became used to his snoring, his snorting and other noises. Actually, his noise was comforting to me because I had not been acquainted with anybody who had sleep apnea, and I had heard horrible tales about somebody with sleep apnea actually dying because he stopped breathing; "He swallowed his tongue." I didn't believe anyone could swallow his tongue, but I sure could believe that people with sleep apnea did occasionally die in their sleep.

As I returned from one of my nightly visits to the pee tree, I sat on the edge of my bed listening for Bill. I heard nothing. I listened intently for almost a minute and still heard nothing. So

I flipped the light switch on and ran over to feel his arm. It was still warm, so if he were dead it had to be just recently. He still was not breathing. So I shook him and hollered, "Bill! Bill! Wake up!"

"What's wrong?"

"I thought you were dead." Great sigh of relief and return to my sleeping bag. Once he got his C-PAP machine that was the end of that. I mentioned that bed placement was important for all of us because by this time a lot of guys were using C-PAP machines and everyone had to plug his machine in. So electrical outlets dictated who slept where.

On the occasion of one of our earliest trips I had just tucked myself into my sleeping bag and was on my way to nah-nah land, when I felt Bill Stoub drag a shirt across my forehead. "Hey! What are you doing?" I heard mumbling from across the room and realized that he had done nothing. He was still in bed. "What had I just experienced?" I slept rather fitfully for the rest of the night. Next morning I related my peculiar tale to my comrades and we realized that our cabin had become infested with four-legged fuzzy little creatures better known as mice and one of them had run across my forehead.

We sent out a call to Dennis and he supplied us with a half a dozen mousetraps. That night, we set a number of traps and as we were sitting at the card table we heard a snap. We had the interloper. Somebody got up, flipped the dead mouse outdoors, re-baited the trap, washed his hands and returned to the card game. We were all happy. Fishing had been lousy, and catching a mouse was the best thing that happened to us all day.

"Who's deal is it? It's yours JP." Snap, a few chuckles and, "We got another one."

Same deal, threw out number two, returned to the table. JP dealt and we played a hand and then it was Mick's deal. "Okay, diamonds are trump." Snap, number 3 just bit the dust and this brought overt laughter, we were on a tear. After a few more card games, a few more margaritas and 2 more snaps we were rolling in the aisles with laughter. We had a far better day catching mice than we did catching walleyed pike.

39

The Missing Plug

The drain plug is a critical part of every boat larger than an eight foot pram. I assume this is historically true, since boats have not always had electric bilge pumps. One sure way to get water out of the bottom of the boat is to pull it up on land, or on a trailer, and 'pull the plug.' If you had positioned the boat so that the stern was the lowest point, pulling the plug would allow all the excess water to drain out from the bottom of the boat. For very small boats it was usually easier and quicker just to flip the boat over, as I used to do with Bob Bailey's boat on Warner Lake. While at Wintering Lake, we leave the boats at the dock when not fishing. It's simply too much work to haul them out of the lake onto the trailer every night. And because it frequently rains or occasionally snows, at the Wintering Lake Resort, the first thing we do when setting foot in our boat in the morning is to turn on the bilge pump and evacuate all excess moisture.

That combination of circumstances; the plug, the bilge pump, rain and other sources of water in the boat can set up any number of interesting scenarios. Such was the case with my boat one year at Wintering when I found myself running the bilge pump more than I ran the motor. It was obvious I had some sort of a leak in my boat and so we pulled it out and put it on the trailer. Search as we did, we could not find the source of the leak. We consulted with all the members of our fishing trip, Craig, Dennis and even Tim. No apparent reason. So for the duration of the trip, we pulled my boat out of water every night, pulled the plug and drained the boat. It became quite obvious that if my bilge pump ever failed, the boat would probably sink. At least that is what I thought, so upon returning to the good old USA, I inquired of many professional boat men before I arrived at a solution.

A boat on a trailer is supported by a series of padded supports applied over a fairly large area of the bottom of the boat. By this means, force is applied to the bottom of the boat by the supports; much like the force of pounding of water on the bottom of the boat is transmitted to the struts transversely placed in the bottom of the boat. Weight or force is more equally transmitted, uniformly to the bottom of the boat. I learned that my boat trailer had not been well devised. Although there were the supports at the rear of the boat, in the front of the boat and trailer, the keel of the boat was resting directly on the shaft of the trailer. When driving on the smooth surfaces of paved roads, there is little jarring or bumping applied to the boat.

Traveling that eighteen mile stretch of very bumpy gravel road from Highway 11 to Wintering Lake had literally pounded the bottom of my boat until one of these struts broke. That led to a loosening of all the rivets in that section of the bottom of the boat, which in turn led to unimpeded leaking. So do I get it fixed or take the risk of sinking every time I go fishing? No-brainer. Fortunately, the insurance company helped me pay that sixteen hundred dollar bill to get my boat fixed. All of this to say that it is important to make sure your boat does not take on water.

With that background, we were having a reasonably successful day in Fecta, which is the top lake just before entering Wintering Lake itself. Mick was driving his boat and I was driving mine. We had mixed clouds, which provided some sunshine and warmth, and a fairly high wind directly out of the north. This provided us a drift across a point on the west side of the lake. We have learned that it is certainly possible to catch walleye on a fairly flat bottomed portion of the lake, but elevations and drop-offs usually carry a higher percent of striking walleye. So we were drifting over the point from the north and we would either get hits as we went from ten feet to six feet or on the other side going back down.

It wasn't exactly like we were catching a fish per man on every run, but at least we were having enough action to make our drifting worthwhile. We had previously tried drifting over the flat bottom in the center of Fecta and had zero results. So any hits, even though we missed a lot, were a whole lot better than no hits. Under these circumstances, running a boat was a difficult chore for the captain. Running into the wind determining the flow path of the boat and making sure we did not run aground was a constant chore for the guy running the boat. As per usual, if someone got a hit we threw out a buoy. In the course of the day there were several buoys out and they ended up being the point around which we wanted to drift.

Because of our intense concentration on feeling the hit and striking at the right time, we were inattentive to the position of the buoys, and as a result, ran over several of them, one at a time. Running over a buoy is bad news because there's always the possibility that you will run over the line with the motor and cut it, or if the motor is not running the line will get tangled up in the motor or in the sonar plate. Then we have a mess on our hands. Unwinding the tangled line from the sonar head, or raising the motor up and trying to reach out to the end of the motor to unwind the line is always a pain. Because of this story that I'm now retelling, all of us have been much more attentive to buoys in our drift line.

Fatigue, cold and hunger finally won and we headed home, a twenty-five minute run. Over the sharp S-curve at the run out, over the twenty-five foot hole in the middle of the channel, over honey hole four, a sharp left turn over honey hole three, a right turn across the mouth of Grandma's channel, across the big twenty-five foot hole, around the dead moose, across honey holes two and one and then the home stretch. Always careful when drifting past the buoys at the mouth of the basin, we then dock the boat. The fish cleaners did their job and the cooks did their job and we had the usual wonderful meal that we all anticipated and enjoyed thoroughly.

The standard fare for the evening meal was walleyed pike shaken in a basin of Aunt Jemima's Complete Buttermilk Pancake mix to provide the batter, fried in olive oil and seasoned with Lowery's Seasoning Salt. Soggy for a few of us, crisp for most. Sliced fried potatoes with copious amounts of Texas sweet onions and cold slaw with tomatoes. Vegetables were varied and optional. We tried canned corn, canned peas and a few others but they weren't big sellers. Baked beans with chunks of Polish Sausage became the vegetable of choice. The meal was always topped off with a few choice homemade cookies of several varieties. We never tired of home made cookies.

Breakfast was our only other formal meal and that started off with Richard's boiled Colombian coffee. Richard was always the first man up. And that was followed by the cook's choice; fried or scrambled eggs and alternating bacon with sausage links and toast of Sandy's homemade Swedish rye topped with gobs of butter and some jelly.

On that fateful day we had completed our evening chores and some of us sat down for an early card game. A few guys had other things to do and Larry decided that he had not caught enough fish for the day. So he went down to the dock to cast out for whatever might be cruising. Historically, that had been fairly productive for Larry but it was usually for pike and not walleye. We heard him in the distance hollering, "Hey guys, Mick's boat is sinking!" Not having any idea what to expect, we all jumped up and ran down to the dock to find Larry with his boots off, standing in the back of Mick's boat with several inches of water around his feet. He had a bucket in his hand and was bailing furiously.

We quickly realized that this was a losing proposition so we ascertained that Mick's boat was still floating and we were able to move it around to the launch site, back his trailer in and dragged the half sunken boat up on to the trailer. As we slowly and carefully pulled the boat and trailer out of the water we immediately perceived the problem; there was no plug in the back of the boat. There was no chain on the plug so it was gone. After some discussion we realized what probably happened. As we had drifted into the marker buoys, we figured that one of the buoy strings got wrapped around the plug and we inadvertently pulled the plug as we retrieved the buoy. And if you ask us today, we will stick with that story. No one has ever confessed to pulling the plug on Mick.

<h1 style="text-align:center">40</h1>

Notes to Bill from the Guys

Bill,

My first trip was in the summer of 2008. The experience was awesome: great weather, great northern outdoors, great fishing and great fellowship! The impact that trip had on me was a chance to meet and get to know great Christian guys! Bill, your trip was not really about great fishing, but great friendship among Christian men. God bless you and thanks for including me!

Jim Visser

Bill,

The trip... Going to Canada to fish the first time was so foreign, frightening and exciting all at the same time. It is now the trip I look forward to the most. Some of the feelings that the memories of the trips stir up for me are: challenging, wet, cold, tiring, discouraging, competitive, rewarding, fellowship, margaritas, up and down and out, peeing on trees, tires, in cans, listening for bears as we walked with Winter, seeing bears up close and personally with the West Virginia guys, fish fries, fried potatoes without onions, eggs and bacon without onions, friends and community, my first rod and reel that you helped me buy, my first tackle box full of who knows what and only Jerry Kasper knows what's in there. Thank you, Bill. It would never have happened without your passion and pursuit of our friendship. It is the best trip I have ever been on for men. You have given me so many fond memories that have and will last me for a lifetime. You da man... And you are my friend and I do love and appreciate the impact you have made in my life and my son and my grandsons lives.

Love you, JP

Bill,

My first trip was the spring of 2004. I fished between you and Bill Stoub and it was a riot, never laughed so much in my life. I had not fished much since my teenage years and needless to say I had a blast. You and Bill were very helpful to a foreigner from Texas. I was even accused that it was because no one could understand me that we were stopped on the border and fined. The trip has given me an opportunity to develop relationships outside of my every day circle of life. I have made some dear friends. Men can have fun as boys again without pressures. Bill, you have given each one of us a blessing by your dedication and generosity of yourself in pulling off these trips. Most of us have never experienced what we have on these trips. I have got to know you as a man with a heart as big as all Texas in serving others. Thanks for being a true friend. I hope we can continue these trips for many years. Thanks again.

Richard

Bill,

You are always a pleasure to fish with. I especially enjoy your sense of humor. Your walleye and potatoes are 2nd to none. Often I've eaten out at a restaurant and said, "This isn't as good as Bills'." I look forward to our next trip together. Hopefully I can get clued in on some of your "honey holes". Thanks for all your hard work that goes into every trip. It doesn't go unnoticed. Thanks.

Matt Moon

Bill,

I just want to thank you for inviting me to join you guys at the Wintering fishing retreat four years ago. I wasn't able to join you guys the first year, but you very graciously furnished me with maps and contacts and even your "honey hole" locations. My sons, Corby and Andy and I had a mountaintop experience at that camp and we talked about that trip often. The next year I was able to join the rest of you. That was a fantastic experience. You have always treated me like a son and a good friend and I think of you whenever anyone mentions fishing. Your organization and time, and sacrifice in preparations that you began months before our leaving is so greatly appreciated. I know what that is like, I am usually the one who has to do all that stuff for my kids and family. The fact that you always made sure that no one is ever left out or in need of everything is above and beyond. From any special food needs or wants to clothing needs. Several times I have needed outerwear and you made sure that I was adequately protected from the cruel Canadian weather. Two of my five near death experiences in my life happened at Wintering. One was being caught out on the lake with my two boys in an electrical thunderstorm and the other was the black bear camp episode with Bill Stoub's son-in-law (Dave). You guys were playing up and down and Dave and I were praying for God to come down and rescue us. Bill you are much loved and appreciated by me and if there ever is anything I can do for you please call on me.

Your good friend, Mick

Bill,

The dominant memory is of the first time I went up there with you, Bill. It was just the two of us and the folks back home were making book on who would come back! In those days we stopped over night in Wawa and continued on Saturday morning, leaving time for fishing in the early evening when I was introduced to "honey hole # one" and caught walleyes. We used one of Dennis's boats... For the last time. And we got the cabin in the back forty and drove to the boat docks! I think that was the time we missed the turn off at White River and decided to continue to the next northbound road. It turned out to be gravel! We had a blowout driving that road. What a mess that was. Another memory is when you, Frank and I went up in the fall. I don't remember what year it was when we tied into the perch at Grandmas Lake. What a blast! I have some photos of the catch. Was that the time I ran the boat aground? Then on the way home, the OPP stopped us for a safety check for seat belts and open alcohol. You didn't have your seatbelt on in the backseat and there was a half gallon of wine open in the back to the car. They asked if we'd been fishing... We had a boat we were towing... and we said yes and they asked us to see the fish, pull to the side of the road. Turned out he was the fish and game man. We thought we only had eleven walleyes along with one hundred and forty-eight perch and told him so. So he counts the walleyes and swishes around for perch and finds another walleye. We were still legal but he checked those perch hoping to find more walleyes to no avail. Our last memory... Was at the bridge to the USA and we got checked and were all right. You had gone in to get your tax money back and we were asked twice more if we'd been checked already. We said we had been and where waiting for you. Finally you came out and we were on our way. We told you the story and you said "Good thing they didn't check the little cooler cause I forgot to eat the cold fish on the way to the border." These are great memories and I have lots more of other trips with you. Thank you so much and know that you are loved. You are a great fisherman and a dear friend!

Bill Stoub.

Bill,

My first trip to Canada with you that I recall was when you asked me if I would go up to Canada and check out this fishing resort that someone had told you about called Wintering Lake Resort. We went up in late August or early September as I recall. On the trip we spent the night sleeping at a scenic Lookout north of the Sault in the back of your vehicle. We caught walleye on that trip but I remember most was the 150 Perch that we caught at Wig Lake. We had so many fish that we had to stand on the boat seats. I think it took us 4 hours to clean the mess of fish. There have been many memorable moments on the trips that we have taken to Wintering. The Fellowship, fishing and food have been really great. I always remember that I went with you on a trip to the Western UP to check on a fishing resort that you were thinking of taking your grandkids to. The fishing wasn't very good but we sure had a great time. My first experience steelhead fishing was with you when we went up to your cabin at Baldwin and floated the Pere Marquette. What a blast that was. Bill I really appreciate your friendship and being included in these trips that we have taken together. Your hard work in planning the trips and your interest in me as a friend is greatly appreciated. I love you Bill.

Larry Moon

Bill,

The first time that I went up to Canada with the guys was in May 2006 I think. You had invited me a couple of times be-

fore that. I had not been fishing much at all since fishing with my dad in grade school and high school days. Cane poles and bobbers for bluegill and perch. So I do not consider myself much of a fisherman. You were very supportive in showing me how to catch Walleye Pike and how to try for perch back in grandmas Lake. The chance to spend some more time bonding with the guys especially the SALTS leaders was great. For me the best part of the trip is up and down games. Bill, thank you so much for being the moving force behind those fishing trips. Without your drive and sponsorship I would not have had the opportunity to connect more with the guys.

Jim Keller

Bill,

I am back and saw God do a real work in Greece,and in me.

I was not getting emails when I was away but Carol texted me and told me to open my emails and she warned me I would get a good cry from reading the things Bill wrote about me. (and I did cry tears of joy)

I do think of that week as being the most "male" I ever remember. It was the first time in my life that I was invited to be one of the guys for a week. It was really more than that because they were all safe men who knew my story and invited me anyway. It has turned out to be the last time I had that kind of experience so that makes the memories even more precious.

To answer your question, yes you can share my story. Thanks to everyone who played a part in making my story!

Dan Colley

In Memory

Fisherman Friends Who Have Passed On

William Isaac Burdick (grandfather)
Andrew Sprague Burdick (father)
Doug Wendzel
Bob Bailey
Wayne Schense
Frank Amtower
Lloyd Cook
Howard Davidson
Dr. W. Duncan Rowe
Dr. James Glessner
Dr. Marshall Patullo
Dr. Jack Crawford
Dr. Carl Nagel
Dr. George Bennisek

Proof #1 B&S

Made in the USA
Columbia, SC
25 April 2017